CATCH THIS!

Going Deep with the NFL's Sharpest Weapon

TERRELL OWENS

with STEPHEN SINGULAR

SIMON & SCHUSTER

NEW YORK ● LONDON ● TORONTO ● SYDNEY

SIMON & SCHUSTER
Rockefeller Center
1230 Avenue of the Americas
New York, NY 10020

For information about special discounts for bulk purchases,
please contact Simon & Schuster Special Sales:
1-800-456-6798 or business@simonandschuster.com

Designed by Julie Schroeder
Manufactured in the United States of America

1   3   5   7   9   10   8   6   4   2

Library of Congress Cataloging-in-Publication Data
Owens, Terrell, 1973–
Catch this! : going deep with the NFL's sharpest weapon /
Terrell Owens with Stephen Singular.
p.   cm.
1. Owens, Terrell, 1973–   2. Football players—United States—Biography.
I. Singular, Stephen.   II. Title.

GV939.O82A3 2004
796.332'092—dc22   [B]   2004048724

ISBN 978-0-4516-3168-5

For my family, as thanks for their support
and always being with me:

Alice Z. Black
Marilyn Owens
LaTasha Scales
Sharmaine Stowes
Victor Stowes
Charvinski Scales
Terique Owens
Kaleb Stowes

Acknowledgments

Over the course of my career in the National Football League (1996 to present), certain of my actions as a professional football player have drawn a lot of attention from the media, in particular from certain media outlets and specific persons. Unfortunately, the decision often was made to paint my actions in the most negative light and to conclude that I must be, among other things, a bad person, a bad teammate, or a bad influence or force in general. Interestingly, most of the media members who have consistently passed judgment on me as a player and as a person do not know me nor have they ever taken the time or made the effort to get to know me. After several years of living through this persistent and cruel treatment, I and many of the people close to me decided that it was time for me to tell the world my side of the story. Well, here it is—my life as it has been lived to date. After you have read this book, I hope you will conclude that as far as Terrell Owens is concerned, the old saying does hold true: *"You cannot judge a book by its cover."*

As with most things in life, many people did an enormous amount of work on this book but will never receive the credit or recognition that they deserve. Accordingly, I want to acknowledge and thank each of them here.

I must first acknowledge God, through whom all things are possible. The first person I must thank, as with most things in my life, is my mother, Marilyn Heard. Marilyn played an integral role in the education of the author(s) as to my upbringing, my hometown, my family, my faith, and many of the decisions that have shaped my life. As this book shows, she always stood proudly beside me whatever the situation and I love her dearly.

I must also thank my maternal grandmother, Alice Black. As most know, she continues to suffer from Alzheimer's disease, and thus was not able to contribute personally to this project. However, as the pages of this book reveal, my grandmother remains one of the most important influences in my life, and her influence on this book was substantial.

A special thanks must go to my friend of the past nine years, David Joseph. David's commitment to me and my family has never wavered and as a result ours is a true friendship. This book demonstrates that David has been there through all of the highs and lows and, most important, always stood up for me and supported me. Our relationship is so much more than client-agent, and for that I will always be thankful.

I want to also thank my friends Theron "Coop" Cooper, Carlos "Pablo" Cosby, Anthony Shaw, Antonio "Pokey" Graham, Roderick "Big Unk" Tuck, Antonio Minnifield, and Andres "Chub" Hicks. Not only has each of these gentlemen always stood beside me and given me support but each also contributed to this book by taking the time to provide the authors with information and stories about me and our shared experiences.

I also must acknowledge and thank my personal trainers and friends James "Buddy" Primm and Melvyn Williams. Buddy and Melvyn have been instrumental in my development as a world-class athlete and in keeping me consistently healthy. I respect them as professionals who do an outstanding job and, more importantly, as friends.

This book was originally slated to be published at the beginning of the 2003 NFL regular season but was delayed because of unforeseen circumstances. Accordingly, the persons and companies involved in the information collection, drafting, shaping, editing, publishing, and marketing of the book had to put in what amounted to an extra year's worth of work. I thank them all for their dedication to this project and for never wavering from their commitment to get the book published.

To that end, I would like to thank my literary agent, Reid Boates, for bringing the expertise to locate the right editor, publisher, and author and for navigating us through some difficult times on the project. I would also like to thank Steve Singular who did a miraculous job of picking up this project midstream and being able to complete the project in a short period of time. Steve was able to do this because of his tireless work ethic and because of his dedication to the project, which is evident through his commitment to go anywhere at anytime to further the project.

Our editor, Jeff Neuman, kept us all focused on the end goal for the past two years. He took Steve Singular's manuscript and molded it into this book. Simon & Schuster was a great partner to work with because of its willingness to originally commit to this project and because of its commitment to staying the course until completion. Finally, I would also like to acknowledge Richard Weiner's efforts relating to the project.

I would also like to thank Jason Knight and Jodi Miller of Joseph Athletic Management for their efforts in doing a lot of the little things that must be done to get a manuscript completed and a book published.

Finally, I would like to thank everyone who played a role in my free agency and in getting me to what I hope will be the NFL Promised Land—*Philadelphia.*

CATCH THIS!

PART ONE
THE SOUTH

I

A COUPLE OF YEARS AGO, I went back home to Alexander City, Alabama, about an hour's drive south and east of Birmingham. I don't go home much anymore, but my mom still lives there, along with a few old friends. I was eating at a local restaurant when a white family came in and sat down a few tables away. Their son was about three years old and had a high, loud voice, the kind that grabs your attention. He kept pointing at me.

"Who's that nigger, Daddy?" he said. "Who's that nigger over there?"

I tried to ignore him, but that was impossible.

"Who's that nigger, Daddy?"

I've been trying to ignore insults like that ever since I was very small. I'm dark, and I grew up hearing racial slurs from everyone— both black and white. Other black kids called me "Shine" and "Purple Pal." You can guess what the white kids called me. From the time I was a child, I had to learn not to react to people's stupidity and cruelty, even when that's all I wanted to do. I had to learn to let things go and to control myself, and I was trying to let this go in the restaurant. I just wanted to finish my meal, leave these people and this town behind, and not come back home again anytime soon. But the kid wouldn't be quiet.

"Who's that nigger, Daddy? Who's that nigger right there?"

Someone else in the café decided to stand up and walk over to the family's table and tell them that I was Terrell Owens, Pro Bowl wide receiver for the San Francisco 49ers, who'd grown up in Alexander City and played ball at the local high school.

The family looked stunned to hear this, and it shut the boy up, at least for a short while. His parents were so embarrassed that they turned away from me and talked between themselves. But then I heard a sound and saw the kid approaching me.

His parents had sent him to my table for my autograph. I was, I guess, the most famous person Alex City had ever produced. When the child got to my table, I looked right at him and didn't say anything, but very slowly and neatly wrote out my signature, using my best handwriting and putting the number *81* on the piece of paper. I always do this when I give out an autograph. I was raised to be polite, to forgive and to accept and to go on. I've tried to do that my whole life—with myself and my family and others. That's why I gave the boy my autograph. I wanted his parents to know that it wasn't the kid's fault that he was acting this way—no three-year-old knows this stuff unless someone has taught it to him, so he didn't deserve to be punished. Racists aren't born but made, one child at a time, one word at a time, and until adults break this chain of ignorance and hatred, it will never stop.

I also wanted his parents to know, just as I want the National Football League to know, that they don't get to define me or to control me or my feelings. That's my job, on the football field and in life. They don't get to tell me when to give an autograph or when to celebrate or when to cry. I'm the only one who can decide what's right for me—and I'm willing to pay the price for being who I am. My grandmother and my mom taught me that I need to walk through this world with a strong mind and a big heart, so that's my goal. I don't always reach it. Sometimes I stumble, and sometimes I come close to falling, but then I refocus and try to learn and get better.

I've been doing this for as long as I can remember.

* * *

Football is not the most important thing in my life. It's not even the second most important thing. It's faith, family, and football, in that order. I don't think of myself as a professional football player but as an athlete who ended up in the NFL. I wish it were different. If things had gone the way I wanted them to, I'd be playing pro basketball now instead of football, and then my mom could see my face whenever I made a basket or grabbed a rebound or blocked a shot. She's the reason I started celebrating in the end zone in the first place: I wanted her to see me on television. She watched the 49ers games down in Alabama, and the only way I could make sure that the camera stayed on me was to score a touchdown and then do something nobody had ever done before. This led to dancing on the star in the middle of the field in Dallas, and that led to Sharpie and to shaking the cheerleaders' pom-poms. Who knows what will happen next? Before each game, I tell my mom to stay tuned for something new.

In the NBA, I could express myself naturally on the court without causing a national crisis, but the NFL—the No Fun League—isn't like that. It's a lot like the military, where everyone is supposed to fall in line and be like everyone else. I'm not like anyone else. My family wasn't like anyone else's, so I wasn't raised like other people. I was raised to be myself and to tell the truth and to take the consequences for doing that. I'm not going to keep quiet or stay inside a box, the way many pro athletes do, even some very famous ones who've told me that the best road was to be politically correct at all times. That was best for *them,* not me. The NFL can't deal with me—because they never know what I'm going to do next.

After I scored the winning touchdown against Seattle on *Monday Night Football* and then signed the ball with a Sharpie, some people in the NFL and the press called me an embarrassment to the sport, shameless, selfish, egotistical, and worse. Seattle coach Mike Holmgren took a major shot at me, and so did football commentators from coast to coast. You'd have thought I committed a crime, like some other players we could talk about in pro sports today. We've got guys charged with rape, with drug abuse, with beating their wives and girlfriends, and with murder. We've got rap sheets all over the league, and I brought disgrace to the league by carrying a pen in my sock and autographing a football? A lot of people in America have lost perspective about sports, and about life. Some of them are filled with judgment and even hate. Many have forgotten what love and acceptance are all about—not to mention having fun. They forget that football is entertainment, and they have no idea what an athlete goes through to get into the NFL, let alone get into the end zone on *Monday Night Football*. If they did, they might feel like celebrating, too, when something goes right.

After Sharpie, the media began writing and talking about me as if they know who I am and what I stand for. They don't. Like many NFL owners and league executives, they don't know where I came from or what I believe in. They don't want to know too much about the hired hands who make their football machines go. They want us to do our jobs and stay in our places and shut up. They don't want to see or hear anything that will make them think very much about the people who work for them. The press can't understand that when I went to the star in Dallas, I wasn't trying to taunt anyone but was thanking and honoring God for all the blessings I've received and for all the things I've been able to do for my family. They want athletes to be role models for young people, but when I try to tell them about my spiritual foundation, they don't want to know about it. Real faith makes them nervous. Real life is too big or too scary compared with a football game. Athletes aren't supposed to be real people, only trained entertainers, but reality can get in the way of a good story or a cheap opinion.

I always tell people that if they really want to know who I am, they should look deeply into my eyes, because the reality and the truth are there. I'm a person just like yourself, with a heart and a history and a lot of feelings about my past. Look into my eyes, and maybe you'll understand why faith and family are so important to me and why football is just a way of serving them. Look into my eyes, and maybe you can learn where I'm from and why I want to celebrate after scoring a touchdown.

   Look and listen.

I GREW UP in a true company town. I attended Benjamin Russell High School and visited the Adelia Russell Library, the Russell Medical Center, and the Russell Retail Store. Like everyone else in my family, I worked at the Russell Athletic Mill, a group of cement and brick buildings with tall smokestacks that shoot steam into the air twenty-four hours a day. My grandmother, Alice Black, worked at this plant, and so did her husband, Simmie Black. My mom, Marilyn Heard, worked there for almost twenty-five years. Our story, like the stories of so many other families in the town, is wound around the Russell Mill. You can't understand my life unless you know what it means to live in a company town.

You need a little history, too. Alexander City existed before the Civil War, once the U.S. military had driven off the Creek Nation Indians who'd lived in this part of Alabama. The Creek met their final loss at the famous Battle of Horseshoe Bend, right outside town. In 1865, 399 slaves were freed in our county, and then the Ku Klux Klan quickly became popular. Klan members rode through the night and terrorized the local black population by forcing the men to lie down in the dirt in front of their wives and children, while hooded white men measured them for coffins. They let them live if they promised not to vote in the next election.

In 1902, a fire broke out in downtown Alex City, as people there call it, and destroyed all the businesses and many of the homes. That same year, Benjamin Russell opened a textile mill at the edge of town, with six knitting machines and ten sewing machines. The workers at his plant made ladies' and children's underwear. Later, they began sewing athletic gear, and the Russell Athletic Mill became by far the region's biggest business. By 1998, the Russell Corporation, which has never been unionized, employed almost 18,000 people and had annual sales of more than $1.2 billion. The corporation also owned the local bank and much of the land around the huge lake outside the city limits, Lake Martin.

A couple of decades after the plant opened, my grandmother came up to Alex City from southern Alabama. She'd been picking cotton for a living but wanted something more for herself and her children. Being inside a factory beat laboring all day in the fields. She was also trying to get away from her past and from the past of many black people in the South. When she was twelve, her mother disappeared, and this was the most important event in her life. Her mother may have run away or been murdered or died of other causes; one day she was there, and the next she was gone, leaving a hole that could never be filled. My grandma never found out what happened to her, and this would haunt her until she was an old woman. It made her fearful of many things and deeply protective of her family. She didn't trust anyone easily and almost no one beyond her blood relatives. She raised her children with great strictness, not letting them do many things that other kids and teenagers could do. When my mother's younger sister, Elizabeth, couldn't take it anymore, she ran off to Michigan as a teen and never came back.

My grandmother treated us grandkids the same way. I was born on Pearl Harbor Day, December 7, 1973, and my mother and I lived in Grandma's home on the north side of Alex City. The house was tiny with a small backyard. My grandmother disliked almost everything that was new—new appliances, new ideas, new people—and she constantly let you know that. She made the rules, and nobody ever won an argument with her. It would have been hot inside those

Alabama walls in the summertime no matter what, but Grandma made it a lot hotter by shunning air-conditioning and keeping all the doors and windows closed. She kept the blinds down. She kept the sunlight out. She didn't want anyone coming in or leaving the house. She wanted you to stay home with her so she could see you at all times and correct your behavior. The only place we were allowed to go, besides school, was to church several times a week, a couple of blocks away. After church, we walked back home and sat in the house by ourselves. She didn't believe in using the telephone or watching television, so I never saw cartoons or other kids' programs. The one show she liked was *Wheel of Fortune*—and years later, when I appeared on this program as a guest, I froze up from the memories of seeing it with her.

In the wintertime, if we got cold and my mom crawled out of bed to turn up the heat, Grandma immediately got up and turned it down. If you used too much bathwater, she came in and shut off the faucet. If you opened the windows in the summertime, she closed them and lectured you on letting bugs and flies come into her house. If you talked back to her, you got a whipping. The only time you could relax was when she got depressed thinking about her mother and started drinking—but if she drank too much, you might get another whipping. Sometimes she'd drink so much that she'd pass out, and we'd sneak out of the house and try to get back before she came to.

We couldn't have other kids over for sleepovers, and we couldn't sleep at anyone else's house. I grew up feeling very isolated inside that house and envious of other kids. I wasn't just envious of their freedom; they were learning more about dealing with outside people, while I was learning how to be alone. Many of them had fathers, and I didn't even know who my dad was. As a teenager, my mom had broken through all that strictness she was raised with and gotten pregnant, but my dad had never been around, and nobody ever spoke about him. As far as I knew when I was very young, he didn't even exist. No one talked about this, because it wasn't that unusual. My grandma hadn't known much about her father, and my mom hadn't known much about hers, either. Their dads weren't there when they were children, and the women had to bring up their families by themselves. It was just the way things were, and we had to accept it, like Grandma's rules.

One year, I got a bicycle for my birthday, and I couldn't wait to ride it all over town, but that was never going to happen. Grandma let me ride it to the end of the driveway and back to the front door, over and over again, until I'd worn out a patch of ground. She wouldn't let me dribble a basketball in the house, because it made too much noise and got on her nerves. She didn't want us listening to new kinds of music, because gospel sounds were good enough for her and other music might lead to trouble. Across the street, kids were always playing basketball or football, but I couldn't go over and join them. She'd watch me get right to the edge of the curb and try to step into the street before yelling at me to stay in the yard. Everything had to be a certain way: neat and clean, controlled and contained. Kids had to be polite and quiet, well behaved. In Alex City, they call this being "mannerable," and that's what you were expected to be.

Looking back, it would be very easy to criticize my grandmother, but that isn't how I feel about her today. She told me a lot of things when I was young, and most of them have come true. It's almost as if she knew that I was going to be in the spotlight someday and would need her advice. The best place to turn for it would be inside myself, so that's where she put a lot of things when I was a boy. I never realized all this until I became an adult. It's kind of like the way a lot of football players feel later on about the men who coached them. When they were playing, they thought the coaches were too tough, too demanding. They complained about men like Vince Lombardi, George Halas, or Bill Parcells. But when they got older and looked back, at least some of them could see the point of all that discipline and toughness. It had helped them win football games and prepared them for some of life's trials. Sometimes, the dislike you feel for these coaches when you're a player can even turn into love.

When I was growing up, my grandmother told me that people

were going to talk about me and get in my business, and there was nothing I could do about this. They weren't going to understand my ways, so I should just accept it.

"They talked bad about Jesus," she said, "so you know they're going to talk bad about you. You might as well get used to it."

You've got to be very strong, she insisted, and make your own decisions, because nobody else can do that for you. You've got to know the difference between right and wrong and always figure out which side of that line you're standing on. You've got to work very hard for everything, because no one is ever going to give you anything. And you've got to tell the truth, even when it's uncomfortable, even when you don't want to. Lying isn't good for anyone or anything. And if you're going to tell the truth, she let me know, you'd better be prepared for the consequences.

As a child, I didn't see either the good things or the storm that was coming my way, but maybe she did. She and my mother used to say that there was something different about me, something that most people didn't observe. They said that from the time I was very small, they knew I was going to need strength and spiritual help.

My feelings for my grandmother have deepened since 1997, when she was diagnosed with Alzheimer's disease. My family has watched her fight this terrible disease, and it's made all of us closer and caused us to draw upon our religious foundation. When I was a boy, I hated going to church with her, hated sitting there on Sundays in that hot old church, but now I'm glad I did. It rooted me in something bigger than myself. The older I've gotten, the more I've been surrounded by temptation, especially when I started to find success in pro football. Everywhere I turned, there was a chance to go astray, with drugs or women or booze or violence or bad investments or many other things. Whenever I was standing at the crossroads, I thought about my grandmother, and she helped me through.

WHEN I WAS NINE, I won the spelling bee for Tallapoosa County. The real glory came the next year, when Alex City decided to hold a Michael Jackson contest downtown. Mom made me a costume, with sequins on the outfit, white gloves and dark shoes, glitter socks, sunglasses, and an Ivy League cap. I didn't have to practice moon-walking, because it came to me naturally. After I performed in front of a couple hundred people and heard their loud applause, the judges gave me the twenty-five dollar prize for my imitation of MJ. I wasn't nervous behind those sunglasses, because I didn't have to look right at anyone. With twenty-five dollars in my pocket, I thought I was rich and got so excited that I moon-walked all the way back to our house. People came outside to watch me and point and whisper my name.

"They're staring at you," my mother said.

"I *want* 'em to," I said.

I liked the spotlight and was thrilled to see the look of pride and joy all this put on my mother's face. She didn't have a father or a husband, but she had a son who wanted to make her feel good. I'd given her pleasure, after all the sacrifices she'd made for her children, and that was something I wanted to do again and again. A few years later, I reached for more glory by trying out for the "Quiet Storm" dance troupe at the high school, but they didn't let me in. I'd have to find my success elsewhere.

Every time I strived for something and tried to better myself, it seemed to cause trouble. In the eighth grade, when I got higher marks than the boy sitting in front of me, he tormented the fire out of me. He was relentless and mean as a snake, making fun of my looks and my skin color, calling me names and trying to get me into fistfights. My eighth-grade American History teacher, Gayle Humphrey, watched what was going on and was always there for me. She told me to ignore the kid and stay focused on my work, and she let me know that I could trust her. Like my grandmother, I had real trouble trusting anyone outside my family, but in time I let Mrs. Humphrey in. I listened to her and understood what she was saying: I had to make a choice; I could either get distracted by someone else's problems, or I could take advantage of the opportunity she was giving me to learn more. If I got distracted, the opportunity might not come again. If I could control myself, I could do more than I realized.

"Don't let the tormentor get to you," she'd say over and over again. "You're better than that. Don't let him win."

Mrs. Humphrey was the first person I ever trusted who wasn't a blood relative.

I stayed focused on my work, and eventually the kid left me alone, but there would be others just like him. I was skinny and not very strong. One time, a boy threatened me at school, and I got so scared that I ran all the way home. Alex City has a small population—about 15,000—but it's very spread out. Many of the houses are so far from downtown that they seem to be out in the countryside. When I got to my grandma's house that day, I was out of breath, but more trouble was waiting for me. Grandma didn't want to hear that I'd run away from a bully. She didn't believe in backing down from anybody. She told me that if someone hit me and I didn't hit him back, *she* was going to whip me. I never wanted to face her, so I began getting into fights and losing them. Other boys just seemed to enjoy picking on me.

I was dark-skinned and serious-minded and shy and socially awk-ward because of my background. Girls didn't know what to make of me, but boys couldn't resist baiting me. When something went wrong at school or in the neighborhood, I usually got blamed for it. The problem was that I wouldn't admit to something I hadn't done or take the heat for somebody else. I'd been taught to speak the truth, even when it might cost me, so that's what I did. I was never afraid to tell the adults who was really to blame, and this didn't ex-actly make me a popular kid in Alex City. They called me "Tattle-tale" and a lot of other things, and there was always another fight to get into. I couldn't back down and couldn't escape, so I just went through it as best I could, but it left me feeling lonely.

I don't remember hearing "I love you" from my grandmother or my mother or anyone else when I was small. I had two younger sis-ters, LaTasha and Sharmaine, and a baby brother, Victor. As they got older, they didn't say these words, either. We all felt it, but we didn't know how to express it.

When I was eleven, I noticed a girl living across the street. She was pretty and friendly, the first girl I was ever attracted to. I knew just how long my grandma would be at work at the Russell Mill in the afternoons and when she would be getting home. I knew exactly how long I could hang out with this girl before I had to be back in our yard when Grandma arrived. I planned my time around seeing the girl until her father, a man named L. C. Russell, took me aside one day.

"You can't be interested in her," he told me.

"Why not?" I said. "I like her."

"That doesn't matter."

"Why?"

There was an awkward silence.

"Because that girl," he said, "is your half-sister."

It took me a while to understand that I was talking to my father. He'd been living across the street for many years, but nobody in my family had ever told me that. When I asked my mom about this, she said that it wasn't necessary to explain everything to me. I was shocked to find out who my dad was, because I'd thought that someone else was my father, somebody who'd left Alex City a long time ago.

Once I realized he was my dad, we started to develop a relationship, but that caused another set of problems. His wife didn't like me and didn't want me in their house and didn't want to feed me, even when my dad asked me to come over and eat. My dad's wife told everyone she was a religious person, but this didn't seem like a very religious attitude to me. She scared me so much I wouldn't go see him. When I mentioned this to my grandmother, she took action. She said something to them and said it directly, the way she usually said things, and after that, my dad's wife began to accept me more. I got to spend some time with my father, and that meant a lot to me, but growing up around him was still painful. Sometimes, he'd promise me Christmas presents and not deliver them. He said he had five other kids to take care of, and they came first.

On summer evenings, my grandma made us come into the house while it was still daylight and brush our teeth and put on our pajamas. We had to be in bed by seven. I'd crawl out of bed and stand at the window and see the other kids in the neighborhood playing hide-and-seek or kickball, running around and shouting and laughing. I'd stare out at them and cry. I didn't understand why they got to stay up later than I did, couldn't understand why they didn't have so many rules. I'd ask my mom about this, but she always said that as long as we were living with Grandma, we had to do what she wanted. And what she wanted was to keep us inside that stuffy house, where there was a lot of praying and a lot of obedience but very little celebrating going on.

From the time I was three years old, my mom had been working at the Russell Mill, trying to earn enough money to get us into our own home. Occasionally, we were able to move out and live somewhere else, but then we'd have to come back to Grandma's. My mother labored at the plant for more than two decades, first as a sewer making the minimum wage of about five dollars an hour, then as a dye maker and a machine operator, and eventually sweeping out the factory floors on the midnight shift. Sometimes, she worked both the day shift and graveyard to make ends meet, and she also made clothes at home for other people in the community.

"I've got to take care of my children," she told me over and over again when I was growing up. "There's nobody I can turn to for a dollar."

My grandmother worked at the Russell plant for about two decades, until she got arthritis and couldn't do the job anymore. They let her go a couple of years before she could draw social security. I worked there one summer as a teenager, making the boxes they put their gear into before shipping it all over America, but it didn't take me long to know that I didn't want to spend the rest of my life in that mill. There had to be something better, I told myself as I watched my mother leave for work and come home sore and tired. One day, I saw her paycheck, and I was amazed. How could she support herself and four kids on her salary? Back then, that seemed like a miracle to me, and it still does. She did it by doing without. She didn't have a car, and she walked all over town to buy groceries and other things, usually carrying a baby on her hip. She didn't own a home, so she didn't have a house payment, and most of the time we lived with my grandmother. She made most of our clothes and didn't pay for babysitters, because when she and Grandma were working at the mill, I took care of the younger kids, feeding them and changing their diapers. We didn't have parties or festivities, not even during the holiday season. My mother stretched her paycheck and made ends meet, but I wanted something better—for her as much as for myself. I wanted her to have a car and a home of her own, so she wouldn't always have to live with my grandmother.

IV

WHEN I WAS A YOUNGSTER, people said I was too skinny and weak to be an athlete. If that weren't enough of a barrier, my grandmother felt that organized sports were a waste of time, a sure way for me to pick up bad influences from other kids. "Keep him away from those sports," she told my mother, but for once my mom resisted her. I was her son and no one else's, and she thought that trying out for the local teams would be good for me. As a freshman, I ran track and played football for the Benjamin Russell Wildcats, but didn't do much. The next year, I played football, basketball, and baseball, discovering that basketball was my real passion, with all other sports a distant second. In football, there was too much standing around. The game was slow and jerky—it stopped and started with each play—while basketball flowed up and down the court. In football, somebody told you what to do on every play; in basketball, you got to *create* your game on the fly. You got to break out of being inside someone else's rules. But people told me I had more potential at football than basketball.

As a sophomore, I'd stand on the sidelines next to our football coach, Steve Savarese, and grab his arm and tug on it, letting him know that I wanted to be on the field. He didn't like this, but I kept doing it, knowing that if he just gave me a chance, I could make something happen. So I kept tugging and reminding him that I was there and wasn't going away.

"Put me in, Coach," I'd tell him, and he'd shoot me an annoyed look.

He gave me a little playing time, but told me that he was worried about me, because he'd seen me hanging out with some of the rougher kids in Alex City, the ones who were into drugs and knew how to make money selling them. He knew we were poor and how much my family needed more income. (By the time I was a teenager, I was spending more and more time away from home. My grandmother couldn't stop me, and my mother was working all the time, so I was free to come and go and got a little reckless with my friends.) He called a meeting with my mother, my teachers, an assistant coach, and me. He told everyone about his concerns and said that I had some athletic ability but needed to work harder at football and to get in better shape. I listened to him and started to push myself by running and lifting weights. During the summer I'd sneak out of bed in the middle of the night and jump rope and mark off forty yards in the street. I'd run wind sprints in the dark while everyone else in my family was sleeping.

Then the coach put me to work at his house, paying me to wash his car, baby-sit his children, and mow his lawn. He even let me drive his car to a school function. One December day, I was doing chores at his home when he showed up with two Christmas trees, one for inside his house and the other for his front porch. He saw me staring at them.

"Coach," I asked, "y'all have two Christmas trees?"

"Yes," he said. "Does your family have one?"

I shook my head.

That afternoon, Coach Savarese took me home and walked inside, where he could see that we really didn't have a tree. We also didn't have any gifts. He drove back to his house, had his kids wrap some presents, and returned to our home with the gifts, a tree, a turkey, and a ham. I was so happy I started to cry.

But I still had to keep tugging on his arm to get into a game.

* * *

Once football season was over, I traded in my cleats for basketball shoes and headed for the court. I practiced very hard, and in my junior year, I was named the most improved player on the team. Basketball was a release from everything I was surrounded by at home and at school and inside Alex City. When I was hooping, I didn't have to worry about taunts or bullies or getting into fights. When I was running on the court or flying through the air or jamming the ball over my opponent (I could dunk when I was sixteen), I felt free for the first time ever. On the floor, nobody could tell me what I could or couldn't do. I thought basketball was my future.

When I was a junior, the wide receiver ahead of me on the football team, Ricky Morgan, got sick, and Coach Savarese let me start in his place. All that tugging had finally paid off. Before the game the running backs coach, Coach Lasseter, had told me I was going to score a touchdown that game. I caught a pass and ran forty-six yards down the sideline for a touchdown, plowing over and around a couple of tacklers along the way. Once the ball was in my hands, I knew what to do with it and had a nose for the end zone. When I was thrown into the action, my natural attraction for the spotlight just seemed to take over. I started getting a lot more playing time and more chances to catch the ball.

Coach Savarese thought I was a much better football player than basketball player. He didn't want me to go out for the basketball team unless I played football each fall. One of his assistant coaches, Willie Martin, had played offensive line for Edmonton in the Canadian Football League; his team won the Grey Cup. He was a huge man with a big heart and a lot of caring for the kids at Benjamin Russell High. When he told me that I had more ability in football than basketball, I didn't agree with him, but I respected his opinion and went to work on my game. He said I had to learn how to take criticism from coaches and understand that they were trying to help me. And he taught me about more than the physical part of football.

"Fear," he said, "is just something that's in your mind so you can overcome it. You can control it and make it work for you. Everybody has fear—it's how you deal with it that matters. If you've got a dream to play sports, stick to it, and don't ever let anybody take it away from you.

"You've got to understand three things. If you make a mistake on the field, admit it. That's always the first step. Then learn how to correct it. That's the second step. Then make a commitment not to do it again. These three things are all you need to know. And don't be afraid of failure, because hard work will get you past it. If you get knocked down and get back up, you've got nothing to worry about. If you don't get up, then start worrying."

The more success I had on the football field, the more I wanted my mother to come see me play. That didn't happen very often, because she was too busy working at night or taking care of the kids, or she couldn't get a ride to the game. Someday this was going to change, I promised myself, because she was always the fan I most wanted to perform for.

As soon as I started succeeding in football, trouble followed right behind. One night, we were riding the bus back from a game, and I fell asleep in my seat. My mouth had fallen open, and one of the guys saw this and couldn't resist. He leaned over me and spit between my lips, right into my mouth. I didn't wake up and never even knew this happened until someone told me about it. I was filled with disgust and couldn't get the image of what he'd done out of my mind. It was so powerful I could taste it. To the other players, it was a big joke, but to me, it became the ultimate personal challenge. As Coach Hicks had said, I could either turn fear and anger against myself, or I could make them work for me. I decided to use this incident to motivate myself to get better at football and to get as far away from this situation as I could. This insult became a part of my deep faith in God.

My faith is not about being a sports hero but about taking advantage of the opportunities God puts in front of me and then using them to help myself and my family. Others might have gotten something else out of all the religious training I received as a child, but this was what it meant to me. It was what Gayle Humphrey had been teaching me in the eighth grade, when she said I needed to rise above my tormentor and keep studying. It was what Willie Martin was saying to me at the start of my football career, when he told me not to let fear hold me back. It was what happened when that kid spit in my mouth. God was going to place things and people in my path, and I could either be defeated by them or use them to improve my situation. The choice was always mine. Do you try to hurt someone with your fists because he spit on you? Do you give up playing football because some of your teammates don't like you or make fun of your looks? Do you walk away from your dreams because everything just feels too difficult? Or do you find another way?

The kid who spit in my mouth will never know how much he helped me.

This mentality started when I was very young and still motivates me today. Every morning, you have the chance to move forward with what God has created or to fall backward into fear and hate and confusion and despair. From the time I was a boy, I prayed for God's blessings, and they kept showing up every step along the way—in high school, in college, and in the pros—just like clockwork. Some people call this coincidence or luck or an accident, but to me, it's all about faith. This process is everything I've tried to talk about when reporters have asked me what's really important in my life, but the moment I try to answer their question, they get that glazed look in their eyes and drift away. They don't realize that I'm trying to tell them something they don't usually hear: my success is not just about football and working hard, but about something more than that. It's about real faith and paying attention to what comes your way and then knowing what to do with it.

V

FOLLOWING THE SPITTING INCIDENT, I was determined to get into the kind of shape I'd never been in before. It was the start of my commitment to being more than a local athlete—a commitment that's never ended. At school during study periods, I'd go into the weight room and lift while other kids were either fooling around or doing their homework. Then I'd lift before football practice and after it. If I had more muscles, kids might think twice about picking on me on bus rides or in the hallways at school. I liked pumping iron and feeling it stretch and strengthen my body.

Early in the morning, Alex City is often covered with a fog that comes off Lake Martin and blows into town. It's a thick, humid soup that sits on top of the buildings and the pine trees and can make it hard to see more than a couple of blocks. Two or three hours of sunlight burn it away, and then the day gets even hotter. I'd get up at dawn and put on my tennis shoes and run all over town, past the hardwood forests and out beyond the city limits. I'd run and see all the people in their cars driving to work at the mill. I'd run past the beautiful crepe myrtle bushes and the big yellow monarch butterflies that are everywhere in Alex City in the summertime. I'd run and listen to the birds stirring in the trees and making their morning songs.

The vegetation in this part of the country is covered with a vine called kudzu. It looks like ivy, and it was brought to the South years ago from Japan to help control the growth of other plants. It took over and grew on top of bushes and trees and all over the valleys and hillsides, up the sides of telephone poles and buildings and on electrical wires and mailboxes. Given the chance to spread, it dug in and kept growing and never stopped. All it needed was the opportunity to show what it could do.

I ran everywhere in the hot Alabama fog, and it felt as if I could run forever. This was a great outlet for me, an escape into another place where I was in charge of my life and could push myself as far as I wanted to. The more I ran, the more I wanted to run and the more I wanted to see what I was capable of. I was putting on weight and adding strength to my legs and endurance to my lungs. My body was changing, and people were starting to look at me in a new way. As I ran, I saw the steam rising from the stacks at the Russell Mill, where my mom and my grandma were still working, and I told myself I didn't want to be stuck in there for the rest of my life with the other people in town. There had to be something more.

One spring, our football team got to visit Tuscaloosa, home of the University of Alabama, a few hours west of Alex City. This was where Bear Bryant had coached the Crimson Tide to national titles, and it was my first chance to see a big-time college football program up close. I was awed watching the players move on the field, seeing how big and strong and fast they were. Everything was much quicker at this level, and everybody hit a lot harder. You could hear the contact and feel it across the field. Everyone was very organized and very serious. It seemed like a whole different game from the one we were playing in Alex City. At the end of the practice, the players gave us their wristbands, and I couldn't stop looking at mine, couldn't stop touching it. I put it on and didn't ever want to take it off. I hated getting back on the bus home that day. Maybe Alabama would take an interest in me and recruit me to their program, I secretly hoped, but I'd barely begun to make a name for myself in Alex City.

In high school, I wore number 80 on my jersey, because my football hero was Jerry Rice, the legendary wide receiver of the San Francisco 49ers. The Niners were at the top of the NFL (they'd won four Super Bowls in the last decade), and Rice was the greatest pass catcher ever. He was one of the very few football players I was aware of. Because my family had been allowed to watch almost no TV when I was little, I'd never had the same exposure to athletes that a lot of other young players did. I'd turned only two sports figures into heroes: Jerry Rice and Michael Jordan. I didn't see college football games on TV on Saturday or pro games on Sunday or Monday night, but Jerry Rice was different; it was impossible not to know something about him. He came from the South and went to a very small school, Mississippi Valley State, but would go on to succeed beyond anyone's dreams, becoming a star receiver with the 49ers and winning Super Bowls with both Joe Montana and Steve Young as his quarterbacks. JR was like Michael Jordan, in a class all by himself. He was known as the hardest-working and most disciplined player in pro football, the one who was setting records that nobody would ever break. When you looked up at the top of the mountain as a wide receiver, JR was looking straight down at you. He was so far beyond anything I could imagine, more like a figure in a movie or a superhero in a book than a real person.

In my senior year, I was friendly with another receiver on our team, Derek Hall. Experts in the area thought he was our best pass catcher, so he began to attract the attention of small-time college scouts. One recruiter, Bobby Johns, came down from the University of Tennessee–Chattanooga, a Division 1-AA school about 220 miles north of Alex City. UTC was the poor cousin of the University of Tennessee Volunteers. UT was a college football powerhouse and had the largest stadium in the country, holding 110,000. UTC had an old, worn-out stadium called Chamberlain Field, seating 10,000 people. The stands on the north side of the field ended at the 30-yard line, because when the school was building the facility, it ran out of money and never finished the job. This was the second-oldest college football stadium in America, and it looked like it. The field sloped up in one of the end zones, which held a stone wall that players could run into after scoring a touchdown. It was common for 10,000 people in Chattanooga to get into their cars and drive several hours to Knoxville to see the Vols play, but Chamberlain Field almost never sold out. UTC had never produced an NFL star and was known much more as a basketball school, the alma mater of the NBA's Gerald Wilkins (Dominique's brother).

In the fall of 1992, the UTC head football coach, Buddy Nix, came down to Alex City to watch Derek play, but I had a good game. Then Bobby Johns saw me play basketball and thought I had some raw athletic talent. I was 177 pounds and stood over six feet and was still working on my coordination—about as "raw" as you can get. Nix believed that Derek could help UTC quickly, but if they took a chance on me, I might develop later on. Coach Nix saw something in me that no on else had and told his assistant that someday I might even be able to "play on Sundays"—in the NFL. Back then, I don't think anyone else in the world believed I could even play Division I-A college ball, although I did get a couple of other recruiting calls from Division II Livingstone College in Salisbury, North Carolina, and Division I-AA Samford University in Birmingham, Alabama; I didn't even know these schools had football programs. UTC decided to offer Derek a full scholarship and me a partial one (I got a grant to cover the rest of my expenses). I was excited about going to college but very nervous about leaving Alex City. As much as your hometown can be a burden, it's the only thing you've ever known. I would miss my mother badly, and my brother and sisters, and wasn't at all sure that I could stick with college and living a couple hundred miles away from them.

"You can do it," my mother kept saying. "I know you can."

I had my doubts, and I was greener than green. I'd grown up so isolated from the world that when I first left for school, I didn't really understand where UTC was or what I was signing up for. Until I filled out all the paperwork and got up to Chattanooga and moved into my athletic dorm, I thought I was trying out for the Volunteers. I thought UT and UTC were the same school.

VI

LOOKOUT MOUNTAIN, just south and west of Chattanooga, saw some of the Civil War's bloodiest fighting. In the fall of 1863, 34,000 soldiers died there, and two years later, the North declared victory and the slaves were freed. Chattanooga went on to become a railroad center and a city of nearly half a million people, but it still feels like a small Southern town. UTC was integrated in the mid-1960s, and when I arrived three decades later, the school had a student body of about 8,000. The place had very little nightlife, which was probably a good thing for me and other young men in the athletic department. I had no car, no girlfriend, and not many social activities, so I had to find other things to do after dark.

One thing I did was call my grandmother and talk on the phone. I told her that I couldn't make it in Chattanooga and was homesick. School was too hard, and I wasn't making any progress in sports. In fact, I often seemed to be going backward. Although Buddy Nix had recruited me out of Alex City, we didn't get along. He didn't believe in playing freshmen, and ever since I'd first encountered sports, I had only three goals: getting into the game, making a difference to my team, and winning a championship. Coach Nix and I had a series of run-ins over my playing time, and I got very little of it under him. Out of frustration, I missed a couple of team meetings, and he suspended me for several games. That year, I caught only six passes, the longest a thirty-nine-yard touchdown throw against Western Carolina. Right after I went into the game against Marshall, a Division I-AA power-house, a defensive back hit me under the shoulder pad and broke my collarbone. It was too late in the season for me to be red-shirted and get my freshman eligibility back, so the year was pretty much wasted. Coming to Chattanooga felt like a big mistake.

If I'd been unhappy and homesick before getting injured, now I was miserable. I called my mom and told her that I wanted to leave UTC and return to Alex City.

"You can't quit now," she said. "You can't walk away from school and that scholarship. Give it time. You've got to keep trying, and things will change."

I let her know how much I was struggling.

"You want to come back here and work at the mill?" she asked me.

"No."

"Then try harder."

We cried, and then we prayed together on the phone. I got down on my knees and prayed with her for guidance and strength.

I prayed with my grandmother, too. I asked for God's help in sticking with this commitment. My grandmother said that this was a test to see how much I wanted to get away from Alex City, attend college, and be somebody.

"You've got to decide who you are," she said, "and how bad you want something."

My mother said that sooner or later, if I was patient and worked hard and kept praying, I'd receive God's blessing. I believed her, but it was still a struggle.

Slowly, my collarbone started to heal, and things began to improve. Action was always the answer for me—action and effort and sweat.

Once I was well enough to work out, I took the same training pro-gram I'd begun using in high school and transferred it up to UTC, except now I was running in a much larger place. Chattanooga sits in the Tennessee Valley, with hills rising on every side of it. Like Alex City, Chattanooga is covered with fog in the mornings, coming off the Tennessee River, which winds right through the heart of town. The sky and the trees are hidden by a blue haze so thick that you can stare right into the sun at dawn without hurting your eyes. I'd get up early and run through the mist, over the hilly campus and down by the river and out past the city limits, where the hills got higher and the challenges harder. The sun was peeking through, and the crickets in Chattanooga were the loudest I'd ever heard; they seemed to be cheering me as I moved along. I'd run through the middle of Main Street, before it got busy for the day, and along the side streets. After a while, other players saw me and asked where I was going. When I told them, they wanted to come, too, and started imitating my work-out. Sometimes I ran with teammates, but mostly I ran alone.

No matter what else I was doing, basketball remained my greatest release from everything else in life. I played in Chattanooga whenever I wasn't studying or on the gridiron. I'd come in from football practice, change from cleats to basketball shoes, and go out to the court for a pickup game in the Roundhouse, where the UTC Moccasins played. Balling was a lot more fun than watching football film, which the coaches always wanted us to do. I never liked studying film in high school or college, and I don't like doing it now in the pros. Way too much emphasis in football is placed on sitting and watching filmed replays of your opponent.

"You study long," somebody once said, "you study wrong."

If coaches want to do that, fine, but players have to get out there and *perform,* which means getting open and shaking off defensive backs and breaking tackles. I felt that I was making more progress in football by playing basketball in my down time than by watching film or reading playbooks. Basketball kept me in shape and helped my reflexes and my lateral movement. It kept me sharp and competitive in all ways. Sports are all about anticipation, reflexes, and instincts, and you use these things whenever you're on the court. You use your strength when blocking out and your hands when making steals. I felt that everything I did athletically helped everything else I was doing, but my coaches didn't agree.

I had only a football scholarship at UTC, but I was determined to make it in basketball at the college level, and I played it twelve months a year. I became a walk-on with the Moccasins and worked my way up to being the sixth man on the squad. Think of me as another Dennis Rodman—I was a little smaller than Rodman, but I could jump, run the floor, play tough defense, and muscle with anybody, and I always enjoyed getting physical under the boards. I played three years of fiercely competitive NCAA basketball against guys like Ray Allen when he was at Connecticut and Keith Booth at Penn State. My role was helping the starters get better during practice, because I was going to give them everything I had; they couldn't coast, and this was bound to improve their skills during games. All I wanted to do—all I ever wanted to do in athletics from the time I was a boy—was play on a championship team. I didn't care what sport it was or whether or not I was a starter. I didn't care if it was a ditch-digging championship. I've never won a title at any level of sports, and that's a big part of my athletic history. I'm thirty and still waiting for a ring. Striving for a championship has always motivated me, but it's also gotten me into trouble, and the trouble would get bigger as I climbed the ladder of success. Another wide receiver, Keyshawn Johnson, told the world that he just wanted the damn ball. All I want is to win.

I got to start six games at UTC, and we went to the NCAA tournament twice but lost in the first round. I cried after one of the losses, stayed in the locker room and cried until all of my teammates had left, cried until someone came in and told me I had to get on the team bus because it was leaving. I didn't even shower that night because I was so upset. I've never cried over losing a football game, not even after the 49ers have been defeated in the playoffs.

The very best memories I have from sports are from traveling with the UTC basketball team to away games. On football teams, there are so many players—about eighty on college squads for home games—that it's tough to get to know many of them. Basketball teams have only eleven or twelve guys and you really develop a bond. The other Moccasins nicknamed me "Skillet," because I was dark and strong as a skillet, and they also called me "Meal Money," because I loved the twenty to forty dollars in meal money they gave us when we hit the road. After being poor for so long, it was great to have a little cash in my hands. I quickly ate through this money or gambled it away on cards in those long hours going to and from the games. Nothing was better than traveling with the guys. When I was a senior, my football coach, Buddy Green, told me not to play any more basketball, because he was afraid I might get injured and harm my chances to play in the NFL. I didn't listen to his advice and believed that if God wanted me to play pro football on Sundays, then I was going to be all right and could avoid getting hurt doing what I loved.

When I wasn't running or playing basketball or practicing football, I hit the UTC weight room—hit it with a true vengeance for the first time ever. The skinny kid who'd gotten bullied and spit on in Alex City was about to be put to rest forever. Inside the blue and yellow weight room in the basement of the Roundhouse, I deepened my commitment to staying in school and making something of myself. Since there was nothing to do at night in Chattanooga, and since I was by nature a night owl, I made that room my morning, afternoon, and evening retreat. I worked out there so much that the staff eventually gave me the combination to the lock on the door so I could go in whenever I felt like it. The walls were covered with mirrors, and I'd look into the mirrors and pump, imagining myself getting stronger with every lift. I watched my shoulders getting bigger and more defined, watched my biceps bulge. I saw the veins on my arms stick out and saw my wrists get thicker. I wanted to look sculpted, and I wanted women to notice this—and notice me. I was slowly coming out of my shell, gradually turning into someone else. The sounds of the weights clanking in that room became my constant companions, and I can still hear that iron echoing today.

The small, intimidated boy who'd grown up as Terrell Owens was becoming another person. A second personality had been growing inside me all along, just waiting to come out. It was there when I'd won the Michael Jackson contest in Alex City and moon-walked all the way home, and it was there when I began getting some recognition in sports. In high school, I'd done little celebrations in the end zone after scoring a touchdown, jumping around or spinning the football on the ground. This other personality wasn't defined yet and didn't have a name, but he'd be different from the old Terrell Owens. He'd have the muscles of an action hero and wouldn't mind being the center of attention. When the game was on, he'd push the boundaries of what was acceptable, but when the game was over and the spotlight turned off, he'd disappear. The quiet, humble Terrell Owens would come back and be the shy person he'd always been. The "other" Terrell Owens first emerged in front of those mirrors in that basement in Chattanooga, and I had no idea where he was going to lead me.

VII

WHEN I WENT BACK to Alex City the summer after my freshman year, I kept up my running workout and my weight program at the local high school. When I returned to UTC that fall, some of the players said it looked as if I had done steroids. Wrong. I never put drugs in my system. Ever. Pills and powders had nothing to do with what I was going through, either then or later on. They're just plain bad for you.

In college, I had a natural growth spurt that coincided with my workouts. I was well over six feet now and approaching 200 pounds. At UTC, I hit the iron with everything I had. At midnight, I'd go into the weight room and think about my mom, who was also working, pulling the graveyard shift at the Russell Mill. Over and over again, I'd read the signs that somebody had tacked up: "The Winning Starts Here!" "Winners Are Workers" and "What Have You Done Today to Beat ————?" I'd look at the blue and yellow stripes on the walls and smell the old sweat that hung inside the room. I'd look into the mirror and tell myself that I was doing all this for both of us, for my mother and myself. She'd gotten me through my first year, when I'd just wanted to quit and go home, and it was up to me to do the rest. Sometimes, I'd talk to my mom and tell her I was going to be somebody.

I'd hear my grandmother's words and what she'd told me so many times when I was small: "Nobody's gonna *give* you anything." At one A.M., when the rest of the campus was studying or nodding off, I was all by myself in the weight room, but I wasn't alone. My mother and grandmother were in there with me, surrounding me with their faith.

In my sophomore year, things got better on the football field. First of all, Coach Buddy Nix was gone, and that filled me with relief. He was replaced by Tommy West, and under Coach West I got more playing time and caught thirty-eight passes for 724 yards and eight touchdowns. From the start, my best football asset was that I could advance the ball after receiving it, and I proved that to Coach West by averaging more than 19 yards a catch that season. I also had my first breakout game.

Marshall was the defending I-AA national champion, and they came to town in the first week of October ranked number one in the nation. It was a perfect night for football, about seventy degrees with a little breeze blowing in off the Tennessee River. I had a feeling that night would be special, and it was. I grabbed five balls for 145 yards and scored four TDs. The last one came when we were behind, and it clinched the game for UTC. People later told me that a nationwide telecast featuring Alabama's Crimson Tide had been interrupted to show what I was doing over at little UTC. My touchdown catches had been for 8, 18, 53, and 69 yards, and the four scores set a UTC single-game record. We beat the best Division I-AA team in the nation that evening, 33 to 31.

All this immediately went to my head. I thought I was going to be an instant star in Chattanooga and that girls everywhere would recognize my face as I walked across the campus and call out my name. Football wasn't a big deal at UTC, so none of this happened, but something else did. On Monday, as I walked to practice Coach West pulled me aside and told me I had not done anything.

The practice area at UTC is called Scrappy Moore Field, named after the most famous football coach in the school's history. Scrappy

Moore ran the program from the 1930s to the '70s and was the only UTC coach ever to beat the University of Tennessee, back in 1958. Scrappy Moore Field sits right next to the Tennessee River, and if I'd grown up thinking that Alexander City, Alabama, was hot and humid, it was only because I hadn't been to Chattanooga in the late summertime. The land around the practice field looked like a jungle and felt like a swamp. It was covered with vines and kudzu and plenty of big mosquitoes, just waiting to attack. At practice, guys regularly threw up from the heat or got the dry heaves or passed out from the humidity. They had to get IVs because their bodily fluids had fallen so low they were in danger of dehydration. Running wind sprints through this heat while carrying twenty pounds of football equipment was enough to eliminate many young men from even trying out for the Moccasins.

Coach West steered me over to the River Walk, which winds alongside the banks of the Tennessee. We went past docked barges and other boats, and for a while he didn't say much. He waited until we were out of earshot of the other players before he cut loose.

"You think you've done something special," he said, "just because you caught a couple of passes against Marshall?"

"No, sir," I told him.

I'd been raised to call people "ma'am" and "sir," and this would continue throughout college and all the way into the NFL. It was my way of staying mannerable, even when I was being chewed out.

"You haven't done anything here yet. Understand?"

I nodded.

"You're nowhere."

"Yes, sir."

It was hot when we'd started this walk, but it felt a lot hotter now. The little ego I'd built over the past weekend had crumbled right in front of me.

"All right. Let's get back to work."

I needed to hear what he was saying—but only once. When you hear things once, it's God way of telling you to make a change.

When you need to hear something more than once, you've got a problem that even God may not be able to fix.

I got the message, and as a sophomore, I was named to the All-Southern Conference first team, but this time the honor didn't give me a swelled head. Coach West had made his point: I knew just how small-time UTC was and how far I had to go to get where I wanted to be. Playing at a Division I-AA school wouldn't impress pro scouts or coaches, although the greatest wide receiver of them all—some people said the greatest *football player* of all time—had come out of Mississippi Valley State, which was farther down South and even smaller than UTC, so maybe there was hope for a guy like me. On the other hand, nobody in his right mind compared himself to Jerry Rice.

VIII

I WAS MAKING a name for myself on campus, but I was also just a normal college kid, with that same old penchant for being around trouble. Because there was nothing to do in Chattanooga at night, we had to make fun for ourselves. A few evenings before we were scheduled to play Alcorn State and their star quarterback, Steve McNair, a couple of my teammates and I were making noise in our apartments next to the football stadium. A security guard came over to quiet us down, and I popped off at him. He'd been giving me a hard time for a year or two, and I'd finally had enough. A piece of my grandmother was alive inside me, and she would only take so much before she said what was on her mind. She'd taught me not to kiss anyone's butt, so I wasn't going to do that with this security guard. I ended up getting suspended for the game against Alcorn State, and all I could do was sit on the bench and watch McNair rip us apart. His first pass went for 60 yards, and his receivers ran right past our defensive backs. I wondered if this was what I'd see every week if I ever made it to the NFL. I promised myself never to mouth off like that again, because it hurt the team.

I could be selfish, too. After two years at school, I decided that I had to have a car or I wasn't going to stay at UTC. Some of the other guys, like my Alex City friend, Derek Hall, had cars, and I could catch a ride with them, but that got old fast. One night, I called my mom and told her that if she wouldn't buy me a car, I was coming back home to stay.

"If you think you've got to have a car to go to college," she told me, "then quit right now."

"But—"

"No, Terrell. I can't afford it. I've got three other kids to raise and bills to pay."

"But—"

"You want to come back here and work at Russell Mill the rest of your life?"

End of conversation.

When I went home for summer break, it was all my family could do to scrape together enough money to buy me good shoes for school. I wore through a pair very quickly, because I played so hard. I was now a year-round athlete, running and lifting weights and playing basketball all the time. I didn't realize that I was putting terrible pressure on my feet by adding weight to my frame and running everywhere. Sports fans often don't understand what the human body goes through to turn someone into a professional athlete, but there's always a price to pay. I was paying it with my feet, day after day as I ran around Alex City and Chattanooga, giving them a pounding that years later would flare up and fill me with pain.

In college, I knew very little about the finer points of either training or nutrition. I started out at UTC by eating the regular fried dorm food, but even I understood that it wasn't very good for me. I gradually made the transition over to the athletic table, which was not always covered with pizza and other greasy stuff. Halfway through summer school, I discovered Ramen noodles, and they became the staple of my diet. I bought them at a store within walking distance of my apartment, and I couldn't get enough. They were good for you, easy to fix, and incredibly cheap. A Ramen meal cost about a quarter, and many times I ate the noodles for breakfast, lunch, and dinner. I still love them today.

Everything I was doing was helping me improve on the football field, though I was still incredibly raw. I understood very little about running routes, blocking, and getting off the line of scrimmage. In high school, all I knew was to catch the ball and run. In college, I was starting to add some skills, but I was mostly relying on the physical ability I'd worked so hard to develop. As a junior, I made second-team All-Southern Conference and scored six more TDs. My longest catch was for 76 yards, and I was closing in on the school records for yards receiving, receptions, and touchdowns. In our game against Georgia Southern, I caught twelve balls. I was figuring out how to use my new strength not just in the weight room but on the gridiron—to get free of defensive backs, to break tackles, to throw blocks, and to run over people. I had a lot to learn about how to finish routes and position myself to make a catch, but once I got hold of the ball, I knew what to do with it. I could outleap most defenders and had enough speed to get away from most players at the Division I-AA level.

At UTC, football was such a small sport that I hadn't yet started to attract the attention of pro scouts or the media, but I was gaining a sense of confidence about my own abilities. Football didn't come to me naturally, but through constant effort and study, I learned and got better. Buddy Green, the coach my senior year, hammered into me that I needed to train harder so I could outrun my opponents in the fourth quarter of a game. The more I improved, the more I wanted the ball. Our offense wasn't built around me or any other single player, so I didn't get thrown to as much as I wanted. This hadn't been an issue until now, but it would become one at UTC and far into the future. Every good wide receiver at every level of the sport believes that he needs the ball more; until somebody throws it to you, you might as well be sitting on the bench. The more my game expanded, the more I had to confront this issue, and it never got any easier.

I'd always thought of myself as a basketball player, but I was discovering that the same athletic skills I used on the court—speed and strength and quickness—could be used in football. It was kind of like lifting weights: I didn't have any idea how good I could become at it until I'd done it for a couple of years at the college level. In the back of my mind, I was starting to wonder how far my football skills could take me.

While I was pushing myself at UTC, my mother was working just as hard down in Alex City, and she was finally able to afford her own car, using a $900 tax refund to buy a 1975 Chevy Malibu. It had always bothered me that when I was in high school, she'd missed most of my football games, and I badly wanted her to see me play in college. Because our games weren't on TV, her only choice was to drive the 220 miles up to Chattanooga. When I told her how important this was to me, she said she would try to get there. This was a real challenge for a woman with three younger kids who was working two jobs, but when she made a commitment to one of her children, nothing stopped her. After working all Friday night, she'd come home; load LaTasha, Sharmaine, and Victor into the Malibu; fasten their seat belts; and head north. I also wanted my grandmother to come, but she never would. To her, sports were foolishness and a big waste of time. A lot of the trip to Chattanooga was uphill and through heavy traffic around Birmingham, and sometimes it was raining or foggy, but my mother just kept driving. There wasn't a moment to waste if she was going to get to the stadium before the opening kickoff, and she was usually there on time.

"We moved up and down the road," was how she described these weekend journeys.

Amazingly, she was never pulled over by the cops, but one time the Malibu's radiator broke halfway to Chattanooga. She quickly found a gas station and got it fixed in time to see part of the game.

I always wanted to do something good on the field so these trips would be worth it for her. I wanted to look over at the stands and see the expression on her face when I made a long gain or scored a touchdown. That was my payoff for all the hard work and hours of practice and lifting weights. She was my motivating force, my rock, and if I could make her proud of me, everything else would be all right. She and I were a team, taking on the world together so that I could move ahead. We never talked about this, because we never had to. We lived it moment by moment and day by day. It was in our blood and a big part of our bond, part of the love that connected us. It was like our little secret, our little dream that was just starting to come true. When she was young, she'd wanted a much more glamorous life than she could ever find in Alex City. She'd had fantasies of being rich and being in movies, but when she was sixteen, she got pregnant with me, and that was when the fantasy ended and reality set in. She had no husband and no support system and had to go to work at the mill to take care of us. She'd made herself into a good parent and a good provider, because that was the opportunity she'd been given. I was making myself into a good football player, not because that was my favorite sport but because it was what God had put in my pathway.

My mom wanted her children to do the things she'd never done. She wanted us to feel free and to be able express our emotions, because she was never allowed to do that around my grandmother. She wanted us to get out of Alex City and enjoy life in ways that we couldn't when we were children and living with her mother. She wanted us to go to college and have careers and not have to work inside a factory the way she'd done. Deep down, she still had some dreams of her own and hadn't given up on all of them. Even though she would be a grandmother before too many more years passed, those dreams were alive and waiting to be stirred. Working out in the dead of night, I was committed to making some of them come true.

IX

BY THE TIME I was a senior at UTC, my combination of size, speed, and strength was gaining more attention. I was something that NFL scouts really hadn't seen before: not a sleek wideout like Jerry Rice but a power receiver who looked forward to running over defensive backs. Once again, I was an All-Southern Conference pick by the coaches and the media, catching forty-three passes for 661 yards and four TDs. I now owned school records for most career receptions (144), most career receiving yards (2,320), and most single-game touchdowns (4). I was given the Scrappy Moore Award as the Moccasins' most valuable player, ending my time at UTC with catches in twenty consecutive games. Scouts recently had started paying visits to Chattanooga, but I still didn't know if I'd be drafted into the NFL. My skills were unrefined, and I knew as much about pro football as I'd known about the college game four years earlier. I was so naive that I thought if a team drafted you, that meant you'd made the squad and had a guaranteed contract. I didn't realize that they could draft you one day and cut you a few weeks later if you didn't perform or fit into their plans. Draft experts predicted that I'd get drafted but not until the second, third, or fourth round.

I'd been selected to play in the Senior Bowl in Mobile, Alabama, which wasn't too far from Alex City. My mom packed the family into a rented van and drove over to Mobile for the game. I was nervous because I knew that pro scouts were watching us closely, but our Senior Bowl coach, Dennis Erickson, seemed a lot more interested in his other high-profile receivers—Michigan's Amani Toomer and Derrick Mayes from Notre Dame—than in me. Toomer and Mayes were already pegged as future starting pro receivers and expected to be first-round NFL picks. I was expected to struggle and maybe wash out before ever making a team. At the Senior Bowl, I watched these first-round picks with jealousy and awe. Some of them had cars, cell phones, pagers, diamond-stud earrings, and girl-friends hanging around. They had agents standing beside them, waiting on them, and getting ready to negotiate their deals.

My coach at UTC, Buddy Green, had pulled some strings just to get me invited to Mobile. A stigma surrounded me, because I'd gone to a Division I-AA school, and players like Toomer and Mayes were far ahead of me in terms of their development as receivers and the competition they'd played against. Compared with theirs, my pass routes were simple and my technique terrible. Our playbook had just a handful of formations. In four years in Chattanooga, I'd faced only a couple of complex defenses, while they'd faced them every week at the Division I level, but once I got to Mobile and began to study the guys ahead of me, it actually boosted my confidence. They knew more about football than I did, but they weren't any bigger or stronger than I was. They weren't much faster and didn't hit any harder. They weren't hungrier. As the week unfolded, I felt I had a chance to make it, and this must have shown on the field. According to newspaper reports, my stock rose during the practice sessions. Nobody expected much of me, and that probably helped. When I got into the game that weekend, I caught a pass for four yards. I was concerned I'd now fall even further in the draft, but there were also signs of hope.

I was getting letters from pro teams that wanted to see film on me, and sports agents were starting to circle. They were a scary bunch. A few were clearly sharks and had to be avoided. Others were harder to read. A couple of them found my dorm phone number and began calling me before morning classes. Since they didn't know my voice, I'd answer and say I wasn't home. Then they began calling late at night and wouldn't stop. After a while, I quit answering the phone. I knew that finding the right agent was very important, especially for someone like me who hadn't had any exposure to the business side of football. Because I wanted to solve the agent problem quickly, I jumped in too fast, signing with a guy before giving it enough thought. Following my senior year in football, everything was starting to speed up for me. I was twenty-two and barely knew how to write a check; to me, forty dollars in meal money was a lot of cash.

I clearly needed help, so I did what I always did in these circumstances: I got down on my knees in my dorm room and asked God to lead me to the right person, somebody who could understand me, my football prospects, my background, and my family, someone I could trust. After praying, I remembered two agents who'd known Buddy Green and who'd come around earlier but hadn't initially made much of an impression on me. Their names were Fred and David Joseph, they were from Greensboro, North Carolina, and were Lebanese-American. From the South like me, they ran a smaller sports management agency, which I found attractive. Even though I'd signed previously with a different agent, something about Fred and David had stayed in my mind. Fred had been a sports agent since the 1970s, before agenting became a big business. Fred had handled receiver Haywood Jeffries of the Houston Oilers, defensive lineman Ray Agnew of the New England Patriots, and tight end Craig Keith of the Pittsburgh Steelers. Being an agent had been a hobby for Fred, who owned and managed his own life insurance agency. His wife, Cindy, worked alongside him in a basement office in Greensboro. That was why it appealed to me.

David had grown up watching his father interact with professional athletes and thought about being an agent but wondered if he could make a living at it. He became a lawyer instead, working in securities litigation in Baltimore. He was very restless, and by the mid-1990s, he couldn't hold back his desires any longer. He moved into his father's office in Greensboro to try his hand at agenting. Within a few months, all of his father's old clients were gone; Agnew and Keith had left, and Jeffries was about to retire. David was like me when I showed up at the Senior Bowl: we had nothing but fire and dreams. After I got rid of the first agent I'd signed with, I started talking more with David and his dad. My key issue with them, as it was with everybody else in my life, was trust—the hardest thing for me to believe in. David listened to me when I spoke to him, and he let me express my thoughts. He took the time to get to know me. He saw that I could be moody and distant, when I go deep inside myself, and he showed me that he could deal with this. He seemed to care. Slowly, I began to trust him. I didn't think he would take advantage of me or double-cross me down the line. He seemed easygoing, but I'd sensed a tough streak inside him. When I decided to ask him to represent me, I hoped he still wanted to.

On December 30, 1995, I called him in Greensboro, just as he and his fiancée were about to go to a New Year's party. He was dressed up in black tie, she had on an evening gown, and they were headed out for a night on the town. I told him that I was getting rid of my agent and needed to talk with him about becoming his client—in person and right now. He asked what I meant by right now, and I said, "Right now." He and his fiancée changed their clothes, jumped into their car, and drove straight through the night to Alabama. When they got to Chattanooga, David let me know that he understood my situation: I was green, I knew nothing about the business of football, I was deeply connected to my family, and they were always going to come first. I wasn't just another prospect looking for a contract but a young man searching for help and guidance. Despite my accomplishments at UTC, I'd never really been a sports star at any level, the way so many athletes are coming out of college. I'd never even played on a winning football team. In my four years at UTC, the Moccasins had won a total of thirteen games. I was getting ready to leave Chattanooga, and nobody had ever really talked to me about turning football into a long-term career. I needed special assistance, and only the right person could provide it.

David saw my hunger and my desire to prove myself to the outside world. I think he had the same set of feelings when it came to trying to succeed as an agent dealing with the NFL. We were both eager for a shot at the big time. He dived right in and started getting to know my family and talking to scouts about my prospects as a pro receiver. Once again, my prayers had been answered: God had sent the right person my way. Now we needed to get busy.

There are only three places where pro teams can watch you work out before they sign you. One is at the NFL scouting combine in Indianapolis, another is at your college, and the third is in your hometown (a player cannot work out at a team's facility). David and I went to the combine in Indy for three days, and they put me through exhaustive drills with the other wide-receiver prospects. General managers, coaches, scouts, and owners also interview prospects to see if they like their attitudes and find them coachable. They test them for speed and strength, they see how well they run routes and catch balls. I performed in front of people from all thirty teams in the league, and David felt I did well, but we knew that many wide receivers were going to be drafted ahead of me—if I made it at all. I had a lot to prove, and time was running out.

Pro Day, normally held in March after the Indy combine, is where personnel from NFL teams come to your school to take a closer look at you. It's their best opportunity to study you in depth before the draft. In March 1996, after the combine was finished, several scouts from the New York Giants, the Green Bay Packers, the Jacksonville Jaguars, and a few other teams traveled to Chattanooga to put me through some drills. The day of my work out was rainy, dark, cold, and miserable. Because of the weather, I couldn't run a 40-yard dash on the practice field. We wanted to do it on the basketball floor at the Roundhouse, but UTC was using the arena that day for something else, so this didn't work out, either. The only choice left was the concourse area of the Roundhouse, where they sell snacks during basketball games. We measured off the distance, and about 10 yards beyond the finish line was a set of locked metal double doors, with handles held together by an iron chain.

I kneeled down and got ready to go, but the cement floor was so slick I had trouble getting traction. Fred Joseph, David's father, was there with David, and they came up with a piece of AstroTurf-like material and taped it to the cement at the starting line, to give my feet a better grip. In spite of this, I didn't get off the line well and ran a poor time on my first attempt. One-hundredth of a second can be the difference between getting drafted and being ignored. I saw the scouts exchanging glances, as if they'd come all the way to UTC to have their day wasted. I knew I had only one more chance in the 40 to make a good impression.

Fred took me aside and looked at me very seriously and said, "You've got to attack the ground with all your strength and power. Try to relax, and don't look up or come up out of your stance until you've run eight or nine yards. Stay down and explode out of your start."

I nodded at him, worried that I was blowing my best opportunity to show what I could do. Our eyes met, and something happened inside me and between the two of us. I suddenly put on my game face, which Fred had never seen before. I've got another gear, but I don't show it to people very often. I used it when I was doing all that running in Alex City and all that weightlifting in Chattanooga. Call it determination, pride, fear of failure, grit, the absolute desire to better myself, whatever. It was probably put there by my grandmother and my mother, and in tough or unusual circumstances I draw on it to help myself. Years later, Fred would tell me that this was the most focused and intense expression he'd ever seen on an athlete's face. I think it scared him a little.

I kneeled down to run again, and he leaned over me and said one more thing. "Don't run forty yards," he said. "Run at least fifty."

"Okay."

They don't use guns or voices to start these 40-yard dashes. The runner holds out his hand and then raises it to signal the timekeepers. I took my stance, gripped my toes on the AstroTurf, and waited there for twenty-five or thirty seconds, gathering all the strength and concentration that I could. Then I lifted my hand and took off, putting everything I had into the next five seconds and attacking the ground with all my force. I exploded off the line and didn't ever come up fully out of my stance. As I ran, I kept hearing the last thing Fred had told me: "Run at least fifty."

I didn't stop at the finish line, and I didn't stop when I came to the locked iron doors. I crashed into them with all my strength and power, and the chains broke and the links flew up in the air and the doors popped open. I was standing outside in the rain.

I turned around to see what had happened.

One the scouts, John Dorsey of the Packers, was staring at me with his mouth open. Nobody spoke for a couple of seconds, as if they didn't quite believe what they'd just seen.

"Let's go," Dorsey said to the others, putting away his stopwatch. "I've seen enough." I ran a 4.47, the fastest I've ever run. To this day, nobody remembers my time, but they all remember my busting through those doors.

If you're just watching the NFL draft on television, it takes forever, but if you're sitting around listening for your name to be called by an NFL team, it takes a bit longer than that. Corey Edmond, a UTC assistant coach, had invited my family over to his home in Chattanooga, so my mom, a cousin, my sisters, and my brother were all there with me as the draft dragged on and on. Nobody thought I would get picked in the first round, so we just had to bide our time while that unfolded. There was some chance that I might be taken late in the second round, but that didn't happen, either. By then, all of us were worn out from the sitting and the hoping and the anticipation. The third round started, but still nothing happened. One team after another selected a player, and the third round was almost over, but my name hadn't been called. Now everybody in the house was bored and disappointed but trying not to show it. What if we'd been all wrong about my prospects? What if playing for a Division I-AA school had hurt me even more than I'd realized and none of the teams were going to take me? What if the Senior Bowl hadn't raised my stock with the pro scouts but lowered it? What if I had no future in the National Football League? What would I do for a living? How could I possibly help out my family if I couldn't play football?

A lot goes through your mind when you're waiting to hear your fate. Eleven wide receivers had been drafted ahead of me: Keyshawn Johnson (number 1 overall), Terry Glenn (7), Eddie Kennison (18), Marvin Harrison (19), Eric Moulds (24), Alex Van Dyke (31), Amani Toomer (34), Bryan Still (41), Muhsin Muhammad (43), Bobby Engram (52), and Derrick Mayes (56). Clearly, 1996 was a great receiver draft, and many of these players were pegged to have outstanding NFL careers. And just as clearly, I was even farther down on the list than I'd imagined.

By the end of the day, I'd more or less stopped paying attention to the proceedings on television. It had gone on too long, and I wanted to be outside shooting hoops. As the third round neared its end, I was down on the floor playing with the kids, trying to distract myself from my disappointment. I'd hoped that the Atlanta Falcons would draft me, because that would have kept me closer to home, but nobody believed this was going to happen. According to David, the only two teams left that had shown a lot of interest in me were San Francisco and Green Bay, and both still had a pick left in the third round. The idea of going to Wisconsin and catching passes from the best young quarterback in the league, Brett Favre, was very exciting. His arm was as strong as anyone's, and he was a great competitor. He could scramble, was a natural leader on the field, was a very tough football player, was from the South like me, and could get you the ball any-where on the field, including deep. Everything about playing with Favre was appealing.

The Packers were one of the league's up-and-coming teams, probably on track to win a Super Bowl in the next couple of years. They'd been getting better throughout the early 1990s and were on the verge of a breakthrough. If I could hook up with them and start grabbing balls from Favre, anything was possible. I might be wearing a Super Bowl ring before long and . . .

"With the twenty-eighth pick in the third round," the TV announcer said, "the San Francisco Forty-Niners select wide receiver Terrell Owens of the University of Tennessee–Chattanooga." I was the eighty-ninth pick over all.

My fantasy was suddenly over. As the eighty-ninth overall pick in the draft, I wasn't going north to Green Bay (the Packers had the pick right after the 49ers) but west to California, a place I'd never been. I was startled and confused. I hadn't focused much on the 49ers in the draft, because they hadn't paid any attention to me, and everyone knew they were loaded at wide receiver. They had the best pass catcher of all time in Jerry Rice, and they'd drafted J. J. Stokes in the first round the year before to be their next receiving superstar, once Jerry Rice retired.

My mother and the rest of my family were jumping up and down over the news, but I was still on the floor. They told me to get up and join them, but I was thinking about what might have been.

"Your dream has just come true!" my mom said, reaching for my hand and pulling me up to give me a hug.

I smiled at her, in a daze.

"Your dream has come true!" she said again.

Somebody picked up a camera and started taking pictures of me and everyone else at the coach's house. Then the media began calling and asking me what I thought about going to San Francisco to play for the 49ers.

I was totally surprised and didn't know what to say. All I knew was that I was going much farther away from Alex City than I'd ever been before, and I was going to be homesick all over again. I didn't yet grasp that my life had just changed forever or that my mom was absolutely right: my dream was finally coming true, but dreams don't always come easy.

PART TWO
THE WEST

X

FROM THE MOMENT I stepped off the plane in California in the spring of 1996, I was completely lost. I felt more raw and green when I arrived in San Francisco than when I'd gone up to Chattanooga for the first time. I didn't even realize that the man who picked me up at the airport that day, former 49er star receiver R. C. Owens, was famous for his "alley-oops" back in the 1950s, when he'd leap high for balls thrown to him by Hall of Fame quarterback Y. A. Tittle. As Owens drove me to the 49ers' training complex in Santa Clara, I was more focused on the surroundings, looking around and wondering where all the blond girls and beaches were. I'd thought every part of California looked like the set of *Baywatch*. Then we pulled into Santa Clara, about a forty-five-minute drive east of the nearest beach at Santa Cruz. We were in the heart of Silicon Valley, where the south end of San Francisco Bay runs dry. Almost nobody surfs the bay or the Northern California Pacific without a wetsuit, even during the summer. So much for the bikini watch.

As R.C. showed me around the 49ers facility, my jaw dropped and just kept falling. The complex had been built in 1987 as the NFL's first state-of-the-art training center—Niner players called it the Taj Mahal. This sprawling monument to the team's great success had been constructed by generous owner Eddie DeBartolo, Jr., for his beloved Super Bowl champions (the 49ers had won titles in 1982 and 1985 and would win three more after moving into the facility). Mr. DeBartolo hadn't exactly shortchanged himself, either. His office had football pigskin stretched across the floor like carpet. The office of team president Carmen Policy had suede walls and a marble-lined bathroom. Head coach George Seifert presided over a space so oversized—filled with expensive leather furniture, a walk-in sauna, and a wet bar—that he joked it was too luxurious for any football man. He was more comfortable working in a smaller room across the hall. The plush green practice fields covered acres and were maintained by a groundskeeper who'd been fitted with a fistful of his own Super Bowl rings. The complex had racquetball courts, basketball courts, and a full-length, artificial-turf football field built on top of tons of sand to cushion blows. It was like one of those country clubs I never thought would let me in.

Before getting drafted that April, I'd never been west of Utah, where UTC had played a basketball game. I had no contacts outside the team in the San Francisco Bay Area and was very lonely. Those first weeks in California, I'd call Alex City and do what I'd done four years earlier in Chattanooga: I told my mom that I didn't think I could last another day in this environment. I was worried about making the team and I was depressed. David had to pull me through a couple of long nights when no on else could. He told me again and again that I wouldn't be able to turn a switch and land a spot on an NFL roster. I was going to make the transition to the pros the same way I'd done everything else: through learning more about the game and through sheer hard work. I listened to him, and I prayed with my mother and my grandmother, and my faith got deeper. With God's help, my mom kept telling me, I was stronger than I thought was; I was never really alone and never would be. I could make it in San Francisco, if I tried harder and stopped thinking about quitting. I believed her, but . . . I was an emotional wreck and couldn't let anybody on the team see this.

I was more immature than a lot of young players—I was twenty-two years old but felt about twenty. I'd almost never been involved in a personal relationship outside my own family. I wasn't as comfortable with strangers as a lot of other guys were, and if Chattanooga had seemed like another country compared with Alex City, Northern California and the San Francisco 49ers organization were like another planet. I was not only a late bloomer emotionally, but I was still growing physically. When I was drafted, I wore a size 13 shoe; my feet soon stretched to 14 and then to size 15, but I think they've finally stopped.

I wasn't just a kid from a small college entering another NFL compound and trying to make a pro roster as an unknown (*Pro Football Weekly* had given the 49ers a C+ for taking me and defensive end Israel Ifeanyi in the draft). I was hooking up with the proudest and most successful franchise in sports. Between the end of the 1981 NFL season and the January 1995 Super Bowl, the 49ers had won five championship rings. No other pro football team had ever done that. No team in any sport, except for basketball's Los Angeles Lakers and hockey's Edmonton Oilers in the 1980s, had accomplished anything like this during that stretch of time. When I was drafted, the Niners were not the reigning Super Bowl champs, but they still thought of themselves as kings of the hill. The money was flowing for amenities for the players, and the attitude and swagger of the veterans showed right through their uniforms. Running back William Floyd talked to me about how proud the Niners were as an organization and what it was like to get handed your Super Bowl ring from Eddie DeBartolo (I tried to imagine myself in that position in the near future). I was so intimidated by the star players in the locker room—Steve Young, Jerry Rice, Brent Jones, Ken Norton, Jr.—that I couldn't even speak to these guys. When I talked to the coaching staff or team executives, I called everyone "sir."

I signed my first deal with the team on July 17, 1996, and reported to training camp the same day. The deal included a $270,000 signing bonus and overall it was a three-year deal worth $840,000, including the bonus. My salary was $152,000 for the first year, $190,000 for the second, and $228,000 for the third. Only the signing bonus was guaranteed. My salary for each season wouldn't begin rolling in until I made the team each year and the regular season games started in early September. At training camp, they did feed you and gave you a place to sleep, which was all I needed. The bonus money was more than my mother had been paid for a lifetime of working at the Russell Mill, but I didn't want to think about that or about how much salary I might start earning in the fall. I just wanted to stay focused on making the team.

The Niners didn't hold training camp at their Santa Clara facility but in Rocklin, California, instead. Rocklin is tucked in a boomtown region just outside Sacramento, which means very long and very hot summer days. Growing up in Alabama, I was used to training in the heat, but NFL training camps involve two practices a day, meetings that last forever, and hardly any time for relaxation. You go from seven A.M. to eleven P.M. every day. It's very military. Players grab naps in their college dorm rooms whenever they can, eat and sleep when they're told to, then wake up and do the exact same thing the following day. I wasn't the first NFL player to despise the process or to resent not being treated like a grown man. I wasn't excited about being back in a dorm, either. The rooms were small, and players shared living space and bathrooms, which got pretty rank. Under these conditions, players form a bond—just like in the opening scenes of *Remember the Titans*. In the movie, the coach, played by Denzel Washington, takes his high school team to an obscure location so they can work through their differences and become a team. I could see the value of this process, but early on in camp, I found myself longing for the preseason games and the regular season—if I could hang on till then.

At an early practice, I got some help from several veterans. Safety Tim McDonald showed me how not to push off of defensive backs, which he said would always get me flagged in the NFL. And Jerry Rice—yes, that Jerry Rice, the hero of my college days—told me to stop swinging my arms so much when I ran my routes. I was wasting too much energy on this, and it didn't look good. He showed me how to pump my arms up and down when I left the line of scrimmage and to keep doing this until my route was finished. I couldn't believe he was taking the time to give me advice.

In those first weeks of camp, I stayed very quiet and just observed the older players. I wanted to stay under everybody's radar, at least until I made the team, but that isn't possible when you're a rookie, because sooner or later everyone makes a mistake. Early on at a practice, I couldn't hold on to a pass that hit me right in the hands, and Ken Norton, Jr., was instantly in my face.

"If you expect to make this team," he yelled, "you better start catching the ball!"

Until now, I hadn't realized that Norton's voice was so loud you could hear it all the way down the tunnel leading up to pregame warm-ups. I also hadn't realized how closely he was watching everything at practice. All I knew was that he was a three-time Super Bowl champion (he'd won a pair of rings with Dallas before moving on to San Francisco), the son of a former heavyweight champ, and he'd just screamed at me in front of the entire team, the coaching staff, and all the local media. His words rang so hard in my head that it felt as if the scene were being replayed over and over again on ESPN's *SportsCenter* for the whole world to see.

This guy's won Super Bowls, I told myself as I ran back to the huddle, *and he called me out in front of everyone. I just dropped an easy pass. I'm not gonna last another day unless . . .*

These were common feelings for anyone not drafted in the first round. The pecking order in the NFL was very obvious. The bonus babies—the first-round picks—were given every chance to make it, to start games, and to excel. Everybody else was basically a piece of meat for practice drills. Most third-round picks had the opportunity to stick on special teams, and once the preseason games started, I was given a couple of chances to return kicks, but I never broke one, so I was going to have to make it as a receiver. When I arrived at camp, there was nothing fluid or graceful about my route running. In college, I'd relied totally on power and full-speed ahead, but that wasn't going to work at this level. After I got drafted, David Joseph introduced me to a track coach, who worked with me on getting a quicker start. Since then, I'd brought my number down to about 4.45. I was fast for my size and was already within ten pounds of the weight I play at now, about 225, but that ten-pound difference eventually would give me a lot more strength. I still didn't have the slightest idea about what real receivers do or what a pro-style offense was.

Our entire playbook at UTC held about twenty plays, and it was like a Dr. Seuss book compared with the Niners football encyclopedia. The team has an elaborate system called a "receiver tree," with the trunk of the tree laying out the basic plays and the branches giving you the variations. There were about 120 set plays, not counting every possible option. Learning a new system was like learning a new language, new terminology for every play. Coaches and veterans suggested I try to memorize the plays one at a time, because there were way too many to grasp all at once.

When you're an unknown rookie, the assistant coaches are the most important people at your job. It's like in a hospital, where the doctors make the big decisions but nurses keep the place running. The main person who helped me through the transition from scared kid to pro player was my original 49ers' receiver coach, Larry Kirksey. He fulfilled all the right roles: big brother, coaching guru, and the guy who fought for me in team meetings. It was Coach Kirksey, I later learned, who'd pounded on the team to draft me the previous spring.

"The only way you're going to play a lot," he told me when I arrived at camp, "is if you know exactly what you're doing at all times. And that starts with catching the ball and being ready whenever your number is called."

I got ready by watching film of Jerry Rice and listening to what the TV commentators said he'd done to certain defensive backs. But it was Coach Kirksey staying after practice with me day after day that was the key to my development, along with veteran safety Marquez Pope. The first couple of times Marquez faced me at practice, he flat-out embarrassed me. I went one-on-one with him and couldn't even get off the line of scrimmage. Quez was very physical, and he handled me so easily that I couldn't begin to get away from him. He'd worked with George Chung, a martial arts expert who helps the 49ers with their hand work. After getting thrown to the ground by Quez a few times, I realized I had to do whatever it took, and that meant using my own strength to get a release. I wasn't expected just to run routes and catch the ball but to be as physical and nasty as the people I was competing against. I needed all the muscles I'd been building up over the past five years just to shake off Quez and start my routes.

Coach Kirksey immediately spotted my biggest weaknesses and worked with me every day for two straight weeks, showing me how to make my feet quicker, my hands quicker, and my mind faster. He taught me how to visualize getting off the line with a burst of speed, and then I started to make this happen. I watched a lot of film, studied a lot of technique, and took notes. For a while, my feet and hands and brain seemed to be going in three different directions, and I was so exhausted at night that I went to bed early, but I was gradually learning the 49ers system. I did everything step by step, as if I were starting football over from scratch, and it was a very humbling experience. Coach Kirksey got me through that crucial first training camp, and without him, I might never have made it.

As a rookie, you're not just constantly learning on the practice field, but also absorbing new things in the locker room. Football locker rooms are pretty much the same at every level, a bunch of guys with different backgrounds thrown together and then breaking off into groups. You've got guys who love to tease each other, guys who just want to do their work and go home, and guys who can be both serious and playful. The married guys often hang out together, as do the guys who came into the league at the same time. Guys with neighboring lockers usually get closer, as do guys playing the same position. Watching the Niners that first camp, I was struck by a couple of things.

Because of all the success in the organization, the players were allowed—and expected—to police themselves. If someone came into camp out of shape, he heard about it from the other guys. If somebody made too many mistakes on the field, his ears got burned in the locker room. George Seifert made very few speeches about these things to the team; the veteran players did this for him. The Niners had been winning for a long time, and losing was not acceptable. The players knew exactly what it took to get back to the Super Bowl, and that's all they were striving for. Anybody inside that locker room who wasn't committed to getting another ring was in the wrong place. I'd never been in a championship setting before, and I quickly saw that success really does start with having the right attitude. I also thought that if I could just stick with this team, all their Super Bowl appearances were going to make it much easier for me to play on a champion in the near future.

The second thing I noticed was that pro players didn't just have more talent; they also had a lot more style. It showed in their clothes, their cars, their hairdos, and the way they carried themselves. Although I hadn't developed a style of my own yet, I could see that it was important (except to Steve Young, who had enough skills to look grungy and make it work). People treated you differently if you made a strong statement about your personal appearance. They gave you more respect, because you were letting the world know that you were a success.

XI

NEAR THE END of training camp, offensive coordinator Marc Trestman pulled me aside one afternoon and clapped me on the back. I was going to make the team, he said, but I had to bear down on learning the offense, because I was being penciled in as number 3 or number 4 receiver. His words sent waves of relief through me and lifted a huge pressure from my mind. I was momentarily speechless and paralyzed with gratitude. For weeks, I'd been waiting and wondering when the cut would come, and then I'd have to go back to Alex City and get a job. Now those worries were behind me. I could just focus on football. I'd be on the scout team during practice sessions, chip in on special teams as a kick returner, and study the veterans until I was ready to see action in a real game. I thanked God and realized, for the first time since arriving at camp, just how grueling the past few weeks had been. I phoned my agent and my mother with the news and cried all over again.

Not long after I made the team, a young woman in Alex City called me and said that she'd given birth to an infant boy who was my son. I felt overwhelmed by responsibility. She and I had been together in the past, but I hadn't heard anything about this child until now. Everybody in Alex City knew that I'd signed a deal with the Niners and had survived training camp, so this may have motivated the woman to come forward and contact me. I called David and laid out the situation: I'd become a father, I had major obligations now, and we needed to develop a financial strategy for me to take care of the mother and the son. David told me to slow down, and he began asking all the right questions. The main one was simple and straight-forward: Was I absolutely certain that I was the boy's dad? Why didn't we call the woman and tell her that in order for the child to be covered for health insurance under the NFL's collective bargain-ing agreement, the infant had to have a blood test to determine that I was his father?

This wasn't true, but it was a brilliant maneuver. My instincts about David being the right agent for me were starting to pay off. While I was learning new moves on the field, he was picking up new ones as a sports agent. We got the woman to agree to have the child tested, and the father turned out to be someone else. I was off the hook, but I had been involved with this woman, and I did feel some sense of responsibility toward her and the boy. I gave her some money, and my mother ended up baby-sitting for the child in Alex City from time to time. All this was a great lesson for me. I had some money now and more visibility than in the past. I needed to be much more aware of everyone and everything around me. From the day we'd met, David had laid down the law to me: never go to bed with some-one you can't trust, never have sex without a condom, and never drive after you've had a few drinks. I told him that I'd pay attention now and be more careful.

Throughout training camp, I'd kept a close eye on what jersey num-bers were available. I'd always liked 80, but that wasn't available, for the same reason that I'd liked it: a fellow named Jerry Rice. Brent Jones had 84, Ted Popson 85, J. J. Stokes 83, and nobody was allowed to wear John Taylor's old number 82. For some reason, I didn't like 89, but when Mike Caldwell got cut, I gravitated toward 81. I could never have imagined that a few years later, when I visited celebrities' homes, they'd want me to bring them this numbered jersey as a present.

After we broke camp, I found a small apartment in the Bay Area, which was all I could afford. I was stunned to see how much rent people wanted for a couple of rooms in the Bay area. I was still very lonely, and everyone in my family agreed that it was a good idea for my cousin to come up from Los Angeles and stay with me for a while, just so I could have a companion. The only people I became familiar with outside the Niners' facility those first months were the workers at nearby fast-food spots. I couldn't cook, and neither could my cousin. I wasn't yet schooled in proper nutrition and was trying to save money, so I began eating at McDonald's or Burger King every night. It was convenient and cheap. I was determined to avoid expensive habits and other temptations, and I sent money from every paycheck back home to my mother.

If I joined a teammate for a night out, booze and girls were everywhere, but I usually said no to both (the fatherhood episode had really shaken me up). I didn't drink in college, because I never drank much in high school. After Friday night high school games, guys would get six-packs of beer and start to down them, but this wasn't anything I wanted to be a part of. It's just how I was raised. People accepted it and left me alone. Alcohol can be very dangerous. My 49ers teammate, free-agent return man Vinny Sutherland, got in a car accident while driving intoxicated. It really bothered me that he'd put two other draft picks at risk by driving them after he'd had too much to drink. He jeopardized not only their football careers but also their lives and their families.

As an NFL rookie, I hadn't had much more experience with the opposite sex than I'd had with drugs and booze. For a single guy, the NFL was a totally different world. Women just showed up, and it was a whole new land of opportunity. I don't want to sound crude or politically incorrect, but it's kind of like shopping: you go in and buy something, but when you get to the next store, you find something else that interests you more, so you want to take the first thing back. And what NFL rookie wouldn't want to explore something like this? I had to keep reminding myself that this was the chance of a lifetime and not to let anything, including bad romantic involvements, mess it up.

My biggest personal challenge was not drugs or alcohol or women but all the mood swings I went through during the season. I was constantly up and down, and it was enough for me to try to deal with this, let alone anyone else. I've often wondered if I will ever be able to find a female who could understand and accept not only what I have to do to get ready to play football but how the game affects my personality. My intensity is something I was born with, and I can't just get rid of it. Being a competitive professional athlete has only deepened this within me. If I ever won a Super Bowl ring, I might become a little less intense—but I might be just as hungry for a second one. Throughout the season, I ache with the desire to win, and I'm usually not lovey-dovey when I come home from practice or when I'm sore from the last game or focused on the next one. My family and my agent know this about me, and they've learned to leave me alone.

The biggest release from tension and the most fun I had that first season came on Tuesdays, the traditional day off for NFL players, when I'd slip off to a recreation center in Oakland to play pickup basketball. As had always been the case, hoops were my escape, my solace. I felt most at home on the hardwood floor. The 49ers never knew I was balling like this, and I didn't think they'd care about a third-round draft choice getting in a little basketball. With the training facility, the rec center, and McDonald's, I kept a very low profile.

When I wasn't practicing or memorizing the playbook, I'd catch myself looking around the spacious 49ers locker room, which seemed bigger than my high school gym. At UTC, we used old wooden lockers set inside a cramped and musty room. The Niners locker room was done up in scarlet and gold, bright and airy and full of open space, designed to accommodate a roster full of strong personalities. My locker was right next to Jerry Rice's. A few feet away was Steve Young, who came off as something of an absentminded genius. Steve never brushed his hair, always wore grunge-style clothes, and said goofy things to me right from the start. I was too shy to approach JR, but I rarely took my eyes off him and listened to every word he said.

I'd wander through the hallways at Niners headquarters and see mementos from each of the team's five Super Bowls and pictures of the heroes: Montana, Lott, Rice, and Young. But by the fall of 1996, no one on the team seemed truly at ease, because it had been almost two years since DeBartolo had hoisted a Lombardi Trophy. The standard of winning was so high that even a rookie like myself could pick up on the whispering among the staffers about who might take a hit if we didn't win in 1996. Change was in the wind, and it was going to affect everyone, including me.

Steve Young's best friend on the 49ers, all-pro tight end Brent Jones, was a couple of stalls to my left. It was clear from their talk that most of the offensive veterans were unhappy with the conservative play selection under the defensive-minded George Seifert. George rarely spoke to his players during the workday, but his name was constantly brought up on my side of the locker room. Back in college, I'd heard players complain about coaches, but most of it was just whining about the length of practice or the heat. This was different and much more serious. I listened now in silence, acting as though I wasn't shocked by their candor.

Defensive players ruled the roster. Near my locker were the muscular defensive linemen Bryant Young and Dana Stubblefield. They didn't say a lot—in public—but had subtle and not so subtle ways of letting you know if you screwed up. Sometimes, they made offhand remarks in your direction. Other times, they yelled in your face. The weight room was their domain, where they would corner you and set you straight. This area was custom-built for the players' every need, and I lifted there every day.

There was a lot of talk about people's personal lives, both inside and outside the locker room. When I showed up, people whispered that Steve Young was gay. A few years later, there were rumors that his quarterback replacement, Jeff Garcia, was also gay. I ignored all of these rumors. Unless I've seen something like that with my own eyes, I don't pay any attention to what people are gossiping about. I know that Steve is happily married, with a beautiful wife and two children. I've met Jeff's girlfriend; they're totally in love. Yet those were the two main questions I got asked all the time after I joined the team: Is Steve Young gay? Is Jeff Garcia gay? I tell people it's not worth responding to, and if that doesn't satisfy them, I suggest that they go ask the people involved. Things like this taught me not to pay any mind to the totally stupid rumors that fly around famous athletes. The more famous you are, the more idiotic they get.

The two stalls bracketing the entrance to the bathroom, showers, pool area, and hydrotherapy tubs were occupied by linebacker Ken Norton, Jr., and strong safety Tim McDonald. Their positioning in the locker room symbolized their jobs on the field. Nothing got past these guys, and ditto for cornerback Merton Hanks, who was located near McDonald. As if that weren't enough, you couldn't get to the equipment room, the players' lounge, or the main doors to the practice field without getting eyeballed or heckled by the huge offensive linemen. I was sure that was why all-pro tackle Harris Barton and guard Jesse Sapolu were situated right by these doors, while tackle Derrick Deese held court at his locker next to the players' lounge. The whole place felt rigged to teach a rookie how to behave now that he was a 49er. You were expected to work your butt off, to control your emotions, and to show respect for the veterans. You weren't expected to call attention to yourself except by what you did on the field, at least during your first season. You were expected to take the game as seriously as these Super Bowl champions did.

Even if these men hadn't been famous football players, it would have been difficult for me to talk with them. I already had a reputation for being withdrawn and set off by myself. I couldn't open up to anybody. While the other guys were eating in fancy restaurants, I was going solo at Burger King. While they were having a drink together, I was playing basketball by myself. While they were talking with their wives or girlfriends, I was thinking more about my mother and my grandmother, who was becoming too old to work at the Russell Mill. Her health was failing, and everyone in the family was concerned. Her memory seemed to be leaving, and her behavior was getting erratic.

I knew that others on the team saw me as distant, but I didn't know what to do about it. Because of my background, it always had been hard for me to trust anybody or get close to outsiders. One time, I asked my mom about this on the phone, and she said, "It's just how we were brought up. We never had any say-so in how things were, and we had to keep our mouths closed. We had a lot of fear over this as we got older. My brother, Victor, was so afraid of Grandma that he used to sit in a corner and not move or make a sound. All this affects you when you become an adult. I've had to work on myself about this. You want to be alone and by yourself, but people don't understand this. It's not that you don't like others, but we were raised in isolation, like we had a shield around us. You have to learn to come out of this and to interact with the world in a new way. It takes time to figure out who you really are.

"I've been called moody, too, because sometimes I just don't want anything to do with others. The more popular you get, the more you're going to have to deal with this. Other people aren't going to understand the way you act, so be prepared for criticism."

XII

ONE PROBLEM THAT HAD STARTED in college was only getting worse in San Francisco. My feet were constantly sore from all the route running at camp and from the pounding they took to keep me in shape. As I put on more weight and put more pressure on my feet, the pain went deeper into my muscles and bones. My feet eventually hurt so bad that I would not get out of bed in the middle of the night to go to the bathroom, because the pain was too great; it took at least fifteen minutes of standing up and moving around to get the blood circulating and ease the pain, and I never wanted to be up that long in the night. So I'd just lie in bed and try to ignore the other pain that was building up in my bladder.

I took some real shots in those first preseason games, when they let me play on special teams on kickoffs, getting smacked around by defensive backs and linebackers who were trying to make their own teams. I didn't mind that, because I just wanted to be on the field. Nothing was perfect, but everything was moving in the right direction. I started the season on the bench and was certain I'd be there throughout the year.

Wrong again.

Through rookie camp and the first part of the 1996 season, my best friend on the team was the receiver the 49ers had taken to be the heir apparent to Rice, former UCLA star J. J. Stokes. The 49ers had given up two first-round picks in a 1995 trade with Baltimore to move up and select JJ. At the time, it looked as if the rich had just gotten a lot richer, but injuries slowed JJ from the start. And despite his obvious physical talent, he was having a tough time matching up with the Rice legend. Some people wondered if his heart was really into eventually taking over Rice's job. Watching JJ, I felt lucky, because nobody expected anything out of me, and the pressure was all on him. He and I were opposites. He was all polish, L.A. smooth, a natural ladies' man who'd been raised very comfortably in the San Diego area. While he was used to the good things in life, I didn't buy them even when I could afford to. But we both had quiet personalities and were soon hanging out together during the day, even though his job was up for grabs.

In San Francisco on October 20, 1996, the Niners played their seventh game of the season, against the Cincinnati Bengals. Until now, I'd only been on the field in garbage time, catching a total of three passes for just a few yards. I was a third- or fourth-string receiver with little chance of seeing more action, but no football season is ever predictable. In the week leading up to October 20, JJ broke his wrist at practice, and I was suddenly scheduled to start. This reminded me of what had happened in high school when Ricky Morgan got hurt and I took his place at Benjamin Russell High. In college, Buddy Nix came down to scout Derek Hall and ended up recruiting me for UTC as well. Now I was getting my chance at the highest level of football. Would I rise to the occasion or fall back into obscurity?

The Bengals game was almost a complete disaster for me. In the first quarter, we fell behind 7 to 0 but were starting our first good drive of the day. Steve Young threw me a pass, and I'd run for 17 yards when their free safety, Bo Orlando, stripped the ball from my hands and knocked it loose. Bengals linebacker James Francis recovered it on our 41-yard line. Walking back to the sidelines, I heard boos and catcalls directed at me personally from about 67,000 people. If I'd thought that Ken Norton, Jr.'s voice was loud after I'd dropped a pass in practice, I was now getting it from tens of thousands of angry fans. By the time I reached our bench, I felt as if I'd shrunk a few sizes inside my uniform. I wanted to run off and hide, but there was nowhere to go. On the sidelines, no one said much to me, and I felt like the invisible man.

Things quickly got worse. Five plays after my fumble, the Bengals marched in for another touchdown, taking a 14-to-0 lead. They soon scored again to go up by 21. By now, everybody on the 49ers was getting booed, but my mistake had started the collapse. I'd let down the team, and the game looked over before halftime. Only twice before in 49ers history had we been this far behind and come back to win.

During the second half, we cut into their lead, and I kept praying for a shot at redemption—just a chance to make up for my blunder, just one more ball thrown my way. In the third quarter, Young took me aside and told me that I had to get open, because with JJ out of the game, the Bengals secondary was putting all their attention on Jerry Rice. Nobody was going to be worried about me—until I made them aware of my presence on the field. If the Bengals could take Rice out of the game through double or triple coverage, we were in deep trouble, but if I could shake free, Steve wanted to get me the ball.

"If you don't step up now," he said, "it's going to hurt the team."

Early in the fourth quarter, with the Niners trailing by seven, Young threw me a deep pass, but it was too far, and I couldn't get under it. I was disappointed all over again but when I got back to the huddle, Steve said he wanted to try the play once more.

He waited until the next series and then sent me on the same route, deep and toward the sideline. When I saw the defender playing me on my outside shoulder, I adjusted and dipped to the inside, even though that wasn't the route I was supposed to run. Steve saw me, made his own adjustment, and threw to where I was going. The ball was coming down toward me, right into my hands. I raised my fingers, blocked out everything else, and used all my concentration to focus on catching it first—and then preparing to get hit. But the hit didn't come, and I kept running and running all the way into the end zone, a 45-yard reception and touchdown that brought us to within a point of the Bengals, 21 to 20. The extra point would tie the game.

When I reached the end zone with the ball, I remembered that my mom was watching the game down in Alabama, and she was all I could think about. Something inside me kicked in that had never kicked in before. More than anything else, I wanted my mother to see me on TV. I wanted her to know that I'd scored and that it was time for us to celebrate, all of us, my mother, my brother and sisters, myself, my grandmother, and everybody who'd watched me come up through the ranks. Something took over my body, and I began to dance in a way they do in Atlanta called the "bank head bounce dance," where you move your shoulders back and forth. I knew this dance would keep the camera on me a little longer, my mom would get to see me celebrating, and that would make her feel good.

This was the first time Terrell Owens stepped aside and somebody else came forward: "TO," the professional football player and entertainer who'd just been waiting for his chance to emerge. He'd gotten his shot at redemption and made the most of it, and he didn't want to hide anymore but to show his feelings and his moves to the world.

Later in the fourth quarter, the Niners drove deep into Bengals territory, and this series, Steve Young decided to run the ball instead of pass. He was a great running quarterback, but he'd been dinged up earlier in the game and was not at full strength or speed. He was coming around the left end, where I was lined up on the outside, and I saw Bengals cornerback Jimmy Spencer charging in for the tackle. I lowered my head and rolled him, the way I love to roll people when I'm throwing a block in football. He folded up right in front of me, clearing the way for Steve to blow past and run 15 yards into the end zone. The extra point made it 28 to 21, and the 49ers had completed one of their three greatest comebacks ever.

After the game, Steve was happy with me for catching the tying touchdown pass, but he may have been happier about the block I threw that sent him in for the final score. I guess I'd already earned a reputation for toughness among the veterans on the club, but until now, nobody had talked about it. I'd earned that reputation by blocking downfield, running crisp routes, catching passes over the middle, breaking tackles, and plowing over people after I'd caught the ball. I had a mean streak on the field, and my teammates were starting to take notice.

"To me," Steve told the *San Jose Mercury News* after the game, "Terrell Owens is the kind of kid who, if you say something he doesn't like, he'll punch you in the face. He's got a nastiness to him like John Taylor, and I like it."

Taylor had been a key part of the 49ers teams that won four Super Bowls in the 1980s (Dwight Clark and Freddie Solomon were the first great receiver combination for the Niners, followed by Jerry Rice and John Taylor). Any comparison between Taylor and me was good news, and I was amazed by Steve's comments. My intensity on the field and my standoffish qualities in the Niners locker room had let people know that I may not have been the easiest person to talk to, but I was tough enough to play in the NFL.

A lot of receivers don't like going over the middle or getting hit, but I just see it as part of the game. Legendary offensive line coach Bob McKittrick told me something before he passed away, words I will always keep close to my heart. He said I was one of the most physical receivers he'd ever coached, especially blocking downfield. The Niners had plays where I'd pull up and block linebackers, even take on a defensive end to slow him down at the line. Defensive backs are another story. I like to abuse them every chance I get. We're usually in a situation where the receivers are exposed while trying to catch the ball, so defenders try to knock us out at any opportunity, but you can also see me cracking back on linebackers on screen plays or taking out a DB on a long run. I love going downfield and clearing space for the ball carrier, and teammates love seeing that when the tape is reviewed the following day. It's fun to wipe out an unassuming defensive player—and the bigger, the better.

The hardest hit I've ever been involved with came when I took out Mike Jones, a linebacker with the Saint Louis Rams at the time, while we were running a screen. I peeled back and blocked him, and he never saw me coming. I can still feel that one, and it was good. The perfect hit usually means that the hitter barely feels a thing, as if you go right through the other guy. My next-hardest hit came on a reverse, but this time I ran head-on into several huge linemen. For years, Bill Walsh used star receivers on the reverse, to keep the defense honest. It spreads the defensive backs out, ensures that the linebackers can't drop too far back into coverage, and sets up all sorts of play-action possibilities for later in the game. Plus, it makes opponents study more tape. But I'm not a running back, and that reverse left some bruises.

That first Sunday against the Bengals, I caught four passes for 94 yards and the touchdown. Fullback William Floyd told the press that I reminded him of himself when he was a rookie because of the fire I showed on the field. Offensive coordinator Marc Trestman told the *Mercury News* that after I fumbled in the first half, he was determined to get me the ball again.

"Like in basketball," he said to the paper, "if a young shooter misses, you've gotta keep giving him the ball. I had no thought about saying, 'We can't throw to Terrell anymore.'"

I called my mom right after the game, and she said that she'd seen me dancing in the end zone and had really enjoyed my show. My dream, she reminded me once again, was starting to come true.

My performance against Cincinnati kept me in the starting lineup for the rest of the year. I ended up making the most starts (ten) by a 49ers rookie receiver since Gene Washington's fourteen back in 1969, starting more games than Niners greats John Taylor,

Dwight Clark, and Jerry Rice. After catching the ball, I busted a couple of long runs and finished the season with thirty-five catches for 520 yards and four TDs. A few football experts besides Steve Young were now comparing me to John Taylor, and the San Francisco media were even learning to pronounce my name correctly ("TER-rell," not "Ter-RELL"). Still, in the pecking order of the 49ers, a Super Bowl contending team, I was way down on the list when Steve Young made his reads and checked off his receivers. When it came time for the playoffs that first year, I was pretty much forgotten. Jerry Rice wanted the ball, especially in the postseason, and JR had a way of getting what he wanted. Steve always seemed to go to his other receivers before he even thought of glancing at me, and I could only look forward to next year. My time still hadn't come.

XIII

AFTER THE SEASON, I went home to Alabama feeling that I was starting to figure out life in the NFL—and what was wrong with it. After Eddie D. left, I had issues with how the players were treated by management. The Niners had been a model franchise across the league for years, but I wasn't impressed with the hours they made us sit in meetings and look at film from old games. A lot of people get put on a pedestal for the "countless hours of film study" they put in, but that never meant much to me. I was always best as a freelance, make-it-happen-now sort of player, as I'd shown with the TD catch against the Bengals. The greatest pass Joe Montana says he ever threw, for the touchdown to John Taylor that won Super Bowl XXIII against Cincinnati in the final seconds, came off a broken play, when both backs lined up wrong and his receivers ran the wrong route. To the casual fan, it looked as scripted and beautifully executed as any other play, but it was their ability to improvise that made things work. This happens all the time in the NFL, but they still want you to study more film. The first day or two after a game, we look at film and reflect on what we're seeing. Receivers watch the game with other receivers and their coaches, and the same is true for the linebackers and other parts of the team. The coaches make their comments, but it always boils down to scoring touchdowns and helping the team win.

Football, I was discovering, was more or less a nine-to-five job. Every weekday except Tuesday, we went to meetings from around nine A.M. until nearly eleven A.M. Then we practiced, ate lunch, and returned for more meetings. I hated the routine and didn't think we should even be at the facility past one P.M. We could have easily finished up by one, but the team always wanted to keep tabs on us. What better way to do that than scheduling more meetings? Just think how much happier we'd be and how much fresher our minds would be if we didn't waste all that time indoors. Why should the veterans have to suffer through all this just because the young guys need to learn it? What exactly can you teach Jerry Rice in a team meeting in the fifteenth year of his career?

As a rookie, I asked JR how he managed to stay alert in meetings while seeing the same plays run year after year after year. He just shrugged. I know they want the repetition to sink in and practice to make perfect, but I struggled with all of this from the day I hit the league. I could sleep for twelve hours and walk into one of these sessions and instantly doze off. Sometimes, I did. Each week, we get playbook inserts, but it's always basically the same stuff, with different variations and names. I could go crazy flipping through the pages of our playbook one more time.

I could also go crazy thinking about fines in the NFL. Getting a $5,000 fine because your jersey is not tucked in, when they're asking guys to play at the highest level of football, is ridiculous. You're out there hitting, you're focused, and who in his right mind is thinking about his clothing? It's just a way for the people with the boss-man mentality to get into our pockets and use the power they have over us, a way of keeping us down. Your first offense is $5,000. Your second is $10,000. That's some people's weekly check (and others' yearly salary). I've had fines rescinded because we appealed, but appealing a nuisance punishment is annoying.

Coaches have to review every situation before someone gets a fine. And here the players are, supposedly giving our all for the coaches, putting everything on the line for the team, but the team doesn't have our backs on this. You're on the field, opponents are grabbing you, and your jersey comes out, and you race back to the huddle to make something happen on the next play, and they're going to reprimand you for that? I got fined for wearing a white body suit *underneath* my uniform because it has a Nike swoosh on it, and everything in the league is supposed to be Reebok. I got fined for wearing a black wristband when everything in the NFL is supposed to be white. Why does it have to be white? Why can't it be black? We get fined for putting our initials or nicknames on our wristbands or headbands. Why? Part of the game is trying to be stylish on the field, but they want to take away our individuality and personalities and make us all the same. It's stifling. Just let us play!

I've never sat down with NFL commissioner Paul Tagliabue to talk about fines, but I'd like to. If I ever get an audience with him, here's what I'm going to say: *While I believe in decorum, even dress codes to a certain level, we don't enjoy the game as much because of some of the picky rules. I'll bet that 90 percent of the guys feel the same way I do. They just don't say anything about it. During the course of the game, you've got guys constantly hounding you. You're trying to get into the swing of things, and you've got the offense or defense assignments to worry about. Your coach is also on top of you. And now we're supposed to be thinking about some guy watching because our jersey or part of the uniform has been altered due to playing the game of football? That's absurd.*

You're out there in the middle of something very intense—and that's football. Your dress code rules would be like trying to redo the chalk lines on the field after every play. We mess them up throughout the game, yet you don't see them fixing the field during timeouts. In football, not everything is going to be pretty—or perfect.

I'm cool with the daily fines that you might get for missing practice or other things. These are at the coaches' discretion and reflect the relationship you have with the team staff. I understand that this fine system was put in place to keep people in line, and it's not as if the coaches abuse the system very often. I've always tried to be on time, so if I'm two or three minutes late, I won't get hit with a fine.

They give us guidelines for all that stuff, and I respect this, but I can't respect all the stupid rulings that come from the league.

You can't even wear a bandanna and nothing can hang out of your helmet. Tell me this: What's the difference between a bandanna, and someone wearing dreadlocks reaching down to his shoulder pads? They're just as dangerous. Next, they'll be telling people to get hair-cuts all at a certain length. What is a do-rag coming out of the back of your neck going to do? Are we talking about a health issue here? No. Personally, I think they're trying to do whatever they can to keep the brother down. I'm serious. Most of these rules are targeted at black players. White people own the NFL, and black guys start at most of the positions. They don't want us dictating how we want to play. They have to keep control of something, so they try to keep control of us, while asking us to give everything we have to the team. Coaches act like your buddies but sit on the various committees that approve some of these rules. What exactly is their goal, to win ball-games or to enforce a uniform code?

In that sense, the league is a joke.

The NFL seems to focus on everything but what is important: the game itself. Can you imagine somebody going into the NFL offices around the league and demanding that everyone has to wear a certain tie every day? Neither can I.

I was also surprised at how the Niners treated us during road games. We'd fly into a city on Friday night, get off the plane, and, ninety minutes later, have curfew at eleven P.M. It was like being back in high school. Major League Baseball doesn't have a curfew. The NBA doesn't, either, but the NFL insists on having one and enforcing it. I understand what they're trying to do, but it's very difficult to relax at the team hotel the night before a game. If you don't go out after the walk-through practice on Saturday but decide to hang out at the hotel, the team won't even let your own family come visit you in your room. If players go down to the lobby just to get out of their rooms, they get hounded by autograph seekers. The security people hired to keep them away from the athletes usually can't hold them back. This is not exactly comfortable, so a lot of players become prisoners in their hotel rooms.

When I arrived in San Francisco, I heard stories about the big-name veterans from previous 49ers teams who paid off the security guards stationed on the players' floors so they could sneak out after curfew and blow off a little steam, but I never saw this happen. Personally, I wouldn't want to be out in public after midnight, and I wouldn't trust anyone who saw me trying to sneak out of the hotel. I also heard stories about coaches who slipped extra cash to security personnel to spy on team members, so it cuts both ways. The best thing to do is to hunker down in your room and try to get some rest.

No matter how early the curfew or how closely they watched us at the hotel, I almost always had a terrible time sleeping before a game. I'm a night owl to begin with, someone who always liked staying up late, whether it was lifting weights in college or watching television or hanging out with friends. So trying to force myself to go to sleep at ten or eleven never worked. I was rarely anxious about the upcoming game, just wide awake with nothing to do. Sometimes, I'd talk on the phone with friends or call a member of my family and talk or pray. Sometimes, I'd watch a movie or read. Other times, I'd just think or pray alone. I often got only three or four hours of sleep, because I do everything at my own pace, with my own little routines. (After games, I always call my mom.) I usually couldn't fall asleep until three or four A.M., which meant that I had to be up at eight to go to the final pregame meetings. I can remember suiting up on just three hours' sleep, but those near-sleepless nights led to some of my best games.

I was also surprised by all the trash-talking defensive backs in the NFL. They called me an "m-f" this and "m-f" that and said things that went way beyond anything I'd heard in college. They'd try everything to slow me down or get my mind out of focus. They told me I wouldn't make the team, talked about my family and about taking the battle off the football field and into the street; some players actually threatening to fight me after the game. From the start, I tried to ignore this, but with these guys, I didn't use the word *sir*.

"Just keep talking," I'd say to them, "and do whatever you need to do. Obviously, you feel you have to talk to get yourself ready to play."

Then I'd trot back to the huddle, but they'd start up again the moment I returned to the line of scrimmage. I'd never heard so much useless chatter.

The sidelines were a regular circus of trash talking. Everybody was trying to take things to the next level—players, coaches, and even the training staff. So many personalities emerged during a game that it almost felt as if computer geeks had programmed us to be different people. Once we put on those uniforms, we changed into someone else for a few hours a week. Then, when we took off the uniforms, we tried to turn back to normal again, but the adrenaline was still flowing. That's when a lot of guys have gotten into trouble, blowing off steam at a club or bar after a game, trying to come down off that rush. Early on in my pro career, I learned to go home after the game or to call my friends and family. Low key. Out of the limelight with little potential for problems.

Some very nasty stuff goes on in the NFL, which fans never see, such as trying to get to the bathroom during a game. It happened to me in one of my first preseason games, after I'd waited until the defense was on the field and felt it was safe to slip off by myself. The dugouts at Candlestick Park had bathrooms, and the first time I went in there during a game, I was thinking, *What if the ball gets turned over and I have to miss part of the next series?* Sure enough, I'm in the dugout taking care of business, and the other team throws an interception. I hear the crowd going wild, so I pull up my pants, race out, and see Zack Bronson returning an interception down the field. I didn't make that mistake again.

I've heard about guys who had to go so bad they just skipped going to the can and did it on themselves. To distract their opponents, they'd tell the other team what they'd done and that it was going to smell. Now, that's funky.

I wonder if they got a uniform-code fine for that one.

You can't prepare yourself for everything in the league. Early on, I got into a prayer circle before a game. A bunch of veterans were there, including Super Bowl heroes Tim McDonald, Merton Hanks, and William Floyd. Everybody joined hands and started to pray. I'm not someone who can quote you a lot of scripture, but I thought being in this circle was a good way to broaden my spiritual foundation and connect with the other players. This would help get me out of my isolation, and I was fairly certain that the farther I went in the league, the more I was going to have to rely on my faith. I'd been raised with deep feelings about how you behaved and humbled yourself when talking to the Lord, and those aren't things you can just turn your back on.

I don't want to call out the veteran who started it, but in the midst of the praying, he said, "God, you know how we talk on the field," and then he began using cuss words that we hear during a game when the trash talking really takes over. He was swearing to the Lord right and left, up and down. He was talking smack to God, and that did not sit well with me at all, even though I try not to judge people. I've got my own flaws and problems, and I know there are things I've needed to do to clean up my own life, but one thing I don't do much is swear. And I never cuss at the Lord. That was the last time I joined that circle, and ever since then, when it comes to pro football, I pray alone.

XIV

I'D STUCK AS A ROOKIE with one of football's best franchises, I was supporting my family, and I'd even found ways to bring pleasure to my mom. Little did I know that everything on the Niners was about to change, from the head coach (George Seifert gone and Steve Mariucci in to replace him) to the owner to the team's front office to my own role on the field. I could never have imagined that I, and not J. J. Stokes, was about to replace the greatest receiver of all time.

The only real interaction I'd had so far with Jerry Rice came when he made fun of my naïveté regarding life in the NFL—from women to clothes to cars to the cheap food I was eating every night at fast-food joints. He and the other players must have thought I was very country. When JR talked about my clothes, I realized how much I stood out in the locker room, but the truth was that my goals in the NFL weren't like everyone else's. My whole purpose in coming to San Francisco at the beginning of my career was to make money for my family. My mother still needed a decent car, a home of her own, and to stop working at the mill for good. Because of all this, I never felt right that first year buying anything extra for myself or eating expensive food. A lot of other guys in that locker room had once been as poor as my family was, so I didn't mind the good-natured jabs. I laughed along with their jokes but wondered if I could ever be like them or develop a style of my own. I never told them that my mother sewed my clothes down in Alex City and shipped them up to me.

Coach Kirksey had told me to study JR's every move on the practice field, so I did. JR was already the NFL's all-time receiver and was about to break Jim Brown's record for touchdowns. He'd made his reputation by pure hard work. No receiver in football history ever got off the line of scrimmage faster than Jerry Rice, who spent tedious hours in the off-season working on his takeoff speed. His desire for the ball was unmatched, and this combination of speed and hunger was lethal. His face and the intense expression in his eyes defined *competition*.

He and I had some similarities, besides coming from unknown Southern schools. After being drafted by the 49ers, both of us had been thrown into an entirely new world (in 1985, Coach Bill Walsh had traded up to get him in the first round). We both relied on an obsessive workout regimen and pure sweat to succeed. The big difference was that JR showed up when the Niners were in the midst of becoming the team of the '80s. I arrived eleven years later, at the end of the dynasty, when the franchise was on the way down. During his first decade in the league, JR was surrounded by a Hall of Fame locker room: Joe Montana (and later Steve Young), Ronnie Lott, Roger Craig, Dwight Clark, Randy Cross, Brent Jones, Tom Rathman, Matt Millen, Keena Turner, Eric Wright, Ricky Watters, Deion Sanders, Bryant Young, Tim McDonald, Merton Hanks . . . On and on it went, as the team filled holes with free agents like Kevin Greene and Rod Woodson, while becoming the first franchise to win five Super Bowl titles. At one point, the Niners were paying Steve Young $2.5 million as a backup QB. The team had one of the greatest nose tackles in history, Fred Smerlas, playing behind Michael Carter *and* Jim Burt. When I got to San Francisco, many of these players were either gone or on the way out.

At first, I tried to mold my football personality after JR's. Keep to yourself. Do your job. Speak up only when necessary, and lead a very private social life. JR, for instance, never got close to Montana off the field until the very end of their reign together. They connected on the field, though, and I already had some pangs of envy about that. Every receiver on the 49ers and beyond the team wondered what his career would be like playing with Joe Montana. As I studied JR's custom wardrobe, his stylish shoes, and out in the parking lot his group of spotless black sports cars in his custom Flash80 fleet, I tried to imagine what it would be like to have one good car.

JR was like one of his own sleek black Mercedes-Benzes. Smooth. Top of the line and powerful but so finely tuned you could barely hear the engine. He was also as moody as they come—another trait he and I share. Part of this moodiness had to do with the marathon length and the demands of the NFL season. There's so much on your mind that you can't be Mr. Cool every day to everyone around you. And the more your status climbs, the more people pull on you to please them. It took me a while to understand why a lot of veteran players hid on the other side of the 49ers building, hanging out in a staffer's office and eating lunch behind closed doors in order to avoid the media. They were sick of reporters and TV cameras. Imagine if a real estate agent or a dentist got swarmed each day over the noon hour by a pack of media types asking a series of repetitive and often pointless questions. I know that journalists are part of the entertainment aspect of the NFL, but they can make people very moody. Long ago, JR had learned to shut down and do his talking elsewhere.

But sometimes even he opened his mouth and suffered the consequences. I heard about the time, after he'd edged out Montana as MVP of Super Bowl XXIII against the Cincinnati Bengals, when he complained in an interview that he wasn't getting the kind of endorsements other Super Bowl MVPs had. The interview had come on a bad day, and JR was just trying to be honest, but nobody criticized the great Montana and got away with it. Somebody had to pay for this "insult." The truth was that he was not a white quarterback riding off into the sunset with a boatload of national endorsements based on that MVP award. He was a black man still trying to gain equality in the realm of commercial success, yet the damage had been done: Jerry Rice was an ungrateful crybaby.

Not.

Once the season started, there were many times when I stood on the sidelines and could see JR getting angry because he wasn't getting enough touches on the field. He wanted the ball thrown his way and to make plays. What else, besides catching the football, was he getting paid to do? His body English conveyed that as he came to the line of scrimmage, but he didn't complain about it out loud. He kept quiet and did his job—most of the time. Back in 1992, the 49ers were playing Atlanta, and Steve Young hadn't once thrown the ball to JR during a critical scoring drive. He hadn't even looked his way. After the touchdown, JR ran over to the sidelines, headed straight to a table holding cups of Gatorade, and knocked the whole thing over, juice flying everywhere.

"I ain't no motherfucking decoy!" he'd shouted, loudly enough for players, coaches, and many fans to hear.

The incident had become part of his legend and what made him the best ever. When you came into camp with the 49ers as a rookie receiver, you heard this story more than once. And you understood that following this outburst, Young made a point of getting him the ball more. His tantrum had worked.

I didn't really understand this story yet, because I was just trying to get into a game and get my hands on the ball. It was only after I made a few catches in the preseason, and then a few more after the regular season began, that the meaning of this incident sank in for me. The better you get at a team sport, the more you want to contribute to the team's success. Once I stopped worrying about surviving with the Niners and started drawing a paycheck each week, I wanted my hands on the ball more so I could make things happen. Some people call this instinct selfishness or not being a team player. I call it wanting to win, and I saw it burn inside Jerry Rice, and I felt it burn inside myself, and it's a natural process that comes with building your confidence. I can't speak for other positions on the football field, but when you're a wide receiver, this is an important and complicated issue. Linemen can block on every play, and defensive players can always try to make tackles or cover their men. Quarterbacks handle the ball on each down, and running backs usually get their carries during the course of a game. Wide receivers are dependent on many different things—the game plan, the down and distance, the play that's called, the defensive set, the quarterback's attitude and vision, the ability to get open versus another receiver's ability to get open—before they have the chance to touch the ball.

Frustration comes with the territory. It's a huge part of being a wide receiver, even a great one like Jerry Rice, because you aren't going to get the ball that often, not even if you're consistently getting open. Hall of Fame receivers are going to get angry sometimes and throw Gatorade because they don't feel they're doing enough to help the team. They're going to blow up and scream at whoever is standing in front of them. That's how it is when you hate to lose. Watching JR, I was just starting to sense how much he was dealing with as the team's best receiver and how much he wanted to help the team when it was no longer winning Super Bowls.

But I had no idea how much all this would affect me in the future, after he was gone.

XV

FIGURING OUT LIFE back in Alex City was tougher than under-standing the NFL. Before I'd gone to training camp in 1996, David Joseph and I had done a one-year deal with Nike that gave me a small amount of merchandise and unlimited football shoe wear, gloves, and so on. The contract also covered certain athletic apparel. At the end of my first season, Nike wanted to extend the contract, but David thought that before we made this agreement, he should con-tact Russell Athletic. At that time, Russell still had its headquarters and most of its operations and sales divisions in Alexander City (some of these are now in Atlanta). I'd been born in Russell Hospi-tal and attended Benjamin Russell High School, I'd worked at the Russell Mill part-time as a box maker, and my family had labored inside those walls for decades. David felt that it would be natural for me, as an NFL player, to have a connection with Russell Athletic Gear, and I was excited about this possibility.

He telephoned their marketing department and said that before we signed a deal with Nike, we wanted to talk to Russell about building a long-term relationship. I was a homegrown young talent, he told them, and this could be a great opportunity for both Russell and me. They said they didn't do deals with individual athletes but to keep in touch. David soon planned a trip to Alex City and called his contact in the marketing department. The man told him to come by his office, and they set up a time for the meeting. David showed up and waited for the Russell representative to see him. He waited and then waited some more. A couple of hours passed, but the man never showed up or sent out any message. He and David never spoke again.

When I got back to Alabama that first off-season, I heard that some of the same guys who used to bully me were now jealous of my success. They talked about this through their friends, and some other people told me about this noise, but they knew better than to come around and challenge me at this point. I was not a skinny kid anymore, not anyone's victim. All that weightlifting had left its mark on my physique, and you could see my muscles through my clothes. The old Terrell was gone and had been replaced by the man who was becoming TO. That kind of thing is bound to threaten some folks, just as success will always turn certain people off. Several of the local bullies were ripping a few of my old high school athletic buddies for staying close to me, since I'd moved on to better things. You'd think the bullies would have let all this go, but they always need someone to put down and hate. It allows them to keep feeling bad about their own lives. They could have gone on and bettered themselves in some way, but most of them stayed on the same old path, messing up workwise or hanging out on the streets. They're right back where they started—and looking for somebody else to pick on.

After my rookie season, I didn't go back to Alex City as much anymore. I wanted to stay true to my roots, but life was getting more complicated, and I wasn't comfortable staying in the town for long periods of time. A handful of people there meant a lot to me, but most couldn't understand the journey I was taking through the NFL or how much bigger the world was outside Alex City. Success is a tricky thing, especially when you're from a small town where you grew up knowing practically everybody. I remember hearing how Joe Montana always felt that he could never win regarding his hometown in Pennsylvania. If he showed up for an event, he was grabbing all the attention for himself. If he was too busy to go, he was ignoring his roots. Sometimes, it's better just to stay away.

Early in 1997, my grandmother's health seriously began to decline. Going to doctors was something else she didn't believe in, and it was always difficult to get her to take care of herself. After working at the Russell Mill for twenty years, she was no longer able to do the sewing jobs, so they gave her the lighter task of putting labels on products. She was only two years away from retirement and she was in the early stages of Alzheimer's and rapidly getting worse. My mother tried to care for her from her own home, but that was more than she could handle. My mom still had teenage children at home and was working the ten P.M. to six A.M. shift at the mill, yet she'd watch her mother all day before going to her job at night. When she was away, Grandma would climb out of bed and leave the house on foot, trying to walk back to her old home, where she'd lived for almost fifty years. It was the place she knew best and the only place she wanted to be. It was also one of the few places she could remember.

Her memory was fading, and sometimes she didn't even know our names or that we were her relatives. It was terrible to see what was happening to her as the Alzheimer's took hold, awful to see her losing control. I thought that I'd had to be strong before this in order to crack a roster in the NFL, but now my family got a whole new lesson in strength and love. It was very good to see the flood of affection that we all had for my grandmother. My younger brother, Victor, once had been very frightened of her, but now his love for her just poured out; one day, he got a tattoo of her name on his right shoulder. I'd grown up resisting all of her rules and restrictions, but now they were helping me ward off certain temptations when I was far away from home and had money to spend. She'd grounded me in trusting in God and taking care of myself instead of relying on other people, and I was very grateful to her for that.

When I heard the stories about what she was going through with the disease and what this was doing to my my mom, I'd sit on the phone with my mother and cry and pray. Alzheimer's takes away your memory, your mind, and your dignity, a horrible thing for any person to face in old age. I thought of all the times in college in Chattanooga or as a rookie in San Francisco when I'd call home and speak with my grandmother. She'd pray with me on the phone and give me all of her support when I needed it the most. Now I wanted to do the same for her. Wherever I traveled, I took her picture, tucked inside a Bible, with me.

As usual, it was my mother who carried the heaviest load. She'd go out looking for my grandma in the middle of the night and track her down and bring her back home. Then she put dead-bolt locks on all the doors to keep her inside. Grandma had to wear diapers and needed to be closely monitored. Sometimes, she had to be physically restrained. My mother couldn't sleep much during the day, because she had to watch her and then go to work at night to pay her bills. She couldn't leave for the mill until my grandmother was in bed and all the doors had been locked down.

When my mother and I prayed about all this on the phone, her faith never wavered. "You have to believe in yourself and in God, and that will take you a long way," she always said. "Our blessing will come, Terrell. Don't ever forget that. Our blessing will come."

If she said this to me once, she said it to me a hundred times. She'd been telling me that for years and encouraging me to live my life every day with that conviction. I went into the 1997 season with those words ringing in my head. If I played well this year and the next, I was due for a new contract, and this time it would not be for the minimum rookie salary. If I could truly establish myself as an NFL player, I could command more money from the Niners or another team and have more for my family and all of its growing needs. My mother was clearly getting worn out from her job at Russell, and with my grandmother's situation calling for more and more care and my younger brother and sister wanting to go to college, we were going to need a lot more funds.

At the mill, my mom had dealt with racial issues in the past, and this had forced her to change jobs there and do things she didn't really want to do. I didn't want her to spend another minute inside that plant; I wanted her out of there for good, and I was the only one with the ability to generate the money to make all of these things possible. That's what I was aiming for now as I entered my sophomore year in the league. I was never playing football just for myself, and when I returned to camp in the summer of 1997, I was a man on a mission, but even that wasn't enough. It would take new opportunities that nobody saw coming—and the kind of blessing my mother had always talked about.

XVI

IN THE 1997 SEASON opener at Tampa Bay, defensive lineman Warren Sapp grabbed JR from behind and brought him down hard. The replays show Jerry's knee sliding off its joint and not sliding back on. Steve Young went down that same game with a concussion. Suddenly, J. J. Stokes and I had to step up and fill in for JR. The Niners had not been without him for a meaningful game for a dozen years, and his absence felt like a hole on the team. It was a strange sight the first time he walked back into the locker room after his surgery, hobbling on crutches. This was a very humbling thing to see. The game can be taken away from you with one hit, no matter how durable you may seem or how much you've accomplished. But it was inspiring, too. JR had taken such good care of himself during the off-seasons that he'd never missed a game due to injuries.

Because he'd always been so healthy, many players copied the things he did. In games, I'd patterned my routes after his—his burst off the line in the first five yards was legendary—but nobody was like him during practice. When I first showed up in San Francisco, he was still adjusting to the transition from Montana to Young, three years after the fact. While the rest of us stood on the sideline talking about movies or women or whatever, he'd be off with assistant equipment manager Ted Walsh (no relation to Bill), catching passes from him. JR always wanted to be in motion on the practice field, and he'd picked Walsh as the thrower because Ted was left-handed, just like Steve Young. JR had spent hours in the training room, nursing bruised shoulders or icing sore hamstrings, but regardless of how dinged up he was, the team always could rely on him to play—until now.

The Niners needed me again, just as they had in the Cincinnati game a year earlier when JJ got hurt. Throughout the 1997 season, a new door opened up in front of me, as had been happening ever since I began playing football. Under coach Steve Mariucci, I started fifteen of our sixteen games and led the Niners in receptions, with sixty for 936 yards. My 15.6 yards a reception was best on the team, and I ranked ninth in the NFL with eight TD catches. I became the first player other than JR to lead the team in receptions since 1988 and extended my streak of catching at least one ball to twenty-six games. People on the team were starting to whisper that maybe the time had come to think about moving JR out of San Francisco for the new receiver on the block. This talk startled even me, because it seemed that he would be a 49er forever, but everything in the National Football League is about change.

When I started playing with the Niners, I'd look around the stadium before the opening kickoff and see all the fans wearing the red-and-white-striped 49ers jerseys. People do this in every NFL city, but the last fifteen years of success in the Bay Area had made it a huge ritual in San Francisco. I'd spot a few number 16s left over from the Montana era and some number 8s signifying Steve Young, but the stands were crammed with number 80 jerseys. JR's number was the clear favorite, not just because he was a great player but because he was the bridge between the first Niners Super Bowls and the later ones. He was the franchise in the eyes of the paying public, and seeing all these 80s made a huge impression on me.

People on TV and radio talk a lot about the game, and they like to criticize anyone who makes a mistake, but many of them are not fans of one team. They get paid to offer commentary, whether they have anything to say or not, and a lot of times they don't. They just blow smoke into the air. They don't really care if you win or lose, but they always seem to have more to say if you lose. The hometown fans are the ones with true loyalty and passion for you and your football team. They're the ones who buy the jerseys and wear them to the stadium on Sunday and pay their own money for tickets and let their feelings out during the course of a game. They're the heart and soul of football, the ones who've built the NFL's reputation as America's most popular sport—the people you really play for.

Coming into the league in 1996, my first challenge was just to make the 49ers, and I did that. During my first two seasons, the next goal was to prove to myself and others that I could play at this level, and now I'd accomplished that. I was starting to think about doing something more on the field and about showing the fans something that would give them a buzz. I wasn't sure what this might be, but my mind was bending in that direction. I was starting to think about developing a style of my own.

With a new contract on the horizon, I was also starting to spend more money. I bought my mom a new Ford Explorer for Christmas one year and I asked David to drive it down to Alex City and give it to her. He parked the car half a block from her home, tied a red ribbon around it, and then asked her to come out and take a look. She was so overcome with gratitude that she began to cry.

"That can't be my car," she told David. "That can't be my car." She said this about ten times in a row, but it was hers now.

Then I bought her a house in Alex City and asked some friends to haul all her old appliances away, so I could replace them with new ones. My mom had never had central air-conditioning or a microwave oven, but was soon settling into her new home.

One day, while driving my used Ford out of the 49ers parking lot, I found myself staring at Bryant Young's white Mercedes and couldn't get it out of my head.

"Man," I said, "I gotta have one of those."

When I told this to David, I know that he felt he should say something but decided not to. I was still making the NFL's minimum salary, and the car alone took about half of that.

One day after the 1997 season, JR took me aside and told me what he thought I needed to know about becoming a public figure in professional sports.

"TO," he said, "at some point, you're going to have to learn to be politically correct. You know, give in, and give 'em what they want."

I didn't say much in response, but these words bothered me.

This was obviously the way he'd done things—the PC way—and it had worked well for him, but that wasn't how I was raised. I've always had trouble with the idea of not speaking your truth. There's no such thing as borderline lying for me. I'm not going to beat around the bush or tell you what you want to hear. I'm not a politician.

"Nah," I told Jerry, "not me."

He gave me a strange look as if he thought I was kidding, but I wasn't. I wasn't of his generation, and I wasn't going to make my mark on the game the same way he did. I didn't really want to be like anyone else and didn't want to present a false image to the world. I didn't, I suddenly realized, want to be Jerry Rice anymore, no matter how great a receiver he was.

A lot of athletes put on a face and then get caught doing things they shouldn't be doing. The public is always shocked when this happens, because they think they know players by watching them on TV. They don't—unless those players make a point of being honest and speaking the truth. There's always a price to be paid for this—free speech is never really free—and many people don't want to pay it. So they just go along with the crowd and keep quiet. My grandmother had taught me not to keep still when I had something to say, not to shove down my truth, and I believed that she was right.

JR may have said this to me because I was starting to get more attention on the field. He was still drawing double or triple coverage, and that left more time for me to get open and get my hands on the ball. Deep down, this probably bothered him more than he would ever let on, but he was trying to be nice about it. At the same time, his temper seemed shorter than in the past. What was lost in the infamous game in Dallas in 2000, when I stirred up so much controversy by running to the star in the middle of Texas Stadium twice after scoring, was another colossal JR blowup on the sidelines, caught by the network cameras but virtually forgotten the next day. That afternoon, Jeff Garcia was not throwing the ball very well, and at one point, Jerry walked over and got right in Steve Mariucci's face on the sideline.

"Tell him to throw a fucking spiral!" JR kept yelling. "A fucking spiral!"

Mariucci stared at him and looked completely overwhelmed. He'd come out of college football, the former head coach at the University of California, and was used to being in control of things. Now he was in the NFL, trying to manage a team that was on the downslide from its glory years, and the best receiver in football history was screaming at him on television. What was he supposed to do? How do you tell Jerry Rice to please go take a seat on the bench and calm down? Mariucci shifted his eyes back to the field, looking more and more uncomfortable, while JR kept yelling at him. No one on the sidelines—and I mean no one—said a word. In fact, people stood back farther and lowered their eyes. Some were in shock, and nobody wanted to get in the middle of this one. Maybe JR should have thanked me after the game, because his outburst would have been front-page news everywhere had I not danced on the Dallas star.

When JR was angry, nobody messed with him, even though he weighed less than 200 pounds. During the 49ers Super Bowl era, the sack specialist Charles Haley got carried away one day, joking with JR by grabbing him and then holding him from behind around the neck and not letting go. After Jerry broke free, he went into the weight room and got a fire extinguisher and came back at Haley with it. This time, people did get in between them, because they could see how serious JR was.

In 1998, JR returned to health and his position as the Niners' number one receiver, but by now, I'd established myself as number two. Steve Young may have been looking at Jerry first as we came out of our routes, but I was next in line. That season, I caught sixty-seven balls for fourteen touchdowns (second in the NFL) and cracked the 1,000-yard barrier for the first time, with 1,097 yards. The most important game of my career wasn't celebrating on the star in Dallas in 2000 or Sharpie night in Seattle in 2002 or the Niners 2003 playoff comeback win against the Giants or even my record-setting twenty-catch game against the Bears, which put my jersey and cleats into the Pro Football Hall of Fame in Canton, Ohio. At the end of the '98 season, we met Green Bay in the NFC wild-card playoff game, and for me the spotlight was bigger than it had ever been.

In sports, it's not always what you do but when you do it. At the end of the 2003 season, we were playing Philadelphia, and 49ers rookie receiver Brandon Lloyd made one of the most spectacular catches the team had ever seen, diving toward the sidelines and reaching out a hand and pulling the ball out of midair. It looked like a magic trick, with the football coming out of his sleeve. The only problem was that our season was already over, and the game was basically meaningless. His incredible grab got some play on the local Bay Area channels, but that was about all. Timing, as they say, is everything.

The Niners-Packers matchup was the most hyped playoff game that weekend in early January 1999. Green Bay had ruled the NFC for several seasons, going to the last two Super Bowls and winning in 1997. We'd lost the last five times the teams had met, including three times in the playoffs. Steve Young badly wanted revenge against Green Bay's great quarterback, Brett Favre. Green Bay head coach Mike Holmgren had been an assistant in San Francisco under Bill

Walsh before going on to lead the Pack to a championship. The rumor mill was saying that he was now ready to leave Green Bay and wanted to return to San Francisco. If the Packers won this game, it looked as if Steve Mariucci, who was locked in a contract dispute with management, might be replaced by the older and more successful Holmgren. Mooch's job, the players were mumbling in the locker room before the opening kickoff, was on the line, even though we'd gone 12 and 4 in the regular season.

Candlestick Park, which they'd renamed 3Com Park, was electric from the moment we took the field. It was standing-room only, and even the people with seats didn't sit down much that afternoon. The first half, which ended with us trailing 20 to 17, was filled with offensive fireworks, but I was having a miserable game. Green Bay defensive backs Pat Terrell and Darren Sharper had been in my face all day, delivering trash talk and vicious hits from every side. I'd fumbled in the first quarter and dropped a couple of passes that killed a scoring drive. I was a big part of the game story—in exactly the way you never want to be. Many people later told me how the network announcers kept saying again and again how much I was hurting the team. This was especially bad because I knew that down in Alabama and across the South, my family and friends were in front of their TV screens for this game. All the people who'd supported me for so many years—my mother, brother and sisters, my high school teacher Gayle Humphrey, my coaches Willie Martin and Steve Savarese, and even the mayor of Alex City, Don McClellan—were glued to their sets pulling for me. And I was letting them down, too.

In the third quarter, I dropped a touchdown pass that I lost in the sun. I felt even worse than before, if that was possible, but the team was beginning to rally. We tied the game with a Wade Richey field goal, and in the fourth quarter, with only 6:12 left, we took the lead with another three points by Richey. It was 23 to 20 as the Pack began a drive, but then our D-back, Darrell Walker, intercepted Favre, who hadn't thrown a single pick in his last three playoff meetings with the 49ers. With a few first downs, we could wrap up the game, but we couldn't even make one, and it was partly my fault: I dropped a third-down pass that would have given us a first and ten. We punted to the Packers, and this time Favre took them straight down the field, throwing a 15-yard TD to Antonio Freeman. They were up 27 to 23 with only 1:56 on the clock.

After dropping this last pass, I'd rolled around on the ground and started talking to Jesus, I was so upset (that's about as serious as I can get). Steve had thrown a good ball, and I'd put my hands up where I thought it was going to be, but it wasn't there. I swear that I'd looked it dead into my hands and still dropped it. Linemen and other players make mistakes all the time, and you only see this if you watch the game film. When a wide receiver screws up, everybody sees it and knows about it, particularly after they instant-replay your drop half a dozen times from six different angles, while three commentators analyze your mistake. All this comes with playing a big-risk, big-reward position, and I wouldn't want to play anywhere else on the field. Following this drop, I stood quietly on the sideline, feeling totally empty and embarrassed and thinking, *If we lose this game, I'm going to spend the entire off-season knowing that it was basically my fault.* I thought the coach would single out one player for the loss, without naming names, and it would be me, and I felt terrible about this. It wouldn't matter what anyone else said about it, because I would know how much I'd cost the team.

Following the kickoff, we took over on our own 24 with 1:50 left. Steve hit J. J. Stokes for 17 yards and came right back to him for a gain of 9. Young threw for 3 more to fullback Marc Edwards, and with only 53 seconds remaining, Steve tossed an incompletion to Stokes. On the next play, JR caught a pass near midfield and ran for several yards before fumbling the ball away. Game over—or that was how it looked to the nearly 70,000 people in the stands. With boos and insults pouring down onto the field, the referees discussed this call for what seemed like forever, before ruling that JR had not lost possession. The drive was still alive. We called time-out with 27 seconds to go and a third-and-4 on the Packer 41. Steve hit running back

Terry Kirby for 9 yards and threw to Garrison Hearst for 7 more. It was second and 3 at the Packers 25. Steve dropped back to pass again, but this one fell incomplete to JJ.

They hadn't called my number throughout this drive, but that didn't really surprise me. I'd had one of those days that you know is going to haunt you for the rest of your career, if not the rest of your life. When I'd most needed to make the big play, I hadn't been able to get it done. On the last play, the incompletion to JJ, I'd been sent out on a double comeback from a slot formation, which has two receivers going straight to the end zone and then the outside guy (JJ) coming back for the ball. It was basic football when your team is behind and time is running out: get downfield, throw it deep, catch it, and score or at least try to get out of bounds. Not only had Steve nearly thrown an interception to Stokes on this play, but I'd been wide open. If he'd just looked my way—touchdown, and we win.

Back in the huddle, I didn't say a word. Things were too intense and moving too fast, and besides, I wasn't in a position to make suggestions. I was still learning my way in the league, and we had a number of other leaders on the team. I held back, because I thought it was best for the club and because I'd had a very rough day. I didn't have the type of relationship with Steve to tell him—or to plead or demand—to look my way. I was sure that now he'd be focused on Jerry Rice, as he should have been, but this would give me a chance to look for the hole that would leave in the Packers defense. Eight seconds remained on the clock, we were down to what could have been our last play of the season, and I was doing my best to ignore what the off-season would feel like for me. Nobody wants the football year to end this way, and this was going to hurt for months to come.

Steve called "All go," which sends all of the receivers into the end zone. As we broke the huddle, I came up to the line of scrimmage and looked straight past my defender and down the field, instead of toward the middle where I was supposed to run. The goal line was 25 yards away. Young took the ball from center, and while dropping back, he bumped into an offensive lineman and stumbled, nearly falling down. This caused the Packers secondary to hesitate for just a moment, as I sprinted toward the end zone, glancing back to see who had the ball.

I looked up and saw it coming my way, falling down through the air, a perfect spiral over my head. I jumped and reached out for it on about the 1-yard line and felt it come into my hands. I gripped it and felt myself getting hit—hard—and landing on the ground. Before I could even figure out that I'd caught the ball in the end zone, everything around me got crazy. I was instantly mobbed by my teammates, and Steve Mariucci ran over and bear-hugged me. I'd exploded into tears and was hugging the coach back, and everybody was screaming my name and pounding me on the helmet. There were three seconds left in the game, but I don't even remember the extra point or our kickoff. The next thing I knew, I was doing a victory lap around the field with my arms waving above my head and tears running down my cheeks and tens of thousands of people standing and cheering me on. When I stopped running, I called my mother, and she was crying, and my brothers and sisters were yelling, and I broke down all over again.

A day or two later I listened to the tape of San Francisco sportscaster Joe Starkey shouting in the broadcast booth, "Owens! Owens! Owens!" after I caught the ball in double coverage and scored the winning TD. People were now calling this Catch II after the most famous reception in 49ers history: Catch I, by Dwight Clark in the 1981 postseason game against Dallas that sent the Niners into the Super Bowl and on to their first championship. With one grab, I'd entered 49ers lore, redeemed my mistakes from earlier in the game, and made everything between me and the 49ers very good. I was a young receiver coming into his own, and the stories written or broadcast about me the following week were overwhelmingly positive. The veterans on the team were appreciative of my work, and the coaches were elated. My contract negotiations were approaching with everyone in an excellent frame of mind. Then we lost the next week in our second-round game against Atlanta, when Garrison Hearst broke his ankle early on, and everything seemed to change once again. My long years of frustration over never winning a football title at any level were not yet done.

But I had more immediate problems to think about.

XVII

AFTER THE '98 SEASON, I was a restricted free agent, and David Joseph approached the 49ers about my new contract. It was an uncertain time for the franchise. The team was undergoing a front-office change (Carmen Policy and Dwight Clark had left for the expansion franchise in Cleveland), and the new management was just getting into place. John York was now the owner, John McVay was the head of football operations, and Bill Walsh still held power within the organization. Under the NFL/NFLPA's collective bargaining agreement, players were eligible to become restricted free agents after their third accrued season and unrestricted free agents after their fourth. Prior to the end of the 1998 season, restricted free agents couldn't be retained by their team with the franchise designation, or "tag," but going into the 1999 season, the NFL and the NFLPA changed this rule. On the very day in February 1999 that I was to become a restricted free agent, the 49ers put the franchise tag on me, which basically took me off the free agent market. To get me away from the Niners now, other teams would have to give up a pair of first-round draft picks, plus a huge unmatched offer, which was more than they were willing to do. I couldn't test the open market to determine my value in the league. On the one hand, the tag was flattering. It meant that the Niners definitely wanted to keep me, and they'd have to pay me the average of the five highest salaries from the previous season at my position, which at the time was $3.5 million for the year. But it also meant that my agent was basically prohibited from talking with other teams about my future. We hadn't seen this coming, and neither David nor I was happy about it, but there wasn't much we could do.

David started negotiating with John McVay, who was also trying to re-sign J. J. Stokes as an unrestricted free agent. The negotiations were much slower than I expected, in part because of their ongoing talks with JJ and because of the 49ers' ownership situation. The Niners' first offer to me was low, almost the same one they'd offered JJ. They were talking about a multiyear deal with approximately a $3.5 million signing bonus, not what David and I had in mind. We wanted longer terms for more money, and we wanted a substantial signing bonus because that's the only guaranteed money in the NFL. McVay's negotiating style was to stall and grind away until the agent and the player get frustrated. The player would eventually relent, or so McVay believed, and settle for less. Early on, David and I had decided that we weren't going to play the game this way. We held our position through February and all of March, as David and McVay slowly began chipping away at the difference between the two sides. They were making headway, but I was getting upset.

In the NFL, if you're a quarterback, contracts usually aren't that much of an issue. Look at Jeff Garcia. I don't want to take money off anyone's table or away from anybody's family, but a few seasons back, when the 49ers gave Jeff an extension worth $36 million over six years, we all knew two things: the team had probably overpaid him (again), and the rest of us were going to get less when our contracts came up. In Jeff's case, he wasn't even the starter yet. Think about the quarterback position. Most of the physical pounding they take comes from game days. They really don't take a beating in practice, aside from the torque on their shoulders from throwing pass after pass. They drop back, make their reads, and pass. Contrast that with all the running around and hitting that running backs, linebackers, defensive backs, and receivers are involved in nearly every day. Not only are we taking the hits during games, but we're taking much more physical punishment at practice sessions, something the fans never see. And in training camp, we practice twice a day for two and three hours for four straight weeks.

Compare that with baseball, and it's ridiculous. Baseball players go to spring training, but the physical work they do is nothing compared with football players. And NFL players generate billions of dollars in revenues, yet we still have a hard time getting paid. Television rights, stadium rights, merchandising rights, and on and on and on. I understand that the NFL doesn't want its league to turn into the NBA, but many pro football players are definitely underpaid. The NFL is a vast industry, but unless you're a first-round draft pick or a quarterback, you're always looking for more dollars.

Take one of the latest busts the 49ers chose at quarterback, Gio Carmazzi, who followed the "great" Jim Druckenmiller. They gave Gio a $500,000 signing bonus, and he never even played for them in a regular-season game. Half a million bucks not to play. My mother would have had to work two lifetimes at the Russell Mill to make that kind of money. So that's another big problem with NFL player contracts: overpaying guys who haven't performed. And then you get into a situation like mine, where the team doesn't want to pay up when it's time to renegotiate yet will pay someone right off the street all that money just because he's projected by the draft experts at this or that. Gio did play at Hofstra, last time I checked, and now he's out of the league, last time I checked.

I can see management's side. There's a huge risk in signing players to lucrative long-term contracts. Plus, some guys can go soft after taking the big money. But look at the risk we take each time we step on the field. It's basically refereed war games, and we're modern gladiators. This all goes back to what Jerry Rice was telling me about becoming politically correct and learning to say the right things. I'm not JR, and I believe this: if enough players stand up, maybe we can change some of this and pay more to the guys who've actually earned it. Maybe someone will eventually listen.

And the NFL players' union? They sit in on meetings and speak about issues but really only do what will benefit their own pocketbooks. They don't talk about what a contract negotiation does to a young player trying to take care of his family. I was very upset when I went up against the 49ers in 1999, and the negotiations felt to me like a direct assault on my mother, my grandmother, my brother and sisters and other family members.

By 1999, I'd been a starter for three years and had proven myself in the league. More catches than any Niners rookie since Gene Washington in 1969. Played better than the first-round pick the team took as its heir apparent to Jerry Rice, J. J. Stokes. Filled in well for JJ when he got injured. Filled in again for JR when he got hurt. And now I was coming off the biggest catch of my career, but the team was balking at paying me market value. Right or wrong, this brought up many things that had happened to me earlier in life and had happened to my family ever since I'd been a child. It reminded me of being buried in a receiver draft class featuring Keyshawn Johnson, Amani Toomer, and Marvin Harrison. By now, I felt that I'd joined the elite from my draft class, and I wanted to be paid that way. Not just for me but for all the people I was supporting. The 49ers thought they were dealing with just David and me, but I felt that we were negotiating for my whole family.

The talks between David and McVay didn't seem to be moving, and then Mooch—the coach I'd been bear-hugging and crying with not very long ago after we beat Green Bay—stuck his head into the middle of things and showed his ignorance. Until now, I had no reason to dislike him, and in fact I liked him a lot. He'd brought more offensive spark to the Niners than George Seifert had, and his future as a coach looked very promising. But he did something coaches shouldn't do, which is to get in the middle of a contract negotiation. There's a reason NFL teams tend to discourage coaches, with the current exception of Mike Shanahan, Mike Sherman, and a few others, to have a role in the general management of teams anymore. Running a fifty-three-man roster is enough of a job without jumping into the money end of things, since you're likely to do more harm than good.

Mooch didn't even know who my agent was and thought David was black (he's Lebanese-American). And he somehow thought it was a good idea to indicate to a reporter that because my agent had never done a big contract, he didn't know what he was doing. Needless to say, that didn't go over too well with any of us.

I think Mooch resented the fact that yet another player was going to be making more than he was. This can be a problem in the NFL, but it doesn't seem to be with the other great coaches who get paid a lot. Jon Gruden doesn't appear to have these kinds of issues with players, and he knows better than to meddle in a contract. Maybe it's because he's won a Super Bowl. (Maybe it's why he won one.) Mariucci came on like a best friend—until the contract talks began. Then it was so confusing that I didn't know if he was my coach, a father figure, or a spokesman for a team trying to low-ball me. Everything that had felt so good a short while earlier now felt out of sync.

He grew up in Iron Mountain, Michigan, and I grew up in the Deep South. We're all different, but he and I were really different, and what was at issue were things most fans never see. A lot of people don't understand what NFL players go through the entire year or what they do in the months when the season isn't in full swing. Fans watch us on Sundays or Mondays and get the finished product. They see us driving that expensive car or wearing that well-made suit, but they don't know what it took to get there or how we feel a lot of the time. Just the physical toll the NFL takes on the body is huge. There are countless stories about sixty-something former pro football players who can't walk or need hip replacements. Even guys in their forties know what this is like: Joe Montana has such bad arthritis that he can't enjoy walking a full golf course anymore. And you know your career can be taken away from you in an instant.

Before I got to the 49ers, the team had a great strong safety named Chet Brooks. He played during two of the Super Bowl seasons and looked like the second coming of Ronnie Lott, even though he was a late-round draft pick. Everyone called him "the Terminator," but right after he signed his first big contract, out went his knee, and he was never the same. Fortunately for Chet, he'd invested wisely, bought his mom a home in Texas, and started a construction business. But most NFL players feel they have little or no say in their future—from the day they get drafted.

After Mooch's remark about David, the 49ers went into damage-control mode. First Steve Young called me, no doubt at the request of his buddy, Coach Mariucci, and tried to sugarcoat the whole thing.

"You know, TO," he said, "the franchise thing isn't all that bad."

The great Super Bowl–winning quarterback was on the line, showing interest in my situation, something he'd never done before. Even though I didn't like what he was saying, his words made me run through a gamut of emotions. I was unhappy with the negotiations so far, but I was encouraged that Mariucci thought enough of me to have his signal caller phone me to try to help. Mostly, though, I was beginning to realize what veterans meant when they talked about the NFL no longer being a game but rather a hard-core business. The family atmosphere that everyone had gotten accustomed to under owner Eddie DeBartolo was disappearing. Eddie's sister and brother-in-law gained control of the franchise, while Eddie became a deposed king. For a lot of the old Niners, this meant only one thing: football in San Francisco wasn't going to be as much fun anymore.

Mooch was half right in what he'd said about my agent—this was David's first big contract—but the coach was also half wrong. David knew exactly what he was doing. As he made plans to fly to San Francisco and hammer out the details of the deal, his father intended to go with him, but a last-minute emergency kept Fred at home. David was going alone into the lion's den of owner John York, vice president John McVay, numbers cruncher Dominic Corsell, and the entire San Francisco 49ers financial organization.

In the South, we have a saying, "He fell in a butter tub," which means that a man who wasn't that rich married a woman who was very rich and ended up richer than his wildest dreams. John York was a Mississippi doctor who married a rich woman and fell in a tub of butter. He wound up owning the 49ers, but a lot of people felt he didn't have the aptitude to run a major league franchise because he didn't like spending money. In pro sports, you've got to spend money to make money—see Dr. Jerry Buss with the Los Angeles Lakers, George Steinbrenner in New York, and Eddie DeBartolo in San Francisco. The butter wasn't really York's, so maybe he wanted to hang on to it.

David was having none of that. The first day he spoke with the Niners brass about my contract, the two sides came up with a set of terms and numbers that we wanted and that they wanted, and they wrote it all out on a blackboard. The next day, when David came back into the room to keep negotiating, the guys on the other side of the table had erased what David had written down. At first, he didn't know what to do, so he did what every smart soldier does in battle. He didn't react, and he didn't panic. He didn't say anything, except that he needed to step outside for a few moments, which he did. He called me on his cell phone and told me what was up, and I encouraged him the same way he'd been encouraging me on the field for the past three years.

He went back inside and acted as if nothing had been erased. He talked about his side of the board as if all the terms from yesterday were intact and we were going to get what we asked for. He called their bluff. They quickly backed down and gave him just about everything we'd asked for. We didn't get a one-year, $3.5-million deal from the Niners. We got a seven-year deal worth just under $35 million that gave me room to choose free agency after five more seasons. I also got a $7.5-million signing bonus, the largest ever for a wide receiver at that time.

When it was reported that I'd signed a seven-year contract worth nearly $35 million, people everywhere started calling to borrow money. I heard from my old high school classmate Derek Hall, asking for help with an apartment for graduate school. I didn't mind him calling, because of all the rides he'd given me going back and forth from Alex City to Chattanooga when we were in college. If he went to Memphis with his girlfriend, he'd leave me his car, and I'd cruise around town. We'd struggled together back then, so now I was okay with him asking to borrow money for the electricity bill, but I also got calls from people who hadn't helped me at all. The worst one came from the mother of a girl I knew who was in jail; the mom asked me to bail her out. When I declined, she tried to make me feel guilty by bringing God into it. I've tried to assist many people, but in this case, I said no.

Many players have gotten caught up in bad investments, especially after a friend pitches an idea to them. Then the money goes the same way as the friendship—down the pipes. After signing the new deal, I got pulled into a scam when I gave $100,000 to a man who said he was a big-time music promoter. His father was connected with the 49ers, and I knew his dad, so I thought I could trust the son. I'd seen him only a couple of times when he told me that he was getting my new neighbor, recording star Kelly Price, involved in his promotional business. I'd just moved out to Atlanta and thought that if Kelly Price was doing it, it must be all right. She got ripped off, too. They can't even find the guy now, because he's on the run.

My mother and brother and sister have felt the burden of my football fame, too, and that's a shame. They've been approached for money the same way I have, and people have acted as if my family members had access to my bank account. At times, I knew my mom wasn't telling me all the horror stories, but I'd find them out anyway. People have put her in such an awkward position that she's cried to me on the phone about it. She, too, just had to say no.

The best part of my new contract was insisting that finally, after more than two decades of hard work, my mom was going to walk out of the Russell Mill for the last time. She didn't have to punch their time clock anymore—and I felt better about that than about anything else I've ever done for anyone.

I was glad I'd stuck with David when lots of other agents were trying to lure me away. The guy from Greensboro had learned his trade, and our relationship had paid off big-time for both of us. I'd taken a chance with him and won, and I'd gambled on my talent in the NFL and won there, too. Now I was getting ready to take more chances on the field and to play a different and larger game. Let Jerry Rice and the others be PC and do it their way. TO had worked hard for the money and was getting ready to celebrate.

Other things were changing too. In the winter of 1999, I played in Magic Johnson's Celebrity basketball tournament at the Forum in LA and held my own against the competition. In the locker room after the game, a man recognized me from the Packers win (he'd won a $100 bet because of my catch) and he called out to me to say hello. He was hanging with a couple of musical celebs, including Snoop Doggy Dogg. The man's name was Anthony Shaw, and he asked me what crowd I was going to party with later on that night. Despite my three years in the league, I was still a shy kid from the country.

"I'm from Alabama," I told him, "and I'm rollin' alone."

He laughed and said that I needed to be with his crew because they were headed to a party in Hollywood. I wound up with Shaw and Snoop that night, and a few months later I saw Shaw with Puff Daddy Combs at another party in Cancun. We spent more time together and got close. I was starting to meet famous people. More important, I was also building friendships with two other men— Theron Cooper and Carlos "Pablo" Cosby—who hung with me when I went down to Atlanta, which was becoming my off-season home. For the first time since leaving Alex City, I was developing real relationships with others and coming out of my shell. I'd been isolated long enough. The Catch II had changed not just my career but my social life. Shaw, Coop, and Pablo, along with two old friends from Alex City—Roderick "Big Unk" Tuck and Antonio "Pokey" Graham—were guys I could open up to and tell about my past and growing up with my mother and grandmother. They were people I could relax with and have fun. At night we cruised and met women, went dancing, and let ourselves unwind. Until now, I hadn't been that confident around women (or men) but all that was starting to fade. My friends were bringing me to a place I'd never been before, and it was great to hang with them.

I was having a lot more fun with them around me and was starting to think about spreading my wings on the football field. Sometimes, I talked about this with Coop or Shaw. One day I said to Shaw, "People are gonna know me now. I'm gonna be somebody."

My world was opening up and these guys were a key part of that. I could trust them and could speak the truth to them because I knew they could handle it, no matter what it was. I had new good friends and I was going to need them more than ever in the years ahead.

PART THREE
SHOWTIME

XVIII

IN THE FALL OF 2000, a few days before the Niners arrived in Irving, Texas, to play the Cowboys, an idea popped into my mind. Throughout the past two decades, San Francisco and Dallas had been heated—and hated—rivals. Back in 1981, Dwight Clark's famous Catch I had symbolized a shift of NFC power to San Francisco after years of domination by Dallas. When Charles Haley was traded from the Niners to the Cowboys in the early '90s, it triggered a shift back toward Dallas, which won three Super Bowls in the middle of that decade. The ultimate move came when Deion Sanders won a Super Bowl during his one year at San Francisco in 1994 and then went straight over to Dallas to lead the Cowboys to another championship. Anytime these teams got together, even if one was down, it felt like a personal war. Plenty of players and coaches were still on both teams from all those NFC title games, and it was no secret that former 49ers president Carmen Policy couldn't stand Dallas owner Jerry Jones. Because of all these things, I wanted to do something special if I scored on the Cowboys. I also wanted to spark the Niners, who were having a rotten season. By late September, we hadn't won a game.

I didn't tell my teammates about this idea before the game, but I did mention it to my receivers' coach, George Stewart. He'd replaced Larry Kirksey as my closest contact on the team, someone I'd come to trust and rely on for all kinds of help and support. When I was feeling so much pain in my feet that it was hard to practice, I told George. When I wanted the ball thrown my way more during a game, I let him know. He was as near to a friend as a player can have on an NFL coaching staff, and we were tight. After I told him what I had in mind if I made a touchdown, he just shrugged and said, "Do what you gotta do." He didn't tell me I was crazy and to stop thinking about doing this kind of thing. He didn't alert anyone else on the staff that I might do something outrageous. He acted as if what I'd said was not important, so I was set to go.

With about three minutes left in the first half, I caught a touchdown pass that put us up by 14 to 3. Once the refs had signaled the TD, I ran out of the end zone and all the way to midfield and stood on the famous blue Dallas star, the symbol of "America's team" in the NFL. The 49ers had never liked that phrase "America's team," and neither had other players around the league; it made the Cowboys sound a lot more special than they were. I didn't look at the Dallas bench, and I didn't taunt. Standing on the star, I raised my arms to the crowd and looked up at the sky and gave a very brief prayer, giving thanks to God for all the blessings I'd received. Then I stared into the end zone, where about 5,000 people were staring back at me and pointing. Over on the Niners sidelines, the players were either laughing or cheering me on. I'd given them and the Cowboys and everyone in the stands something to think about: the 49ers were struggling this season, but we weren't intimidated by the Cowboys or anyone else. And they weren't going to keep me from celebrating inside their own house. Interestingly, not one coach or administrative person came to me when I got back to the sideline and told me not to do that again. In fact, it was just the opposite: I got nothing but pats on the back. Also, the men in stripes did not throw a flag on me. A few minutes later, Dallas running back Emmitt Smith scored, and he copied what I'd done but took it farther. He ran to the star, kneeled down, took off his helmet, and scowled over at the Niners bench.

Late in the fourth quarter, the Niners put together another drive and took the ball inside the Cowboys 10. I lined up against defensive back George Teague, who tried to cover me one-on-one in the end zone, but I did to him what I'd been doing to D-backs ever since college. I basically picked him up and threw him to the ground. George didn't like that, but there wasn't much he could do about it. Before he knew it, I was running another route and catching my second TD pass of the day, one that took our lead up to 41 to 17. I sprinted for the star at midfield again, and as I began another celebration, Teague came out of nowhere, moving at full speed, and knocked me down, jolted me right off the blue star. He was running his mouth, and other players began pushing and shoving, but I ignored them, went back to the star, and kept celebrating. I wasn't trying to start a fight, and I wasn't going to jump into one now—but I wasn't going to back down, either. I came to dance and thank God, so that's what I did.

Then bedlam took over. Next thing I knew, I was standing in the locker room with a towel wrapped around me, and Niners owner John York was staring at me with a fierce look of disapproval. I didn't like that one bit. When somebody stares at me, I feel like a tiger in a cage. York didn't come over to me or say anything, but for the first time, I got a sense of how upset people were with me, not just people on the Dallas side but people everywhere throughout football. Until my dancing, the story of the game had been that Jerry Rice had blown up on the sideline and screamed at Mooch about Jeff Garcia's passing touch, but that was ancient history. All anybody wanted to talk to Mooch or anyone else about was TO's celebration. Everyone forgot the fact that my intention before the game had been to push the Niners toward a much-needed victory. Lost in all the hysteria was that we'd gone into Dallas and spanked the 'Boys in their own crib, by a score of 41 to 24, but who cared about that?

The 49ers were about to suspend me for a week without pay— that cost me $24,294—and the great debate was on. When hell breaks loose, you never know who's going to support you. Former

Bengals wide receiver Cris Collinsworth, a Fox-TV analyst who would annoy me for years to come, said that the officials should have put a stop to all this early on by flagging me the first time I went to the star. They didn't do that, so they were to blame for not taking control of the situation before it got out of hand. Terry Bradshaw, the former Steelers quarterback with four Super Bowl rings who also works at Fox, seemed to be in my corner; I guess he'd never liked the Cowboys that much, either, and he understood the idea of trying to fire up your team through action and emotion. But then Fox sent James Brown down to Alex City to interview me (I went there for my suspension), and he did what most commentators do when they interview you. He wanted me to apologize for my behavior, and I just don't do that, for him or anyone else. I made a decision to celebrate on the star, I ran it by my coach first, and he didn't try to stop me, so I went ahead with my plan. Why should I have asked forgiveness of James Brown or anyone else? He wanted me to say on TV that I wasn't going to do anything like this again, but I wasn't raised to lie or make up stories, so I didn't go along with him. I wasn't sure what I was going to do next, but I did tell him one thing that seemed very difficult for him to understand.

"I've got something creative coming up," I said. "I'm gonna have fun with this. I'm not gonna make fun of others, but I'm gonna have fun when I play football."

To me, it wasn't a lot more complicated than that, but to millions of others, I'd done something horrible, something worse than other things that athletes are accused of, such as drug abuse, domestic abuse, rape, and murder. When I decided to run to the star, I didn't realize that I'd get about as much negative attention for this as Ray Lewis got when he was on trial for murder. The attention didn't bother me that much, but it really upset some members of my family. I remember calling my mom the next day to tell her I was coming home for a while because I'd gotten suspended from the team. I wasn't suspended by the NFL but by my own coach—the same coach who, after the game, said he never even saw me run to the star in the middle of Texas Stadium, twice, after scoring touchdowns. Seventy thousand people in the stadium saw me but not Mooch. My mother saw it, too, down in Alabama, but she didn't think that much about it until I called to say I was coming back to Alex City. If ever there was a case study of how the media influence perception, this was it. When the tide turns against you, there isn't much you can do except stand back and let it go until it runs out of steam. You can't explain yourself, because the public isn't interested in explanations. It's interested in venting its anger.

People who initially thought what I did was cool started listening to everyone else and then jumping the fence. Suddenly, I was a disgrace to football, an embarrassment, and a troublemaker. I had no class—even if I was just a guy trying to jumpstart his team. Veterans in my own locker room privately had to take sides or straddle the issue. Politics exist in any work environment, and most of my teammates kept out of it, which was probably the wisest thing to do, but a couple of veterans bashed me right off the bat: Ken Norton, Jr., and Ray Brown. This was strange, because Ray Brown and I were friends, but he was just doing the politically correct thing that Jerry Rice had told me to do. Brown and Norton were team leaders and trying to keep management happy, but in the long run, their behavior didn't help them. While my role with the Niners was growing each year, they were soon shown the door by the franchise, because they were expendable. After 2000, Ray Brown had to sign with Detroit to keep playing. Ken Norton, Jr., basically had to retire. Trying to please management hadn't saved their jobs or prolonged their careers. Sometimes, you have to say what you feel, politically correct or not.

Things were tough enough when the former great Niners safety Ronnie Lott also took some shots at me, and that seemed to open the floodgates. Other veterans chimed in, and suddenly I felt as if I was in my own little world, and that was a problem. If football teams really are a family—and that's what the 49ers want you to think— then aren't you going to have love for every family member, unless he's done something drastically wrong? The Niners like to say "team this" and "team that," but then you come up with something fun to do in the end zone—I've never done dances that are obscene or flipped off the fans or grabbed my crotch—and all of a sudden, this is taunting and unacceptable and an attack on the team and the NFL.

The Niners hadn't said anything a few years earlier when I'd had Steve Young doing the bank-head bounce dance. Here's a Hall of Fame quarterback, Super Bowl MVP, the great-great-great-grandson of Mormon founder Brigham Young, and we've got him going, and it was fun. That was all right, but Dallas wasn't. Merton Hanks had his funky chicken-neck dance for all those years with the 49ers, and everyone thought that was cool. That could be classified as taunting, too, but nobody seemed too bothered by this.

On the other hand, a couple of my teammates stood up for me right after the game. One was Pro Bowl safety Lance Schulters. Another was linebacker Julian Peterson. In fact, Schulters stated that when I went to the star he was all "jacked up," and that after Emmitt did it he was going to intercept a pass and score so he could go to the star too. The best line emerged from Denver. Future Hall of Fame tight end Shannon Sharpe, who'd cultivated an image where he could say whatever he wanted and nobody got that upset, said, "Hey, you don't like what Terrell Owens did? Keep him out of the end zone." Lance and a handful of other guys went on record saying it wasn't that big a deal, and the Cowboys and their fans had overreacted, and the media were making more of it than it was. But it wasn't the Cowboys or the fans or the press who decided to punish me. It was the people I worked for inside the Niners organization.

The day after the Dallas incident, the 49ers brass called a press conference to announce that I was being suspended for one game, the equivalent of a $25,000 fine. My behavior, they insisted, was not part of the Niners tradition and would not be tolerated. Then my agent got a call from Bill Walsh, the legendary coach of the Niners during their first Super Bowl run in the 1980s. Bill told David that Coach Mariucci had made the decision to discipline me and that he, owner John York, the franchise's administrative personnel, and the coaching staff were all backing this decision and the fine. The team, he explained, was doing the right thing for everyone. If the 49ers acted first and dealt out the punishment in-house, the NFL would back off and leave the situation alone. With that off his chest, Walsh launched into a tirade, saying that he would trade me if he could.

David handled him the same way he'd handled the franchise during the 1999 contract negotiations: he called his bluff.

"Okay, Bill," he said. "Why don't we get some teams on the line, or why don't you give me permission to call them about a trade?"

Walsh immediately backed off—so fast that David would later say it was comical. Walsh was just posturing. He wanted no part of trading me; he just wanted to puff out his chest and express his emotions.

At the end of this tirade, David asked him to help me deal with the media firestorm surrounding the event, but Walsh blew off this request. From there, things got uglier between me and the organization. I was banished from the team facility for seven days, so David asked if I could go to Atlanta for a while and cool down. Everyone agreed to this, and I headed back home, but that put an end to nothing.

It is very interesting to contrast this with how the Cowboys handled the situation with Emmitt Smith and George Teague. The Cowboys did not hold a public press conference wherein they publicly criticized Emmitt's and Teague's behavior; moreover, any discipline was handled in-house between the team and the players. In other words, the Cowboys diffused the situation and made the decision to stand by their players publicly. The Niners, on the other hand, chose to publicly hang me out to dry, to give me no public or private support, and to fan the flames of criticism through their actions and statements. If it had not been apparent before then, it was now clear that these Niners were not the Niners of old, and that they were now more concerned about public relations and in being politically correct than they were in supporting their players in winning.

By Wednesday, I was taking a beating in the press from coast to coast. Talk-show hosts everywhere and their callers were dog-piling on this one. David phoned the 49ers to ask if they would give me a verbal vote of confidence, but they refused. Then David blew up at them, asking why nobody there was willing to stand up for me. The next day, Walsh finally came out and made a halfway supportive statement on my behalf, but the damage had already been done.

At the lowest point that week, Mooch called me and the team called David and asked if I would return from Atlanta—for the team picture, of all things—a day early. They even offered to pay for the flight. David recommended that I turn down this offer and stay in Atlanta until the suspension was over. I couldn't have agreed more. The team could work out its own problems with photographs. (I'm not in the 2000 team picture.)

By the time I'd served my one-game suspension, the whole thing had opened up a series of issues that were hard to close. For one thing, it didn't help my relationship with Mariucci, which was already rocky. I felt that without the media's influence, Mooch might have stood by me, but he'd caved in and gone along with my punishment. He began telling me that I had a lot of ability but I should pattern myself after Jerry Rice, the very same JR who'd cursed him out on national TV that same day in Dallas! That's something I hadn't patterned myself after. Nor had I been like Keyshawn Johnson, who wrote a book called "Just Give Me the Damn Ball!" After Dallas, I never felt that Mooch wanted to use me as much as he could have. The image of the Niners, or maybe his image, was more important than using the tools he had to win.

Following the suspension, some players stayed clear of me for a while. In the NFL, you're away from home a lot, and your teammates become the people you rely on. You think they're your friends, but something like this happens, and they come out against you in public, and you have to reassess everything. At least I could still play football, and that's what I looked forward to the most during the next few weeks. Getting onto the field again and making plays and helping the team win became the center of my focus.

The only ones I knew I could always turn to were my family and my new friends. Typically, my mom looked at the whole situation, heard all the criticism, and put it in perspective.

"What's the big deal?" she said. "What is so important about all this?"

She simply couldn't understand how so many people could get so upset over somebody standing on a star in the middle of a football field. To her, that seemed like a very small thing. Maybe that's because of how she grew up and what she'd been through in her own life.

David eventually appealed the team's decision to suspend and fine me. Normally, this would have been resolved quickly, but the 49ers put off a hearing on the issue until the next spring, when one was scheduled during a mini-camp. By then, the dust had settled, the media had moved on to other things, and David and I just wanted to get this behind us so I could prepare for the 2001 season. The Niners, on the other hand, intended to hold an open, public hearing in San Francisco so that everything could be dug up once more and everybody could relive the ragged emotions of it all over again. David thought this was a terrible idea and tried to persuade the team to settle the matter in private and move on. They wouldn't listen, but just before he boarded the plane to fly west and attend the hearing, he pulled out his cell phone and dialed their number one more time. It was very bad business, he said, to air this dispute now when I just wanted to get back to playing football and helping the Niners win another championship.

This time, they listened and agreed to a compromise: They would cancel the hearing and give back half the fine, adding about $12,000 to one of my paychecks. And I'd try not to enrage them again.

XIX

BY THE END of the 2000 season, everyone knew that JR was leaving the Niners and I'd become his replacement. That was the first year I was selected to the Pro Bowl, after setting career highs with ninety-seven catches for 1,451 yards and thirteen touchdowns. At some point, the team began making a conscious effort to get me the ball more. And, of course, I wanted the ball more. What NFL receiver doesn't? A few teams have been able to have two first-rate receivers work well together, such as Michael Irvin and Alvin Harper of the Cowboys or Lynn Swann and John Stallworth of the Steelers, but for this to go smoothly, both need to be at about the same point in their careers. The Niners tried to ease this transition from JR to me, yet everyone knew what was happening. It started with little things, such as them still using JR as a primary receiver but trying to work me into open space, much as they'd done with John Taylor when he starred opposite Rice. Then it became apparent that we both were ready to be the one, and somebody had to go. Jerry never let any of that interfere with our friendship, and we never had any arguments or run-ins.

The torch had been passed, and you could tell by his body language that JR was upset about not being more a part of the game plan, but he didn't complain about it. Yet there was tension between him and the coaches. Maybe it was because my performances had gradually begun to overshadow his, and then the Dallas star game put a strain on our relationship. Neither of us had ever expected me to be the one who would, in essence, force him to change teams before he was ready to retire. It was like Steve Young pushing out Montana. The team made a decision based on youth and money, and besides, there's only one football. It was an awkward situation, and I'm sure I'll be on the other side in a few more years. I hope I can handle it with as much class as JR did, especially toward the end.

At the close of the 2000 season, the 49ers offered him $1 million to retire with them, but the team was coming off a 4-and-12 season and had already said good-bye to him at Candlestick Park. His last game that year was unbelievable—not for him but for me. We were playing the Chicago Bears, who were so bad they couldn't even get the ball past midfield against our young and full-of-holes defense. The strategy that day was to go to Jerry as often as possible and to send him out in style. I believe the 49ers hierarchy was secretly hoping that he would be so happy and consumed by the emotion of this game that he would take that $1 million and retire the way they wanted him to. The 49ers were still stung by the way Montana and Ronnie Lott and Roger Craig had all finished their careers elsewhere. It was JR himself who made the best point about his last game as a Niner. If they'd gotten him the ball as much as they said they would, how easy would it have been for them to turn right around and say good-bye to him? They don't call him the Man for nothing.

As the Bears steadily double-teamed JR that afternoon, refusing to allow him to go off, Jeff Garcia kept getting me the ball. I was cool with this, even though it was Jerry's day. His family was on hand, his daughter sang the national anthem, and a podium was set up after the game for him to address the crowd, à la Lou Gehrig. The whole team had prepared themselves for this. It was *his* moment, and the game plan was to honor him during his final time at Candlestick Park in a 49ers uniform. Nice touch, but football is not a predictable sport.

The problem was that I was the one making all the catches. Five, then ten, and then I broke my personal record of twelve with more than a quarter left to go. It reached the point where, during the second half, most of the attention had turned away from him and toward me. I soon broke JR's personal best of sixteen, set in 1994, and was possibly on pace to break the all-time NFL record held by Tom Fears, who'd grabbed eighteen balls with the L.A. Rams back in 1950. We were leading the Bears 17 to 0, and some people thought we were piling on Chicago just so I could get the record and JR could catch a few more passes. Late in the fourth period, I caught number nineteen and then got number twenty to finish off the game with 283 yards, sending my jersey from that day to the Pro Football Hall of Fame in Canton, Ohio. A totally different story line was being written for JR's final game in San Francisco, but again he handled it with nothing but class. He always used to say, "Man, they ran Joe Montana and Ronnie Lott out of here. You think I'm going to be any different?" Before long, I was saying the same thing. They ran Jerry Rice out of here; you think *I'm* going to be any different? All this is a natural occurrence in the NFL. Even Montana put up his best numbers as a Niner after Bill Walsh traded for Steve Young.

JR and I worked through all this without a lot of conflict, but unfortunately, I couldn't say the same thing about my relationship with the Niners head coach. Almost everything that happened after the Dallas flap opened a wider gulf between me and Mooch. My twenty catches against Chicago in December 2000 were part of the problem. Usually, when the coach comes in and talks to the entire team during the week, he doesn't say anything earth-shattering. In the fall of 2001, we were 4 and 1 and off to a terrific start. Imagine our reaction when Mariucci started going on and on about Chicago before our rematch game with the downtrodden Bears that season. He basically said that we weren't going to embarrass our opponent by running up the score. We weren't going to beat them as badly as we could, and he told me that I probably wasn't going to get twenty catches against them again.

Hearing this, I was stunned. Everybody knows that in pro football, games can change dramatically in a matter of minutes, if not seconds. Houston blew a 32-point second-half lead to Buffalo a decade or so ago in the playoffs. Tampa Bay recently let a 21-point lead over the Colts slide away with four minutes left on *Monday Night Football* and then lost in overtime. You can't take anything for granted until the game is over; if you do, you're not showing respect for the skills of your opponent. But Mooch saw things differently.

He told us that he had colleagues on the Bears, guys he'd worked with in the past, and he still considered them good friends. He didn't want to be in a situation where he would shame another team, especially when his pals were coaching across the stripes. In this case, the reference was to Bears coach Dick Jauron, one of several assistants on Mike Holmgren's staff at Green Bay who parlayed that experience into an NFL head-coaching gig. So what happened when we took a lead that Sunday in Chicago? What was the plan after we went up 14 to 9 at the half and then 28 to 9 in the third quarter? Mooch got conservative, very conservative. Jeff Garcia hurt his knee, which was one factor, but everybody knew what was going on. We started running the ball instead of throwing it or just throwing short passes instead of stretching the Bears' defense. Mooch had been right: I wasn't going to break any records today, and no one was going to accuse him of hurting Chicago's feelings. I caught four balls in the first quarter as we took the lead, but then they stopped coming my way, and I grabbed only two more the rest of the game. Trust me, I wasn't the only one upset, either by his speech about his "friends" or by his play calling that day. Our sideline was filled with grumbling and moaning.

The more conservative we got, the more the Bears clawed back into the game. We still didn't throw the ball downfield, and on two separate occasions, when our lead was slipping away, we ran it into the line and helped their momentum and their rally. They kept coming and eventually tied the game at 31 to 31, sending it into overtime. I was so upset by all this that on the first play from scrimmage in OT, I lost concentration on a pass play, and the ball bounced off my knee and into the air. The Bears safety, Mike Brown, picked it off and returned it for the winning touchdown. I talked to reporters after the game and told them that we'd blown the game by allowing our offense to get way too tame in the fourth quarter. I was angry at the team for losing, at Mooch for his play calling, and at myself for not catching the ball that Mike Brown ran in for a TD.

When we got on the team bus, I was still steaming at Mooch, but then we learned that Jeff Fontana, the son of longtime team business executive Sandy Fontana, had been gunned down while making a routine stop as a rookie police officer in San Jose. While going through police training, Jeff had worked at the 49ers facility. Suddenly, blowing the game to the Bears didn't matter, but none of that stopped the media from peppering me all the following week—especially that Wednesday, when we took a half-day to attend Jeff's memorial service. I tried to explain to the press the entire sequence of what had happened with the Bears, but all anyone heard was that I said Mooch had let up on his friends and that the 49ers lacked a killer instinct. Here's part of the transcript.

Reporter: "Knowing the whole situation now, with the injuries and everything, do you still feel that the offense should've run plays at the end of the game to put the ball in the end zone?"

TO: "I'm not going to bite my tongue. Like I said, we need to develop killer instinct for whatever reason. That's it. I said what I had to say. I'm not going to backtrack on what I said. I said what I said Sunday, and that's what I meant."

Reporter: "Did you talk to Mariucci and have him explain it to you?"

TO: "What can anybody say? Everybody is trying to get us into that 'Terrell said this,' and Mooch reads it, and then it's a whole big argument again. Don't even try to bait me like that. It's not working."

Reporter: "So did you mean that it wasn't necessarily those two plays of sitting on the ball but the attitude of the offense in general?"

TO: "To be honest, it was killer instinct. Whatever. Like I said, if Steve Spurrier would've been down there, he wouldn't have kneeled down on it. That's the same thing I said Sunday."

Mooch held a conference call with the media after the memorial, and only those quotes were read to him. He stayed calm, until he read the papers the next day. Then he fired back, calling my statements ridiculous, and "the rift" was on. Battle lines had been drawn between Mooch and me, and neither of us felt like backing down. He started telling people (off the record) after I criticized him for the Chicago game that I'd run the wrong route on the play that Garcia got hurt on. He was insinuating that Jeff hurt himself, behind the line of scrimmage, because of something that I'd done downfield. Even if I did break my route—and that is what we're trained to do—I had no control over what was going on with Jeff, but Mariucci had the Bay Area media hanging on his every word. He was the good-looking young college-coach guy from California, and I was the villain.

Maybe he didn't like me getting more attention than he did. Maybe he didn't like that I said he should size up his talent better, so I could contribute more to the team. My job was to go out there and catch balls and score points. How hard is that to understand? That's what bothered me the most when people reported on all this. They said I should go talk to the coach if I had a problem and that I shouldn't be airing it in public, but this is the head coach of an NFL team. I shouldn't be doing his job, telling him to use his players so the team could win more games. A lot of people said that I'd gotten big-headed because of my new contract, but the money only made me want to step up my game. That's all I talked about—how I was going to earn every penny by making more plays than before.

I felt that it would be ridiculous for me, under any circumstances, to walk into the head coach's office and tell him what to do or to question him about why I was not getting the ball in certain situations. Didn't they come in early every day to prepare film and create a game plan for the players? Wasn't he seeing the same things that I saw on the field? Looking back now, I appreciate more than ever assistant coach George Stewart, who was my closest connection on the team throughout all this turmoil. I couldn't have made it through the 2001 season without him. I talked to him in depth about wanting the Niners to have a killer instinct and about my playing a larger role in the offense. There wasn't much he could do about some of this, but he could listen, and he did, and it was very important to me. NFL assistant coaches are so valuable—and underrated—and I was very lucky to have Coach Stew follow Coach Kirksey with the 49ers. He knew exactly what the Niners' problems were and how everything had started to go sour during my contract negotiations, how things had gotten much worse with the Dallas incident, and how my relationship with Mooch had crashed after the Chicago media war of words. Following that, I just stopped talking to the head coach but relied more than ever on Stew.

Not talking with Mooch was not a problem from my end. Let him just call the plays, and let me run them. If he had something to say to me, he could tell my position coach. In 2001, Coach Stew really earned his money. It got so bad that when I passed Mooch in the hallway, I'd stare right through him. Weeks after, I kept his media comments criticizing me out in a prominent place, displayed for all to see. They motivated me the same way that I was once motivated by a high school teammate spitting into my mouth. They both made me want to play better.

Mooch was always more concerned with his image than he was with winning a Super Bowl. While he spent at least thirty minutes a day chatting up the local writers after practice, I stopped talking to all but two of them, even off the record. Mooch was like the guy who hired him, former team president Carmen Policy, who devoted a lot of his time in his office to doing interviews, which drove the real football people like Bill Walsh nuts. Walsh did his share of interviews over the years, but he was much more in control of himself.

I heard Larry Roberts was having fun with the Super Bowl media before the 49ers headed to Miami for Super Bowl XXIII. Roberts played defense for the team and said he was going to come up with the equivalent of the "Ickey Shuffle" if he made a big hit on Cincinnati's Ickey Woods during the game. It was all in good fun, but when these comments were relayed back to Walsh, he said, "Oh, no, he did not say that." Then he disappeared inside the locker room to talk with Roberts. Minutes later, Roberts came out and said he wasn't planning any such thing.

Whenever there was a problem, that's all Mariucci had to do: take control of the situation. Instead, he'd talk on and on, always trying to spin the stories his way. He'd go off the record with the local writers all the time, swaying their copy, and in my case portraying me as bad for his team. So I just shut up whenever he came around. Never before had a player and a head coach gone almost an entire season without speaking to each other. It wasn't that difficult for me, but I could tell it was eating him up.

Everything Mooch did made Stew look better. The reason I never told anyone until now that I'd tipped Stew off about my plan to go to the star in Dallas was that I never wanted him to suffer for that. He'd helped me every day he coached me at the 49ers just by being someone I could trust, and I wanted to give him that trust in return. During the 2003 Pro Bowl, I was fined for missing a practice. The wire reports went out, grouping me with Simeon Rice, who'd also missed a practice. The press made it sound as if we were out partying and just blew off a practice, which is silly, because they barely practice for this game. I wasn't partying; I was in my hotel room, distraught because George Stewart had left the 49ers. The team had basically said he could stay on with the organization, but only if he went back to coaching special teams. So much for the NFL helping to promote black coaches. Stew was leaving for Atlanta, and I was so stunned that I couldn't do anything but sit in my room and think about how much I was going to miss him. I got fined for doing this, which was another joke. Somebody had to slap me with another fine because I was mourning the loss of the one coach who'd really had my back, George Stewart.

The tougher things got for me in football, the more I fell back on the two bigger things in my life: family and faith. I listened to more gospel music. I prayed on the way to the game, on the team bus, in a cab, or if someone else was driving me to the stadium. Some of the best games I've ever had were based on what I was praying about right before kickoff. In the NFL, they have mass and chapel for players on game days, and you can attend these services before or after breakfast, but I usually pray on my own or with one other person. The 49ers chaplain, Earl Smith, was usually right there praying alongside me, as he was for everyone else who wanted this. Fans have no idea how vital someone like that can be to players on a team. Earl passed out little scriptures to read before each game, and he'd hand me verses about being strong and staying in control of myself and feeling close to God when adversity was all around. I'd read these words right before going out on the field, and it always seemed that he picked just the right one for what I was experiencing at that time.

Earl was everywhere—on the sideline, at the training complex— and he saw a lot of what was going on with me and with others on the team. He knew the inner struggle that athletes go through in preparing for games and throughout the long season. To have someone who can detect that and find the perfect message for you at the right time is very valuable. I know he doesn't work for the money, but this man needs a raise.

At the end of the 2001 season, following a Niners loss to Green Bay, Mooch and I finally hit bottom. The Packers had pushed our offensive line around, and their defense had gotten to Garcia and was able to break his rhythm. I had only four catches, and after the game, I called my agent from the locker room, and again from the bus on the way to the airport, and again from the team plane. The more I talked, the more upset I became.

"Get me the fuck out of here," I kept saying.

David couldn't believe it. He'd never heard me swear like this, but I was very angry and disappointed with the end of our season. This wasn't about me and Mariucci but about giving the team a chance to win a championship. I'd trained all year, every year, in order to help us get in position to go to the Super Bowl, but I wasn't getting the ball at critical points in the game. If Jerry Rice, after winning a handful of rings, could still burn with enough competitive fire to blow up in the coach's face on the sidelines because he wanted more catches, so could I. But I didn't want to do that, so I asked to be traded. Then I asked the Niners to put me on the expansion list, as the NFL was growing from thirty to thirty-two teams. Then I asked them to release me, but that didn't happen, either. As the off-season started, things were so bad that something had to give.

In February 2002, David set up a meeting in Santa Clara with John York, general manager Terry Donahue, and me. They asked us if we wanted Mooch to be present, but we said no. He was waiting in the wings if we decided to call him in. We didn't. York and I had never really talked to each other, and this was long overdue, especially after his staring at me following the Dallas game. I still hadn't gotten over that. We met at a sports bar in a local hotel and things were very tense on both sides, and I thought the ice might never get broken. But gradually we began to communicate, and I saw that he was willing to talk about the past, and he saw that I just wanted to get a championship for his franchise. It's absolutely amazing how much sports and winning mean to grown men. Underneath all that competition is an incredible amount of feeling about wanting to be a member of a successful team and to bring pride and joy to your group—to feel like a champ for once in your life.

I never understood how intense and driven I really am on a football field until they put a microphone on me during one game. We were playing the Atlanta Falcons and staging a comeback, when I literally forgot that I was wired for sound. They aired the piece at halftime of the next _Monday Night Football_ game, and when I saw the tape, I realized that I'd totally forgotten about the mike. The person on the field didn't even seem like me, because I was so focused on doing my job.

When I ran off the field after not catching any passes, offensive coordinator Greg Knapp said, "Keep your head up. We're trying to get you the ball."

"Shit," I said. "Y'all ain't trying hard enough."

I talked to myself the whole time on the field, running routes and saying, "Jeff, I'm open!" Then I'd come back to the huddle and say something like "Damn, I was open!" Or "Jeff, I'm open!"

On the field, I was like the engine of the team—an old-fashioned engine that burns coal. You have to put coal in the engine to make it run, and I'm like that coal: dark-skinned and capable of making things go. If I catch the ball, I always feel I can do something special with it.

"Man," Garrison Hearst once said to me, "why don't you ever have any turf burns?"

"Hey," I told him, "I try not to get tackled but to get into the end zone. If you ain't getting tackled, ain't no need for turf burns."

Garrison laughed, but he knew I was telling the truth. We played a game in 2001 against New Orleans, and the first two passes I caught went for touchdowns. Those were the only balls I caught that day, and I never touched the ground.

Several weeks after my meeting with York and Donahue, Donahue called David and said Mooch wanted to get together with me. Thereafter a breakfast meeting was set up at the Atlanta Airport Hilton for April 1, 2002, April Fool's Day, which seemed appropriate after all we'd been through. I agreed to meet with Mooch but only if David was there. Mooch didn't know that David was coming, and when he saw us walk in together, he looked surprised and confused. He did what he always did in this kind of mood: he stuck his fingers through his hair.

After we made some small talk, I excused myself from the table, and David explained to him that he was only there at my request. If David couldn't stay, the meeting was off. Mooch agreed to this condition, and I came back into the room. We all sat down, and David made us talk about a lot of uncomfortable things: the contract situation in 1999, Dallas, the loss to Chicago, the way we'd handled the media, and my future with the Niners. Both of us listened and tried to learn. Once again, David had risen to the occasion and played a much larger role than just working with dollars and deals. It wasn't an easy meeting, but it was an important one, and we basically agreed that as long as Mooch and I were both still with the 49ers, we would resume speaking with each other for the good of the team. This seemed to work during the 2002 season—until the very end.

Mooch got what he wanted: a cleaned-up image that he could manage his star receiver, along with a photograph of the two of us hugging in the *New York Times* as we opened the new season against the Giants.

The cameras stayed on us throughout the 2002 season, and the misperceptions remained. In a game early on, Jeff came out and threw two interceptions. People saw me gesturing while I was talking to him and assumed I was fussing at him, but that wasn't the case. I was telling him, "Don't worry about it. You've thrown picks before, and it basically hasn't affected the outcome of the game." I didn't want him to get down on himself because, like a lot of athletes, he's naturally very self-critical. A few weeks later in San Diego, our placekicker Jose Cortez missed a couple of field goals. Derrick Deese got so upset that he jerked Jose's jersey. People looked at this and said, "Oh, Deese is picking up his kicker," but I was ripping Jeff's head off.

XX

FIRST OF ALL, I don't dislike Jeff Garcia, but I can't help but think what it would have been like to play with Joe Montana. That's human nature, especially since I play for the San Francisco 49ers and broke in with Steve Young. I totally respect Jeff for what he's accomplished to this point. He wasn't even drafted by an NFL team; he went to Canada to make a name for himself and then had to fight his way onto the 49er-roster. Steve Mariucci felt that Bill Walsh had crammed Jeff down his throat. Not only did Mooch bench Jeff at one point, but he sent into action Rick Mirer, by that time an NFL journeyman and a player Bill had signed basically to be a steadying influence on Steve Young (who was hurt at the time). That was when Bill and Mariucci just about stopped talking to each other. Then word leaked out that Steve Young had iced Jeff Garcia, much the way Young had once complained Montana did to him. Long before I ever arrived in San Francisco, the Niners had a tradition of being a soap opera by the Bay.

When Young was coming up, they said he couldn't read a defense properly, not until 1992, when Mike Shanahan broke it down for him after replacing Mike Holmgren as the 49ers offensive coordinator. Prior to that, Steve relied on his running ability first. Some of the tape from Steve playing at Tampa Bay actually looked as if he was running for cover before he even took the snap. When he got to the Niners, Montana refused to relinquish his starting position, and it got so bad that Steve asked to get into some games as a third wide-out. The 49ers actually had scouting reports on Young as a running back when he was leaving BYU, but it was still embarrassing to see Steve line up and run down the field on a post pattern with the Niners, just because he wanted to get on the field but Montana wouldn't step aside.

Nobody doubted that Steve would come to be regarded as the greatest running quarterback in NFL history. The problem was that he needed to slow down—his nickname was "Crazy 8"—in order to read defenses, make his checks, and utilize all his weapons. He was the first to tell you that he couldn't win a Super Bowl until he realized that he had to get the ball out of his own hands and into someone else's. In fact, he tutored my man, Mike Vick, about that very subject during the 2002 off-season. Too bad he couldn't have passed this knowledge along to Jeff.

After taking over the 49ers reins, Garcia faced the same type of problems that Steve Young had. First, Jeff had to win over the players, then the coaching staff. While it's likely that no quarterback in pro football history had a tougher act to follow than Steve Young—Montana was not only an icon on the field but was revered in the locker room for being down-to-earth and watching everyone's back—Jeff had plenty of veterans to woo. Starting with Young. No one could believe it when Jeff let slip to *USA Today* that Young had actually iced him during his final season with the team. The Niners hierarchy knew about this and kind of chuckled at the irony, while the local media had a field day with it and Jeff issued an apology.

When Steve went down with a concussion that would prematurely end his career, Jeff clearly was unprepared to be an NFL starter. He hadn't gotten the proper coaching or playing time, so he relied on pure guts and instinct. He gained nothing but respect from his teammates, especially for the way he took on hits without regard for his body. We're not talking about one of these huge and ultra-strong modern quarterbacks; at just over six feet with his cleats on,

Jeff can barely see over the line of scrimmage. In his second season with the Niners, some inside the organization started calling him "the Stunt Man." You'd watch him take off out of the pocket and refuse to slide and get creamed by a huge linebacker, and you'd figure that he'd never get up. Time and again, Jeff pulled himself up from the turf and went back to the huddle. It was like watching a *Rocky* movie.

Ultimately, he turned himself into a Pro Bowl–caliber performer. Like Steve Young, he figured a way to get the ball out of his hands. The coaches helped, breaking away from the West Coast offense tradition and inserting the shotgun formation just for Jeff to get him in more of a comfort zone. He'd used the shotgun at San Jose State and in Canada, but he took so many hits with the Niners during the 2001 season that he looked like a mummy after games. We'd be showering and getting changed, and Jeff would walk by, his shoulder draped with Ace bandages and ice, his ribs covered with more Ace bandages, his knees, ankles, all the same. How could I get upset with someone who was giving his all like that?

Most often, I got annoyed with Jeff for sticking with the conservative play calls the coaches sent in from the sidelines. We had opportunities where we could do unexpected things, but he was so programmed—to be safe and not sorry—that he wouldn't go outside the box to try anything different. The only innovation he used was called a "smoke," where he'd throw the ball quickly after a one-step drop and let us do something with it, but that became very predictable after a while. We'd catch the ball on this play but barely get off the line of scrimmage.

Jeff and I were cool, but sometimes it's frustrating when I think about how much he gets paid and know that at certain moments he wouldn't challenge the 49ers system and be more innovative on the field. It always boils down to pure trust. Early on, I'd say that to him over and over again: "Just trust us. Just trust us to win together."

I remember sitting with him in the steam room, the two of us alone. I said, "Jeff, I know how coaches are, and I know they don't want you to do certain things. But you can check off other receivers if you feel you can get me the ball."

I wasn't trying to be selfish or ridiculous but trying to help the team win. The bottom line: a lot of great plays were not the ones originally called. You can go across the league, with any team in any era, and if you sit down with someone who knows the plays, they'll tell you about things that worked that were never planned in the huddle. Most quarterbacks tell good stories about the reactions they got upon returning to the sideline after making these kinds of plays. Some coaches blew up at them. Others were thankful. Some even took credit for calling the play when they met the media after the game. It's all about winning games, and this is football, not a science project. There's a certain free form to it all, just like the game in the street—run past that lamppost, turn around, and the ball will be there.

There were reports of a major feud between Jeff and me, but the real point here was that he and I go our separate ways. Did we hang with different people on the team? Yes, but who didn't search out his own friends once the games and practices were over? Did Jeff get upset with some of the things I did or said? Sure he did. Did I get upset regarding his play at times? Of course I did. He's the quarterback. I'm his top receiver. There were games during the 2001 season when everything clicked, and it felt as if we were just playing pitch and catch. The Niners made it back to the playoffs, we both went to the Pro Bowl, and I wound up leading the NFL in touchdown receptions. But other Sundays weren't like that, we disagreed over the best way to win football games, and that tension between us didn't go away. In fact, it was only going to get worse over time, until it reached the breaking point. Losing doesn't usually make competitive people closer

But bad blood? That was pure tabloid. Still, I kept hearing about it, and this "controversy" totally surprised me at first. I'd say to reporters, "What do you mean?" And they'd look at me and ask, "What are you *really* getting at?"

This caught me off guard, and I had no idea what they were talking about. I thought Jeff and I were cool, yet it got to the point where he came up and asked me, "Did I say something?" Or "Was it anything that I've done?"

I'd tell him, "I'm just as clueless as you are. I don't know what's going on. I don't even know where they got their information."

I even asked Coach Stew, "What's going on? Everybody is asking me about this, and I don't know what to say."

He had no answers, either, so I just stopped granting interviews. The NFL strongly encourages its players to be media-friendly, and most have little problem with that; some decent airtime, a few good stories, and all that hard work can pay off in terms of the proper image necessary to land a few extra-income endorsements. When it comes to the local media, it's also commonplace for players to find their own favorites. It's like any relationship: you click with one particular reporter, and then you test him out in terms of trusting him with something off the record. If he passes, it's usually all right to keep telling him things and to help him out with other stories. Or just to talk. Most of the media are decent folk. A lot work hard, and many get paid little in proportion to the service they're providing— that daily link among fans, their teams, and their favorite players.

Most NFL players give a little extra time to the beat reporters, who basically live with the team on a daily basis throughout the season. I'd tried to spend plenty of time with the local press, but then it started to feel as if they were baiting me to get me to say controversial things, just so they could make a headline or sell a juicy item to a national publication. Dallas. Mooch. Chicago. Jeff vs. TO. The locals liked to refer to me as the "Barry Bonds of the 49ers locker room," as if they knew what really went on in our locker room—or knew Barry Bonds.

Before the Dallas incident, Barry was the Bay Area's number one pro sports villain. Even though he'd grown up on the San Francisco Peninsula while his father, Bobby, starred alongside Barry's godparent, the immortal Willie Mays, he'd endured a long-standing love-hate relationship with the Bay Area. He rarely allowed himself to be examined by the daily baseball media swarm, and he'd undergone a very public divorce. He'd absorbed all sorts of unsubstantiated allegations regarding steroid-like enhancements and had never hidden a rivalry with teammate Jeff Kent. He'd also raised more than a few eyebrows by taking over a corner of the Giants plush clubhouse, complete with a leather chair and television set. It was hard for the press to imagine that Barry might be using the chair for therapeutic reasons or to watch the screen to help him play better baseball. He was only on pace to become the greatest home-run hitter (and the greatest baseball player?) of all time.

My public image, like Barry's, was that of an aloof athlete who was totally into himself. He's quiet, like me. He has a mischievous grin, also like me. I've spent time with Barry, and he's told me that he understands what I'm going through and to just stay focused on playing the game. He didn't judge me, didn't talk down to me, didn't even try to advise me, which I appreciated. We were able just to talk about our experiences and compare notes. He said that the day you stop thinking others are going to understand you is the day you start to perform at your best. Then you're free to get better. It was a thrill to be with him and to grasp a little more of what he'd been through, to get below the surface with him and to see and hear the real man. He hurts just like the rest of us and doesn't have all the answers for how to be famous and private at the same time. He told me that through the years, he'd missed out on a lot of endorsements because of his media image. Because he kept to himself and never allowed the public to get close to him, reporters just started writing whatever they wanted to.

By the time it got to the stupid story about Garcia and me, I'd had enough, so I shut out the local media. They whined to the 49ers public relations staff, but I held my ground. They tried pleading with me, but I wouldn't listen. My life became much better with this new policy. I finally did start granting interviews again, but only after games. I figured that would be enough to get them through the week. Of course, if someone like Bob Costas or Suzy Kolber or Andrea Kremer came to town, they'd get all the time they needed, because a lot of the national media had always treated me with respect. So I gave it right back to them—because that's what I'd been raised to do.

As I became better known in the NFL, I gradually turned into something of a spokesperson for awareness of Alzheimer's and efforts to get more funding for victims of this disease. With my new contract in place, I was able to put my grandmother into assisted living, where she was given drugs that dramatically helped her condition. She was no longer in bad moods all the time or trying to escape from her living situation or creating havoc for my mother. ESPN's Andrea Kremer was aware of my family life and did an excellent TV feature on me and my grandmother. During the show, I visited my grandma in her new residence and talked with her about how she was doing now. She joked with me and sang a song on camera, and this brought tears to my eyes. It was still painful to watch her dealing with this illness, but it was also very good to know that she was much better than she'd been in the past. I never realized how much I loved her until I saw her get sick.

I'd always have time for reporters who wanted to do these kinds of stories, about real people living real life, with all the joys and sorrows that come with being part of a family.

XXI

IN THE SPRING OF 2002, a school classmate and former teammate from Alex City, Cedric Kendrick, called me while he was passing through Atlanta. He woke me up from a nap and said he wanted to see me, but I was too tired to get together with him. Later that week, he died when a train smashed into his car. A good friend can be here next to you one minute and gone forever the next. Since that happened, I've made a conscious effort to be happier, to spend more time with people, and to talk and hang out with people I meet in social situations and with the guys in the locker room. I talk to football security personnel and other team workers. I've tried to connect more with my teammates and to play dominoes with the equipment guys. These small steps were a kind of tribute to my dead friend and represented my desire to be a bigger part of the team.

As I was going back to Alabama for Cedric's funeral, I had a lot of time to think, and I kept returning to my original sports dream: playing pro basketball. I was twenty-eight and hadn't tried to pursue this yet. What was I waiting for? Did I think getting onto a professional hoops team was going to get easier as I got older? I picked up the phone and called David, asking him to look into it. As usual, he made things happen, and before long, I was headed north to Glens Falls, New York, to play for the Adirondack Wildcats of the U.S.

Basketball League. I dedicated my season to Cedric, whose death had pushed me to do something I'd wanted to do my whole life.

I had been thinking about pro basketball again ever since I had a conversation with Shaquille O'Neal. Throughout my time with the Niners, I'd play in their celebrity games, which were supposed to be just fun, but I'd slam a few home, and things would get a little competitive. The itch to play hoops was still there. At a celebrity event in Saint Louis, Shaq and I teamed up and were going through warm-ups when he started throwing me alley-oops, and I went up and stuffed them. Later, we were sitting on the sideline, and he said, "You should try out for pro ball." I waited two more years to take his advice.

I had first met Shaq in 1997 when I went to a Lakers game with Merton and Marva Hanks. Mert got me into the locker room, and I had my picture taken with Kobe Bryant and with Shaq, and then we all posed with Jerry West. Later, after Shaq and I teamed up at that celebrity basketball tournament in Saint Louis, he told me, "Whenever you're in L.A., just holler."

I was overwhelmed. He was the biggest celebrity around, literally and figuratively, and now every time I'm in L.A., he welcomes me into his home. Sometimes, you just click with people, celebrity or not.

Getting to know Shaq only made me more determined to pursue pro basketball as a second career. Whenever I say that I think I'm better at hoops than at football, people tell me I'm crazy. But I got myself to this point as a football player because I worked very hard at it—and with the help of great position coaches and mentor-like teammates—and I think the same effort at basketball would have the same kind of payoff. In football, I had to learn how to catch the ball from different positions and different quarterbacks, had to learn body control, how to run precise routes, how to set up a defender. Obviously, I'd have to learn a lot of other techniques as a professional basketball player, but I believe that making the transition to the NBA would be easier for me than becoming an NFL player. I can guard anyone—quick guys, big guys—I can use my strength as an advantage, and I can jump out of the gym. The 49ers never wanted me to play hoops in the off-season and were dead set against me trying out for the USBL, but I consider basketball a tiny risk compared with how guys on the team go to winter resorts and ski down mountains. Besides, nothing in my contract says I can't ball during the off-season—though if I get badly hurt doing it, I'm kissing the rest of the contract good-bye. But I didn't care; after Cedric died, I just decided to go for it. By May 2002, I was in Glens Falls and playing for the Wildcats. I competed against Oliver Miller and some other guys with NBA skills, whose paths hadn't led them to the highest levels of the sport.

The man who really made my hoops dream come true was the Wildcats' general manager, Mike Sweet, who was at first a little reluctant to get involved with me. He had good reasons to feel that way. The year before, he'd signed Vikings receiver Randy Moss to play for the Pennsylvania Valley Dawgs of the USBL, and that was just about enough to make him never want to deal with another NFL player. Randy had acted like, well . . . Randy Moss. He flew into Pennsylvania on a private plane, which the team had to pay for, and he quickly began asking for star treatment. He demanded to know when he would be playing and how much, and he was standoffish with the other guys on the team. He lasted exactly two games before quitting, not to be heard from again. Mike Sweet felt that his experiment in mixing NFL stars with minor league basketball players had been a failure, and he wasn't anxious to try it again—until David told him that this time around everything would be different.

When I got to Glens Falls, I adjusted to my new teammates so that they wouldn't have to adjust to me. No private jets, just a room at a downtown hotel, a rental car, an agreement to sign autographs after each game, and no demands on my part. My slogan was "Low maintenance all the way." On road trips, I didn't order special food but ate pineapple and tuna out of a can. I didn't want to come in and grab anyone's spotlight, and it was almost like being a walk-on at UTC again, except that they paid me $500 per week (which I donated to some local charities on behalf of the Wildcats). Our first game drew a pretty decent crowd. They'd promoted the fact that I was in uniform, so this was good for the franchise. Later, there was one game when I didn't get in—we lost a close one—and both Mike Sweet and the head coach, ex-NBA player Michael Sanders, thought this would upset me, but it didn't. I told them that I understood they were trying to win, and if keeping me on the bench helped that effort, so be it. I'm many things to many people, but I'm not Randy Moss.

When the Wildcats traveled to Pennsylvania, I rented a big van for the team so we could have a little more room and comfort; the guys really appreciated it. Nike had sent me shoes to play in, and of course, they sent a lot more than I needed. I gave them away to the other players who had the same size as mine. No one called me "Meal Money" anymore. The hotels we stayed in weren't exactly NFL-caliber, but they weren't bad. And after a while, my teammates began to understand that I really did love being with them, and this was a better experience for me than for anyone else.

I played four games and scored a total of 12 points in the USBL. I was rusty, but every now and then, my skills would return, I'd soar in for a jam, and someone would come up and say, "Man, you can ball." That was all I wanted to hear. When I played my final game against the Valley Dawgs in Pennsylvania, this guy had a breakaway dunk, and I chased after him, then went up and blocked his shot. The crowd went absolutely wild, and I can't get that sound out of my ears. If it's in God's plan, I'll return to pro basketball. I had plans to get a tryout with my hometown team, the Atlanta Hawks, and I've built a gym at my house. I'll be in there working on my game, morning, noon, and even late into the night, just as I did at UTC to turn myself into a football player. When I'm alone in the gym practicing, it's my zen. I get into a zone and imagine myself playing in the NBA. I challenge myself mentally, and then I go back to work. My life has shown that you should never, ever limit yourself based on what others think and never quit dreaming your dream. Don't stop creating or enjoying yourself just because some people say you shouldn't.

XXII

A FEW YEARS BACK, when the Niners scored, we'd do a routine together in the end zone, but then the NFL implemented the "no group celebration" rule. No more letting three or four or five guys have fun after a TD—couldn't allow that to happen—so I set out to find my own creative expressions for a score. In the weight room over by the mirror between lifting sets, I'd try to practice something for the upcoming week. I always felt I could score at any time, and I wanted to be ready with something new. I never know when it will hit. I could be watching a video, playing pool, or blasting the stereo, or something on TV may strike me. The inspiration for touchdown celebrations can come from anywhere. After Dallas, everyone had suggestions for me. My friends would call before games and tell me what to do, but sometimes you plan and plan but never make it to the end zone. In the 2002 season, I was going to "strike the pose" for the Black Hole in Oakland, but Garcia didn't throw to me that day.

When the Niners played Seattle on *Monday Night Football* in '02, I didn't even start to formulate a plan until the night before. It was a big event for the Seahawks; they could get back into the division hunt with a win, and it was the first *MNF* match-up in their new downtown stadium. One of their cornerbacks, Shawn Springs, and I are good friends. My friends Greg Eastman and Jimmy Farris told

Shawn that I was going to score on him in the game, ragging him a little bit. Then Greg Eastman told me, "TO, I know you're going to score. I know you're going to get to the end zone about two or three times. You gotta give me a ball." He said he wanted it as a memento for his house. I thought about giving him a ball if I scored, but the rest of the plan didn't hit me until the end of the third quarter in the actual game. The idea came to me out of nowhere. I didn't tell anyone about it, but I went up to Donovan Dressler, one of our equipment guys, and said, "Doc, I need a Sharpie." He got me one, and I said, "You're not getting it back." He walked off without a clue about what I meant. Nobody saw me put it in my sock as I went back into the game.

Later on, everyone wanted to know, why my sock? Hey, we don't have pockets in our pants, so what else could I do? I tried tucking it up my shoelaces, but it didn't hold, and I couldn't wedge it down my pant leg, so I just stuck it in my sock, between my ankle and my Achilles. It fit perfectly, and it didn't bother me at all. I had two pairs of socks on, so it stayed in place, unnoticed for that possession. I thought about getting tackled and wondered if I could hurt myself or somebody else with it, but everything seemed to happen just right that evening.

With seven minutes left in the fourth quarter, I ran down the left sideline, outleaped Shawn for the ball—using my basketball skills—and made it to the end zone for a 37-yard score that proved to be the game winner. I went straight over to the field-level seats that Shawn owns, pulled out the pen, signed the ball, and handed it to my friend and financial planner, Greg Eastman (he's also Shawn's financial planner). Greg was totally surprised, and so was everyone else around him, everyone else in the stadium and all the millions of people watching on TV. I wasn't surprised until a short while later, when I started hearing the reaction to the incident.

First up was ABC sideline reporter Melissa Stark. I told her I was just being creative, and I think she thought it was funny. Even Shawn was laughing about it later that night.

"Hey, he had to do something," he said, grinning. "It was his only catch of the night."

Actually, it was my second *touchdown* of the night.

Right after the game was pretty tame, but by the time we landed back in San Francisco, Sharpie had taken on a life of its own. My cell phone voicemail was full, and I had people from other pro sports calling me to offer support. It was as if they knew I was about to get smacked again from coast to coast.

Shaq passed along this message: "Just keep ballin'."

Mike Bibby of the Sacramento Kings called and backed me up, while Guy Torry, the comedian, said, "Man, as long as what you did wasn't disrespecting God, just keep doing your thing."

That last one meant a lot to me as Monday turned to Tuesday and the negative reaction began to build. But this time, none of my coaches ripped me, not even Mooch. "That's just TO," Coach Stew said with a smile.

My teammates had my back on this one as well, especially after the Seahawks started whining about it—including their coach, Mike Holmgren. He told the media, "It's shameful. It's a dishonor to everyone who has ever played this game." Veteran Seahawks Chad Eaton and John Randle were the worst critics. Randle said I was a disgrace to football. This was the same John Randle who'd gotten down and pretended to pee like a dog on a fire hydrant after making a sack. Then there was Sean Salisbury of ESPN. I thought he was cool, being a former NFL quarterback, but he couldn't wait to trash me on the air. I agreed to do live radio with him the next day and did my homework on his career. When he was in college, Rodney Peete took over for him at USC, and he never was a legitimate starter again. Maybe that's why he went off on me.

I did an interview with Ricci Graham of the *San Francisco Examiner* and opened up another bucket of worms by saying the league treats black players differently from white players. As if that were a news flash! I added that these racial perceptions were playing a part in people's reaction to Sharpie and that it was also a generational thing. Duh! Then I told *USA Today* that a lot of players felt the same way I did but were afraid to voice their opinions. I guess that went too far and got too close to the truth, because the Niners PR staff then put out a statement designed to stop the firestorm. Good luck with that. I had no desire to feed the beast on this issue, but the NFL now issued a memo saying you can't have any foreign object in your sock on the field during a game. I'll have to frame that memo.

Sharpie Web site hits and sales, meanwhile, began skyrocketing. Of course, if Jason Sehorn had done this, Sharpie's representatives would have been camped on his doorstep, while it took them months to ask me to work on a national campaign. At least some people had fun with it, as opposed to the Dallas incident. I've gotten loads of fan mail—most requesting an autograph, pen included. I've had people ask me to sign their arms or chests or breasts (no, thank you) with a Sharpie. I didn't have a major Nike commercial or one with Gatorade or Coke, but things changed after Sharpie.

Of all the endorsement deals I've cut recently, the Sharpie one was the best, because it turned out to be a joint charity venture. We kicked off the Sharpie Metallic Autographs for Education Program in Atlanta, and we're taking it to Chicago, Denver, Saint Louis, Pittsburgh, and San Francisco. I go into summer camps, Boys and Girls Clubs, schools, and other selected organizations. Sharpie sets up an eight-by-ten-foot wall, which then collects signatures. Based on the number of signatures, Sharpie donates cash and matching donations of school and art supplies. It's cool to be a part of this, knowing it will help out kids across the country. When I visit these places, it reminds me of being a child, and it's great to see the youngsters respond to this program. In East Palo Alto, there's a school called the 49ers Academy, and anytime I run into kids from that place, we have a blast playing together. I wish every team had something like this.

I've also done Nike commercials lately, with the young Atlanta quarterback, Mike Vick. He has a great, unblemished NFL image, and Nike chose the two of us out of its 1,200 NFL clients to kick off a new ad campaign. The ultimate for me came last year when Nike picked me to have my own line of shoes. They're called "Vapor," a lightweight specialist shoe for football players to wear on the field, designed like the ones I put on after halftime. Major cool.

Dallas and Sharpie will be hard to top, but the pom-pom move isn't a bad way to get a cheerleader's attention. Even though we're not supposed to fraternize with the cheerleaders, I've gotten to know some of them at different team events. Actually, that's another silly NFL rule. They can cheer for us, but we can't talk to them? It's not as if we're all trying to date them; that's for the TV producers who roam the sideline. It's weird not to be able to speak to them, but that's the ironclad rule somebody somewhere set up for them.

The 49ers Gold Rush Cheerleaders knew that I liked to celebrate scoring. At one point, I told them I was going to do a little split on the field after making a TD, but I couldn't really bring it off. Then I said I was going to do a toe touch, but they said that I should celebrate in a way that involved the cheerleaders. I thought about it for a while and decided that grabbing the pom-poms and dancing was the answer. It was fun, and I got a lot of female attention afterward, even from women who don't usually watch football. They must have detected my feminine side coming through.

When I grabbed the pom-poms from the cheerleader, I didn't even know who she was. A lot of people thought we'd planned this together, but it was spontaneous on my part. And once more, I did it because the Niners really needed a spark. We were down by a touchdown to Green Bay, and I'd just scored, and I was trying to sustain the buzz for our team. But again, the critics couldn't handle it.

ESPN put me on the cover of its magazine, with this script: "Guys are beating their wives, getting DUIs and doing drugs, and I get national attention for a SHARPIE?" I wasn't smiling in the photo, because that's exactly how I feel about the issue. Compared with the important things in life, how you celebrate a touchdown is very, very minor. I haven't flipped anybody off or done any sexual gestures.

Everybody who plays football knows, after all the practices and all the two-a-days, that game days are the most enjoyable. It's not like basketball or baseball, where you play several times a week. In football, you can't quickly rebound from a bad performance. You get only one day in seven to show your talent and have fun at the same time. During NBA games, I like to watch the interaction between the players and the crowd; I see a lot of guys smiling and talking to the fans. But in the NFL, we're so far away from the stands that it's hard for us to do that. Celebrating has always been a way for me to connect with the crowd. I think the fans want to do more than just come to the park and see us play the games or score touchdowns. They want pleasure and escape during those three or four hours out of the house, so even if we lose, they'll have something good to talk about on the way back to the car.

After all that our families go through, after all that our country has been through in recent years, how significant is signing a football after scoring a touchdown or dancing with some pom-poms? How much anger or rage can people spend on this? My only advice for people who don't understand what it means to have a good time or to give thanks for all that God has done for you is this: Chill.

The worst celebrations ever? Those have to be the ones by Steve Young, because when he tries to dance, he has no rhythm at all. Then there was Gus Frerotte. Playing for Washington a few years back, he hit his head on the stadium wall and nearly knocked himself out. That was the dumbest one of all.

XXIII

BY THE END of the 2002 season, my role on the Niners had changed and expanded. I was a veteran now, my ideas about how to win games were getting stronger, and I was having more trouble holding them back. This was my seventh year in the league, and I was starting to play a bigger part on and off the field. One Sunday afternoon that fall, Kevan Barlow, the spectacularly talented young 49ers running back, was walking around the locker room talking to himself and getting more and more amped up. He kept repeating, "Let's go, guys, let's go!" until it made the whole team uncomfortable. The rest of us were all looking at each other and thinking, *Will you please just sit down and shut up!*

Finally, I had to say, "Kevan, take a seat, man. I'm not the only one who thinks you should. It's everybody."

Part of that was youth. It was only his second year in the league, and already the pressure was on him to carry the load. He was starting to split time with the great Garrison Hearst, and the other part was just Kevan finding his own way. How do you get ready to go do something in public, with 65,000 people in the stands and millions more watching on TV? How do you act in a locker room filled with veteran players who've seen it all? Now I was getting to be one of those guys, which was why I had to calm him down. It wasn't the only thing I did in the locker room that season.

In 2001, we had a Pro Bowl safety named Lance Schulters, who then went to Tennessee as a free agent. Not only was he a top-caliber player, but in the locker room, he always used to sing that DMX song, "We Ain't Going Nowhere," right before we'd take the field. After a while, everyone began to expect this and to rely on it. The song felt like a natural part of our game day, and after Lance left the team, there was a void. You could just feel it. You could almost see it when we were about to exit the locker room. It was like leaving the house but forgetting to brush your teeth.

I decided to do something about this and brought in a Bose CD system. I set up the system in my cramped locker-room space and turned on some hip-hop music to fill the void. Immediately, I could see that it was getting a bunch of the guys jacked up, but we've also got some conservative Christians on the team, and I didn't know how they would respond. Some people like country music, you know? (I like hip-hop *and* Jesus.) Basically, I had no clue what would happen if they were getting ready for battle and suddenly heard lyrics that they found shocking.

I started out with the music pretty low (much lower than I play it at home), but then something happened that really pissed me off. The huge defensive lineman Bryant Young, who is black and whom I totally respect as a Hall of Fame–caliber player, walked over and snapped off my music. You could feel the silence filling up the locker room. I didn't say anything, but privately I was hot. I knew everyone was waiting for my response, so I walked over and turned it back on. This time, he left it alone.

Later on, I told J. J. Stokes that if BY turned off my music the following week, I was going to have some words for him. JJ could see what was in my eyes: there could definitely be trouble ahead. I'd gotten to the point where I had a certain status on the team, and that had to count for something. BY had played in the 49ers' last Super Bowl, was considered the best defensive tackle in the game, and was widely respected for his work ethic and his sincere devotion to community service. Still, this was a classic case of old school versus new school, with a little offense versus defense thrown in. That two of the team leaders were butting heads made for even more drama. While BY keeps a low-key attitude, my reputation outside the locker room is as someone who says what's on his mind. Inside the locker room, though, I usually don't say much.

The confrontation never came: my music replaced Lance's, and nobody said a word about it. BY may not have liked my approach, but he knew that this was a team locker room, and players were preparing for a game, and we needed a new ritual. I just happened to step in and give us one. After a while, most everybody started getting into the music. Even the white guys like Sean Moran, Jeremy Newberry, and Brian Jennings were getting pumped up by hip-hop, just like the rest of us. Oh, yeah, there's a black-white thing going on inside locker rooms, like everywhere else in this country. It's not a divide but simply a natural way of people bonding with one another, but the music helped bridge that gap. It was something new and different, and, like Lance's song, people got used to it. As the weeks went on, if it wasn't playing, people would say to me, "T, where's the music?" Even some of the coaches said this. Then linebacker coach Richard Smith and defensive coordinator Jim Mora came in and started getting pumped up by it, too. It was funny to watch what hip-hop can do to a group of oversized men.

I sat out a couple of games toward the end of that season, trying to rest some injuries before the playoffs started. With my absence from the locker room, everyone began missing the music. The equipment manager finally asked me for the discs I was playing so the routine wouldn't be disrupted. He even took my sound system to Saint Louis for a meaningless regular-season finale on *Monday Night Football*. That game had no importance, because we were already in the playoffs and preparing for a showdown with the hated New York Giants.

I'd never seen a pre-game locker room this lively. My music was blasting, and all the players were in motion. The mood was so upbeat it could have been a postgame setting after a win. Yet this was the beginning of our run for Super Bowl 2003, and everybody—I mean *everybody*—was hungry for the Giants. We'd beaten them in our season opener in the Meadowlands and were playing them at home today, but they were favored to win. Bad memories were everywhere. Our game against them back in week one had gotten ugly, especially for me. It was clear that the Giants had targeted me and felt they had to get inside my head to keep me down. I'd led the NFL in touchdowns the previous season, so the book on our offense was simple: pound quarterback Jeff Garcia, and stop TO. That was the first game of the 2002 season and was being shown to a national audience on a Thursday night. It was also a very emotional evening in New York, with the game set up as a tribute to those who'd endured the September 11, 2001, terrorist attacks on the city. My family had flown in for the game, which always makes me play better, and you couldn't help but get caught up in the emotions in the stadium. When a helicopter flew low over the field before the game, I felt chills and started to cry, and most of the people in that stadium broke a tear. During the national anthem, I'm usually so intense and focused on the upcoming game that I can't even *see* other things around me, but tonight was different. Everybody was listening to the words of the anthem and thinking about their meaning.

Then the game began, and there went Giants defensive back Shaun Williams going off at me with his mouth. He was talking trash at levels I'd rarely heard, and he never stopped. He wore out the *F* word and the *MF* word in the first quarter. He ripped everything about me he could think of, reminding me of a windup doll or a chatterbox. It was personal, and some of it—about my team and myself and my family—was downright low. After the game, the Giants defensive backs coach, Johnny Lynn, who used to be with the 49ers, told George Stewart that they tried everything they could think of to get me off my game. Stew passed this along to me to let me know that it really wasn't personal. I knew they were only doing their job, but Williams never shut up. I'd just come back with my standard line: "Why are you even talking to me?"

He'd say, "We can forget these football pads and take it into the streets."

I thought he was serious.

The Giants ran their mouths so hard that they got fined for how they treated me in that game. After reviewing the tape, the league said it was taunting and dished out a handful of financial penalties. Because of all this, I was really looking forward to this playoff rematch with them, and I wasn't alone.

Inside the locker room, we were "crunk"—the players' term for being cranked up and then some. If they gave out an award for a pregame celebration, we'd have won it. We had an edge that day, in part because of what we'd been hearing in the press for the past week. I like to pay attention to the comments made by the so-called analysts leading up to a game, because you never know where motivation will come from. This week, the theme was pretty blatant: the 49ers may be back in the playoffs, but we had holes on both sides of the line, our young defense was all beaten up, and no one had stepped up to establish himself as a bona fide threat opposite me to take off the pressure. Mariucci had never won the big one, and Jeff Garcia was having such an inconsistent year that even he was surprised at being selected to the Pro Bowl.

That's some of what Cris Collinsworth said on HBO, and a few other newspaper stories expanded on this theme. I'd never really cared for Collinsworth, and this just lowered my opinion of him some more. He said that everybody in the playoffs was a contender—except for the 49ers—and that we were pretenders. A lot of players heard about this and started asking how many Super Bowls Collinsworth had ever won. I didn't see the telecast where Collinsworth blew all this smoke, but Coach Stew told us about it in a receivers' meeting, and then things got pretty quiet. A lot of times in the past, I'd wished that I'd been more vocal with my teammates, in the huddle or in the locker room, but I'd always kept still. I was getting tired of being called a pretender, and I had the feeling that we had a chance to go deep into the playoffs and might even get to the Super Bowl.

I know only one thing for certain: we were as crunked for this showdown as we'd ever been. Maybe that was the problem. Maybe we overexerted ourselves with the pregame stuff, right before we stepped out onto the field for the introductions. We started very well when I busted a 76-yard TD on our first offensive play of the game, and the score was tied 14 to 14 after we scored again with six minutes to go in the half, but then the Giants exploded for two touchdowns in the final three minutes of the half, and we left the field feeling completely deflated. I was standing on the sidelines and thinking, *Collinsworth was right—we are just pretending.* It was bad enough that we were getting our butts kicked, but we were also getting trash-talked into the ground—and loudmouth Jeremy Shockey, the Giants tight end, had even thrown a cup of ice on two young Niners fans, almost setting off a fight in the stands. Shockey apologized to them and gave the kids a football, probably to avoid a lawsuit.

The halftime mood in the locker room had dropped about ten notches. It was very quiet in there, and even the hometown crowd seemed to have given up on us. I kept thinking about Collinsworth's comments, and then I did something I'd never done before. I stood up and began to talk, and my voice got louder, and I let it all out. I spoke from my heart to my teammates, telling them that we could still win this game. Usually, another veteran, most likely Bryant Young, took over the halftime locker room, or the coaches would try to motivate us when we fell behind, but this time I did the talking. At first, it felt weird, because I'd never played this role before, in high school or college, but I was finally comfortable enough to do it now. I was going to my third straight Pro Bowl this year, and some people were calling on me to be a team leader. I was ready to try to be that, and I was tired—extremely tired—of losing. It takes a lot just to get to the playoffs, so anytime you're there, you have to lay all of it out on the field, because you never know when you're going back to the post-season. Or maybe you get hurt and never play again. Who knows?

My intensity level had never been higher. I was pumping my fist in the middle of the floor, and everybody was looking at me, even Mooch. I could see him out of the corner of my eye, staring at me and no doubt thinking, *Where's this coming from?*

It just felt right to do it, to try to use some of the fire that had motivated me for so many years to help others get back into the game. This was my coming-out party, and it was completely spontaneous.

"We're either going to contend or we're going to pretend," I told the team. "What's it gonna be?"

In the second half, things quickly got worse. We went down by 21 points in the third quarter, and by now the crowd must have fallen asleep. The loudest noises in the stadium were coming from the mouths of Giants safeties Shaun Williams and Omar Stoutmire and Giants defensive end Michael Strahan. Their trash-talking had gotten even nastier and more personal, with Stoutmire spewing profanities at me every time I lined up on the field. Jeremy Shockey was flapping his lips, too—when he wasn't dropping balls. With the score 35 to 14, Shockey muffed a pass in our end zone that would have put the game out of reach. Then he caught a ball in the end zone but came down with it out of bounds. The Giants had to settle for a field goal, to make it 38 to 14. So much for my halftime speech. Only one other team in NFL history, the Buffalo Bills, had ever come back from this far behind to win in the playoffs.

In the first half, Jeff Garcia had been taken out of his rhythm by their defense, but late in the third quarter, he began to hit his receivers, running the hurry-up offense and playing with frantic intensity. He moved us 70 yards in seven plays, hitting me for a 26-yard score. On the next play, I caught a two-point conversion from Jeff, cutting the lead to 38 to 22. After the Giants couldn't make a first down, they punted to Vinny Sutherland, who called for a fair catch but was then hammered by linebacker Dhani Jones. The 15-yard penalty gave us the ball at the New York 27, and three plays later, Jeff used his legs instead of his arm, running 14 yards for the score. He hit me again in the end zone for another 2-point conversion, and it was suddenly 38 to 30. The crowd was fully awake now and roaring with each play. You could feel the stands rocking beneath them and sense that something unusual was building. The Giants, for the first time all afternoon, weren't swaggering but staggering.

I was tired of Michael Strahan's tongue, so after our last TD, I made a little gesture in front of him just to let him know the game wasn't over. He struck a pose right in my face, pointing up at the scoreboard and then staring at me.

"Look at the score, bitch!" he said.

I didn't say anything but gave him a grin, because I knew that he was getting worried.

Our defense held again, and now Jeff moved us down the field once more, like clockwork, 74 yards in fifteen plays, setting up a Jeff Chandler field goal attempt from 25 yards. He nailed it, and the score was 38 to 33.

When you're crunk, you're crunk. This was the kind of football game I'd always wanted to play in, the kind that could lead to a championship. This was why I'd worked so hard in the weight room all those years, preparing myself for the chance to help my team win. The second half was like being on a thrill ride at Paramount's Great America Theme Park in Santa Clara or living inside an NFL Films canister. Leading by only 5 points now, the Giants put together their own drive and gave their placekicker Matt Bryant a chance at a 42-yard field goal, but he pushed it to the left. We got the ball on our own 32 and began moving into their territory. It was hard to say what was louder now, the Niners fans or the Giants defense putting up a constant whine.

After eight plays, we'd driven to their 13 when Jeff dropped back to pass. I was covered, but he found Tai Streets in the end zone and hit him for the go-ahead score, 39 to 38.

By now, I didn't feel like being called a bitch anymore, and I was ready to blow. The pressure of playing in this great game eventually caught up with a lot of people, including myself. Before we could attempt another 2-point conversion, I pointed up at the scoreboard, so that Michael Strahan, Shaun Williams, Omar Stoutmire, and everyone else would see. I got flagged for taunting Williams, but then he went wild in front of the refs and got hit with an offsetting unsportsmanlike conduct penalty.

With the crowd on its feet and screaming insanely, we went to the line of scrimmage, and Jeff took the ball from center. Looking around to throw, he tossed the ball into the hands of Giants cornerback Will Allen, who thought he was playing college football and could return an extra-point try for a touchdown. I wasn't too clear about the rule myself, and when I saw him running down the field with the ball toward our goal line, I took off after him, using the 4.5 speed I was known for. When I caught up with him, I tagged him with the kind of hit I'd been putting on D-backs for the past seven years and sent him toward the first row of seats. One sportswriter later said I met Allen going 200 miles an hour. I was flagged again—this time for a late hit out of bounds—and then Stoutmire came after me and was finally ready to take the game into the streets, where he'd been pushing it all along. Williams threw a punch at our center, Jeremy Newberry, which got him thrown out of the game.

The game, by the way, wasn't over. We had a 1-point lead, with a minute left to go. After Williams was escorted from the field and Stoutmire quit jawing long enough to catch his breath and players from both teams were separated, we kicked off to the Giants. With absolutely nobody in the stadium sitting down, they started their last drive of the day, moving the ball down to our 23-yard line. With six seconds left, they set up for a 41-yard field goal. It was almost more than I could watch.

On the sideline, I was standing next to Stew, and I said, "If they miss this field goal, it was meant to be. We're going to the Super Bowl."

The Giants had signed a stopgap long snapper, Trey Junkin, who was forty-one and got pulled out of retirement when regular long snapper David Leary suffered a finger injury. Junkin was a graying eccentric from a different era who looked like someone from a Harley-Davidson convention. His snap was so low that the holder, Matt Allen, couldn't handle it. Allen jumped up and tried to throw downfield to Rich Seubert, but the pass fell incomplete, and the Giants went crazy again, charging that Niner Chike Okeafor had interfered with Seubert (which he had).

I grabbed Stew and said, "I cannot believe this. This is unreal."

Time had expired, and players were running everywhere, but no one was certain if the game was over. Whistles blew, referees huddled, and the crowd cut loose at the officials. Was the game over or not? Had there been a 49ers penalty that would give the Giants another try at the field goal? Were we going on to the second round of the playoffs against Tampa Bay . . . or what?

The refs came out of their huddle and made their announcement: the game was over, and we'd won. I was so jacked that I climbed up onto a camera pod and whooped it up with the fans who cheered me on with everything they had. It seemed that no one moved from the stadium for the next thirty minutes. The Giants were too stunned to leave, and we all hung out together on the field far longer than we ever had after a game in my career. But this was no ordinary football game. Jeff had thrown for 331 yards and three TDs, while I'd made nine catches for 177 yards, two touchdowns, a pair of 2-point conversion receptions, one pass completion, and one scuffle that got Shaun Williams ejected from the game.

By the time I got into the locker room, news of my halftime speech had reached the media, and it made for a good story line the next day. In the locker room, I broke my silence with the local press long enough to say that I was very, very proud to be part of a great organization like the 49ers, and I meant that. This was how I'd always wanted things to be when I came to the Niners. For at least this one game, I was portrayed in the media as something other than a villain. I could inspire people as well as make them angry about my celebrations. I was not just out for myself but truly wanted the team to win.

I really appreciated the kind postgame comments tossed my way from Niners like Julian Peterson. I don't know if my words really helped, but maybe they had. Until this game, I'd tried to lead on the field by example, straight from the Jerry Rice playbook: keep your mouth shut around your teammates, work hard, do your job, and hope that others will follow your lead. This game was a turning point for me. Because of what happened at halftime and because we'd gone on to beat the Giants, I felt that it was now all right to express my feelings in front of the team. I was able to act like a veteran and not just play like one. I had a new role to play—or that's how it looked at the time.

The next day, the NFL office reviewed the game and said that it shouldn't have ended as it did, because there were offsetting penalties on the Giants' botched field-goal attempt, but it was too late to go back and change anything. It was on to Tampa Bay to play the Bucs in round two.

Mooch's response to the league's comment that the game should have gone on for at least another play?

"Bummer."

He had no idea that this word was about to describe his football future.

XXIV

I DON'T KNOW WHAT made me turn around and go up to Mooch's office. It was three days after our last game of the 2002–03 season, the one that followed our win against the Giants. We'd lost ugly to the eventual Super Bowl champion, Tampa Bay, and I was still angry about it. I'd dropped by the facility to pick up a few things, and when I was in there, the news hit like a Bay Area earthquake: Mooch had just been fired. Our difficult relationship was finished. I was staying, and he was moving on. People would blame me for his leaving or assume that I was ecstatic about it, but when the news came, I had a bittersweet feeling. You go through trials on sports teams that are hard to put into words. You bond with people without ever talking about it, sometimes without even knowing it. You exchange emotions, hunger, hurt, and dreams. You know some of what they've gone through, which the public never sees, and they've seen you low enough or happy enough to burst into tears. You can't hide this stuff, even if you try to, and by now, Mooch and I knew each other whether we wanted to or not. He'd just lost his job, and I felt for him, because in pro football, you never know who might be next to go.

At the same time, Steve Mariucci and I weren't exactly hanging out during our nights off together, and my anger after the Tampa Bay game was partly directed at him. The Bucs had come out like the Giants the week before and run up a big lead on us. With fifty seconds to go in the half, they were ahead by 22 points, but we had the ball on our 31, and our offense looked as if it might be finally waking up. A lot of the players felt we should try to make something happen in this fifty seconds. Look at what we'd done against the Giants after trailing them by 24 points. Three touchdown drives in just a few minutes. One score before the half against the Bucs, even a field goal, would have sent us into the locker room with some hope, but Mooch went conservative again. He had the team run one play up the middle to kill the clock. He quit on an offense that a week ago had put up 39 points. Jeff must have picked up on the coach's lack of confidence in us; after playing great against the Giants, he threw three picks against the Bucs. For three years, I'd been saying that Mooch was a conservative offensive play caller, and I'd been getting ripped for this from every side. Now he'd been fired, and the national media were saying the same thing. So was the 49ers brass.

After we beat the Giants, Mooch seemed to have a long-term future with the Niners, but he was gone the moment that play was called in Tampa Bay. It was the most nontraditional 49ers play since he'd brought back the shotgun formation to accommodate Jeff Garcia's style, and it left the Niners hierarchy as livid as I was. Mooch had a year left on his contract, but management was never going to give him the type of raise he'd been lobbying for. This was the out the organization had been looking for. Following our 31-to-6 loss to the Bucs, I'd made a bet with my agent about how many days it would take before he was gone. I'd said forty-eight hours, and I was only slightly off.

Less than seventy-two hours after the game, I was leaving the locker room when I noticed one of the equipment managers, Kevin Latique, packing up Mooch's things. It was a weird sight; usually, you see them packing for players who've been cut. I realized what had happened, and I thought, *Terrell, you have to be a bigger person now. Just go say something to him. Anything. Don't let him go without trying to say something to him and finding some closure.* So I went on up to his office.

Only a year before, during our rift, I couldn't have done this, not for a million dollars in cash tax-free, but because of all we'd gone through together, I was pulled in his direction. It's very rare that players and coaches really don't like each other. I didn't dislike him. I just wanted to win, and taking a knee in a playoff game was not the way to do it. The conflict wasn't about our personalities; you can work with people you aren't crazy about. The conflict was about the best way to win football games and championships. I didn't think he could get it done, and I wasn't the only one who felt that way.

I walked in, and there was Mooch, sitting at his desk, talking back to the television. The analysts were buzzing on ESPN, usually a Mooch-friendly network, about how he'd gotten fired. The team's hierarchy had pinned the firing on co-owner John York, who'd upset Mooch even more by letting on that the coach had asked not just for more money but for more power.

"Can you believe this BS?" Mooch said to me.

He was so annoyed that I don't even think he knew who'd come into the room.

I was still so uncomfortable around him that I didn't sit down.

Suddenly, he realized who I was, and he looked as surprised at seeing me in his office as I was to be there. He turned down the volume, and we started to chat. But first there was a beat, as in a movie, where we just looked at each other in silence. Somebody had to say something, so I wished him the best of luck.

"I don't know what's going to happen," he said, and then there was another pause. "Hey," he said, "someday, maybe a year from now, we may be back together again."

I nodded, but I was thinking, *You must be out of your damn mind!*

There was nothing left to do but shake his hand, say good luck again, and leave the room.

When his firing hit the papers the next day, the New York press greeted it with a one-word headline: "Bummer!"

But the story wasn't over.

Within a couple of weeks, he'd made a deal with Detroit for $5 million a year. He'd gone from coaching a playoff team to running one of the doormats of the NFL. On any given Sunday, or Monday or Tuesday, anything can happen in the NFL. I could even go play for Mooch in Detroit—for about $30 million to sign!

A month or so later, I was boarding a plane in Portland after meeting with Nike about an endorsement deal. Earlier that day word had gotten out that the Niners were hiring Dennis Erickson to replace Mooch. I was supposed to take off at seven-thirty or eight P.M., but the flight was delayed. I wasn't in any hurry to take my seat, and my agent and I had talked at the airport for as long as we could before he caught a flight to North Carolina. I'd been hiding out in the boarding area, keeping my head down, because some fans were at the gate, and I didn't want to be hassled. Back in the day, a kid or two would ask for my autograph to stick on their bedroom walls, but now I have to be careful, because the memorabilia creeps have figured out a way to get more autographs. They pay kids to approach athletes in hotels or other places. It's all right, usually—until you see the same kid asking for your signature for the third time in one weekend. You bust on him, and he denies it, but you know the truth, so you warn him that he's had enough.

It's always hard to turn adults down, especially if they have children with them, and hard to refuse teenagers. If you turn just one down, he may go away thinking you're a jerk. But if I go somewhere and start signing, then I can't enjoy myself. The worst is when people come up and say, "TO, I hate to bother you, but . . ."

If you hate to bother me, then why bother me?

"I know you're busy but . . ."

I mean, even when you're eating!

"I hate to inconvenience you, but . . ."

For the most part, I try to be polite, but you can't please everybody, and sometimes you just have to say no.

I'd sat in the airport unrecognized for about forty-five minutes, before getting on the plane and looking for overhead space for my little bag. I slid into my seat and felt a tap on my shoulder. I looked around and realized it was Dennis Erickson, the new head coach of the 49ers, the man taking over Mooch's job.

"Is this a joke?" I said. "Am I on *Candid Camera* or something?"

He just smiled and grabbed my hand.

It really felt as if somebody was playing a trick on me, but I think he was as amazed as I was. I'd only heard about him becoming our coach that morning. He was en route from his office at Oregon State to a press conference the next day in San Francisco. What were the odds of us sitting beside each other on the same flight back from Portland on the same day he was announced as Mariucci's replacement?

Ever since the loss to the Bucs, the Niners had been surrounded by drama, with all kinds of crazy rumors flying in the media. I'd seen this before when George Seifert got fired and Mooch was brought in, but now I was a veteran leader on the team, and people were calling me to ask what I thought about it all. What I thought was that nothing surprised me anymore in the NFL—not after Dallas, Chicago, Sharpie, the Giants, and Tampa Bay. I'd gone from hero to villain, back to hero again, and I'd probably be a villain again soon enough. I'd seen our entire roster get overhauled, watched one of the proudest franchises in professional sports history hit rock bottom, its popular owner run out of town by his own family and friends, and then get back on its feet with an infusion of young players signed by Bill Walsh and John McVay. But I wasn't ready to be sitting next to my new head coach.

When I'd composed myself, I reminded him of when he'd coached me in the Senior Bowl, back in Mobile in 1995.

"You didn't give me any playing time," I said, joking.

He didn't laugh.

"You had Derrick Mayes and Amani Toomer and Mercury Hayes," I told him. "You tried to make them stars, and you did, because Derrick Mayes wound up being the MVP of that game. I barely got any playing time and caught one pass for four yards."

He just looked at me and said, "You know how things are."

We talked a bit, and I kept shaking my head, wondering if he'd planned this meeting to try to get started with me on the right foot.

"Sometimes," he said, "things are meant to be. Just look at it as this was meant to be."

XXV

AFTER THE 2002 SEASON, I wanted only two things: to help make Erickson a winning coach and to help the team achieve the things we hadn't gotten done under Mooch. In order to take us to the next level, I felt that I needed to step up, not just on the field but also as a leader. I also knew some other things: that I've matured late, both as a football player and as a human being, and that my upbringing made for some underdeveloped social skills. I was slow out of the chute when it came to interacting with other people, like a grade school kid in high school, a high-schooler in college, and a college student my first few years in the NFL. My body was still growing, and I was about to turn thirty. So were my emotions and my relationships and responsibilities.

By now, as the world knew, I had a three-year-old son, Terique, a great kid who lived with his mom in the Bay Area. His mother and I weren't married, but I tried to spend as much time with Terique as I could. I designed special rooms for him when he stayed with me in Atlanta or at my home near the 49ers facility. I love being a dad, I've loved being with him from the moment he was born, but I can't lie—at first, this was a very difficult situation for me because of the way I'd been raised, not knowing my father until I was almost a teenager. Terique's mom and I should have planned better before we had a child, but we've been able to maintain a good relationship and have done everything we can to help our son. I didn't have a dad growing up, and the last thing I wanted was for Terique to experience that. I feel that we've made the best of the situation. My son has helped me be less moody and more present with other people. I can be playful and lighthearted with him in ways that I can't with a lot of adults. Anytime he's around, my mood changes instantly for the better. Children pull you out of yourself and connect you very directly to life. My son is helping me to grow up.

Like many NFL fathers, I missed practice when Terique was born. We got the call in the middle of the night, and I was excused for most of the next day. I didn't even have a chance to phone my mom until after he was born, because I was in the delivery room, which was exactly where I wanted to be. From the moment he came into the world, I wanted more for him than I ever had as a child. I also wanted more for myself, both as a football player and as a human being. And I wanted more for the 49ers and our new coach.

Perhaps in 2003, it would all come together, and the last seven years would truly pay off for me and the team. My career with the Niners had been very up-and-down, with me constantly learning to adjust and adapt to changing circumstances. We'd gone from the NFC title game in 1996 to being 4 and 12 two years after that—the end of a dynasty but also a new beginning. I wanted to be a major part of the next Super Bowl victory in San Francisco, a driving force. Maybe the growing pains were finally over, and it was time for something better. As the new season approached, my contract with the Niners was running out, and 2003 would be a make-or-break year for me.

The game had gotten much bigger than I ever dreamed it would. Each time I walked out onto the field at Candlestick Park for home games in 2002, I looked up at the stands, which a few years earlier had been filled with number 80 49ers jerseys honoring Jerry Rice. Now there weren't hundreds but thousands of number 81s up there, from top to bottom and from one end of the stadium to the other. You couldn't look anywhere without noticing them, and every time

I saw this, it almost brought tears to my eyes. Only a handful of people knew how far I'd traveled to this moment. Only a couple of them had been with me the whole way. No matter what some media people had written about me, no matter what they said about me on talk radio, the real Niners fans showed their support on Sunday by putting on these jerseys and cheering for me on the field.

They were a tough crowd, not easy to impress. They'd not only seen the 49ers win five Super Bowls, but they were hard-core football fans. John Brodie had once been the quarterback of the Niners, in the years before their championship run, and I'd heard stories about fans—49ers fans—throwing bottles at his head after he walked (or ran) off the field following a loss. He kept his helmet on until he reached the locker room, because he never knew when a missile might catch him on the skull. In 1996, I'd come into this environment and through sweat and commitment had built my own fan base. Whenever I doubted myself or felt that I hadn't come that far, these number 81 jerseys told me that I had. I wanted to win a ring for these people as well as myself—now.

PART FOUR
THE MELTDOWN

XXVI

FOR THE FIRST TIME EVER, I used all of the winter and spring months of 2003 to recover from injuries. I didn't play basketball in the off-season or travel much or spend a lot of time with my mom and grandmother in Alabama. I made a total commitment to football and to my health, staying in Atlanta and seeing doctors almost every day. The 2002 football campaign had gone against my usual philosophy— "Don't touch the ground"—because in game after game, I'd kept banging into it. Until now, I'd been mostly injury-free, with only a few nasty turf burns (any stadium with old artificial turf should immediately be outlawed; if the NFLPA wants to do something for the players, there's an issue to jump on). This had been by far my worst year in terms of being slowed by injuries. My feet bothered me, as they had since I'd started constantly running on them ten or twelve years earlier. While running a reverse, I managed to separate cartilage from my ribs. I hurt my heel in New Orleans on some bad turf. I jumped up to catch a TD pass and landed on one leg, coming down hard on my heel. I kept playing, but the next day I couldn't even walk. This turned into a four-week process of healing and trying to compensate by not running on my heel. Then other things started to happen. The heel injury moved up to my hip abductor and from there up into my groin, and it just got worse. While trying to heal, there's always the fear of doing too much and reinjuring yourself. My ribs, meanwhile, didn't start to feel better until the off-season.

In 2002, I went for about a month and a half without practicing at all because of the injuries, just playing on Sundays. After taking those weeks off and resting my groin, I was able to practice twice the next month; when I tried to practice a third day, I knew I'd already overdone it, but I didn't want to feel that I was slighting the team. I didn't want anybody questioning whether or not I was really hurt. This is a huge problem in the NFL. You start missing a few practices, and people begin to whisper behind your back. It's just human nature, and some guys will do anything to get out of practice, especially some of the veterans. It's no secret that the repetition can be boring, but I've never tried to cheat my team or myself by missing practice. In this case, I was hurt. Still, there's that little voice inside that says you should get out to the field just to show everyone you're trying. They can't see you working all those hours in the training room. All they see is that you're not at practice, but in the meeting rooms you look fine, except for an ice pack. Resentment seeps in. I've found myself thinking that about other players, so it was natural for me to feel that someone was thinking this about me, especially since I wasn't making any significant improvement.

Enter Mike Hatrack, an Atlanta-area chiropractor whom I'd worked with over the previous couple of years. I'd lift weights, and he'd keep my body in line by adjusting me. My trainer, James "Buddy" Primm of the Personal Training Institute of Atlanta, would monitor me from afar and then ask me questions after he'd hear reports about me on ESPN. Mike was an extension of my training program; Buddy would detect something, call me to talk, and then get me hooked up with Mike for some isolation treatment. My attitude was always the same: Do what works. I'd been getting treatment from the 49ers training staff—Lindsy McLean (since retired), Todd Lazenby, and Jeff Tanaka—for my injury, but I wasn't getting better. All I was getting were stim and ice, and their exercise program was killing me.

So Buddy said, "Get Mike Hatrack out there."

"What can he do?" I asked.

"Listen to me," Buddy said. "I know what Mike can do. Just get him out there so he can work on you."

Mike came out, and it was like a miracle. He arrived on a Saturday in late December 2002, before a huge home game against Green Bay. Both teams were positioning for home-field advantage in the playoffs. A loss for us would make the final two games of the regular season virtually meaningless, so if I could play against the Packers, I might be able to rest until the playoffs without any harm to the team. Worse, the San Francisco Bay Area was getting hit with a storm that brought twenty-five inches of rain in less than a week. It poured for days, and it was cold, at least by Northern California standards. So I could feel the pain even more. Extreme weather conditions will do that to a sports-related injury: heat increases swelling, and cold magnifies pain.

I'd tried to practice earlier in the week, but it just wasn't happening. My first attempt at running came on Saturday. I went out to the field, but couldn't go 5 yards, and it was really frustrating, because this was one of the biggest games of my career. Everything was weighing on my mind. I'd been cooped up inside all week rehabbing, and everyone kept asking if I was going to be able to play, especially my teammates, and all I could say was, "I don't know."

Coach Stew and I would sit back after meetings and talk.

"Stew," I said, "I don't know if I'm going to be able to go. I can't run."

That Saturday, after I went out and tried to run but couldn't, I looked over at Mooch and signaled, "I can't run, man." I was really upset. The doctors wanted to give me a cortisone injection in my groin for the game. I'd taken a small one at the start of the week, so they gave me another one, a mild injection that wouldn't damage any tissue. It felt a little better. Then I hooked up with Mike Hatrack.

Before Mike worked on me, on a scale from one to ten, I was probably a three or four, but when I left him that night, tears were in my eyes from sheer gratitude; I was up to a seven. I know I sound like one of those evangelist healer shows on late-night television, but this was real. Mike broke up scar tissue, moved it around, and worked everything deep. He worked every muscle that was keeping me from releasing the tension on my groin. I almost cried on the spot. I left and returned to the hotel. The first person I saw was Stew.

"Stew," I said. "I'm ready. This was like a miracle."

After our team meetings, Mike worked on me some more, and once again the morning before I went to the stadium. Until now, I'd felt that I was getting the best treatment possible from the 49ers training and medical staff, but then word got around about what Mike had done for me that weekend. We talked about introducing him to the Niners staff, but this was a difficult call. At first, we thought the staff might feel undermined by his presence; people can get very territorial in situations like this, and you don't want doctors to think that somebody is stepping on their turf. You'd think that with all the money these teams spend on their athletes, they'd use the best resources available, but this is a big problem across the league. Teams have their own doctors, but a lot of players feel that they should have their own medical personnel.

After Mike helped me so much, I thought he might be able to help others, so I put my concerns aside, went into the 49ers training room, and talked him up as much as I could. A bunch of guys were soon going to see him: Derrick Deese, Tony Parrish, Ahmed Plummer, Jamie Winborn, and J. J. Stokes. When Parrish dislocated his elbow and his arm swelled up to twice its normal size, he went to Mike, and the swelling was soon drastically reduced. This kind of healing was unheard of, and it had nothing to do with the 49ers training staff. We tried to tell the team how good Mike was, but some people seemed intimidated by what we were saying. *Threatened* may be a better word, so we found ways to get around this. Now all the guys who got healed would come hang with me in Atlanta, then visit Mike's office in a neighboring city. I remember quarterback

My grandmother won first place in a church fashion show. My mother made her winning outfit.

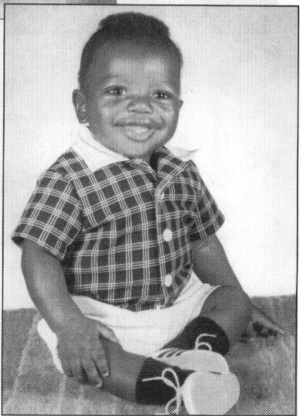

When I first started playing
I was skinny as a rail and
not very strong.

When I was ten I was the $25 grand-prize winner in the
Alexander City Michael Jackson contest. My mom made
me the costume and I won over the crowd with my
moon-walking. That's me in the middle behind those
sunglasses.

Our Christmas picture from 1988. Standing behind our mom, left to right, LaTasha, me,
Victor, and Sharmaine.

Back in high school I thought of basketball as my real passion, with all other sports a distant second. In football somebody told you what to do on every play, but in basketball you got to *create* your game on the fly.

When I was a junior the wide receiver ahead of me got sick and Coach Savarese let me start in his place. I caught a pass and ran 46 yards down the sideline for a touchdown, plowing over and around a couple of tacklers along the way. After that I started getting a lot more playing time and more chances to catch the ball.

Outside my grandmother's house just before the prom, that's me and my date, Metissa, and LaTasha and Charles.

I was excited about going to UTC but really nervous about leaving Alexander City. As much as your hometown can be a burden, it's the only thing you've ever known.

When UTC played Marshall, the defending I-AA national champs, in my sophomore year, I grabbed five balls for 145 yards and scored four touchdowns. The last one came when we were behind, and it clinched the game for UTC. People told me later that a nationwide telecast featuring Alabama had been interrupted to show us beating the best I-AA team in the nation. By the time I was a senior at UTC, my combination of size, speed, and strength was gaining me more attention. I'd even been selected to play in the Senior Bowl in Mobile, Alabama.

"With the twenty-eighth pick in the third round," the TV announcer said, "the San Francisco Forty-Niners select wide receiver Terrell Owens of the University of Tennessee–Chattanooga." Around me are Tammy, Shana, Erica, Carla, my mom, Victor, and LaTasha.

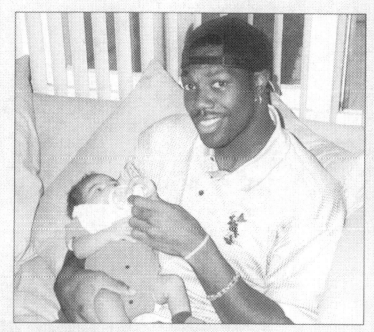

I love being a dad and spending time with my son, Terique. I'll never forget the call in the middle of the night for me to rush down to the delivery room. I was so excited and nervous I didn't even get a chance to call my mom until after he was born.

J. J. Stokes and I sitting on the bench with Jerry Rice.

With seven minutes left in the fourth quarter, I ran down the left sideline, outleaped Shawn Springs for the ball, and made it to the end zone for a 37-yard score that proved to be the game winner. Of course, what happened next is history.

A limo met us at the airport, and we were driven to the Eagles' headquarters with a police escort. When we arrived, fans were holding up signs with my picture that read, "Free TO" and "TO's an Eagle!" They were cheering as we stepped out of the car. At 7:00 P.M. the press conference got under way and I was officially a Philadelphia Eagle. Here I am with Head Coach Andy Reid and Eagles' Chairman and CEO Jeffrey Lurie.

Cade McNown calling me after the first time Mike worked on his bum shoulder.

"Where did you get this guy?" he said. "He's amazing."

I know. I'd improved 100 percent with him in a matter of hours. I still wasn't perfect but was probably two-thirds of the way there. I remember trying to run during the pregame warm-ups against Green Bay, but I really couldn't take off the way I was used to. So I wound up receiving another shot to get me over the edge. They don't shoot you in the injured area but in the butt. Plenty of guys do that, and it got me through. Prior to that, if it hadn't been for Mike Hatrack, I don't think I could have played. We lost to the Packers, but I made an impact. Then I was able to rest the following two games before coming back relatively strong for the playoffs against the Giants. During that time, Mike left instructions for a local masseuse, Kathy Sherrill, to come over and try to duplicate what he'd been doing. I don't think I could have played those last few games without the two of them.

Despite the ongoing pain in my abdomen and groin, I'd gone to Hawaii and played in the Pro Bowl in February 2003, because I felt it was an honor to be selected to participate. Then I went back to Georgia and rehabbed from February through July. All during the off-season, I received shots every other day in and around my groin area to help rebuild tissue and repair torn muscles. The shots loosened up my muscles, but they were extremely painful and regularly brought tears to my eyes. Most of my day was consumed with driving forty-five minutes to the doctor's office and being there for hours. I did exercises in a swimming pool, did strengthening work for my abs. All of this was tedious, but nobody made me do it. I brought in my own doctors, not the Niners' doctors, because I felt they could help me the most. I did all this on my own, because I wanted to be completely healthy for the upcoming season and felt the 49ers now had a chance to be a great team, a Super Bowl team.

When I wasn't spending time with doctors, I prayed about my health and asked God to bless me with a recovered body. I prayed a lot. Fans don't know much about rehab and never see any of this when they look out at the field and watch football players in uniforms on Sunday afternoons. They assume that because we look in such good shape or are so muscular, our bodies must be fine. They had no idea what I was going through that off-season. The pain and all the shots in the groin were bad enough, but the loss of my freedom and movement was a whole other issue. I was tied down in Atlanta and locked into a boring routine. Any athlete forced to heal during the off-season will tell you how frustrating it is. You need time away from football in order to get ready for another season. You need physical rest and mental rest. You need separation from your teammates, your coaches, and your football schedule. You need to let go of the last season and its disappointments so you can prepare for what's next. By 2003, I was very used to the off-season cycle and knew how to manage it, but all that was now gone. Losing this down time made me moody, even cranky some days, but I believed that the extra work in rehab was going to pay off.

A special year seemed just around the corner.

XXVII

IN 2002, WE'D won the NFC West division and tasted what it was like to win in the postseason against a good opponent. We'd shown ourselves that we weren't just pretenders but could contend at the highest levels of football. Teams have to get ready to win titles, and a lot of people felt that the Niners were about to return to glory. The 2003 Super Bowl champion Tampa Bay Bucs had been on the rise for several years before they finally broke through. They'd kept going to the playoffs and losing, until they got rid of their old coach, Tony Dungy, and brought in a fiery younger one, Jon Gruden. Dungy was a good coach, but Gruden was exactly what the franchise needed to take it from a playoff team to a Super Bowl champion. He was fresh and relentless, he got up at three in the morning to start working on his game plans, and he was the extra punch that Tampa Bay had been lacking. Less than a year after his hiring, his players were getting fitted for rings. Change had been necessary in Tampa Bay, and the results proved that.

Change had also been needed in San Francisco. The Mooch-TO rift had become very old news, and I wasn't the only player who felt he had limited our offensive power (just the only one willing to talk about it openly). Maybe Dennis Erickson could provide the spark we needed to get past the second round of the playoffs. Also, for me, 2003 was a special year because my contract ran out at the end of it.

In the winter of 2004, I could declare free agency and test my value on the open market. Players try not to focus too much on this kind of thing, but the truth is that we can't help it. Neither could you, if your work contracts were set up the way ours are. We read the papers, listen to the sports talk shows, and see the numbers rolling around the league, just as everyone else does. We pick up on the rumors flying around the locker rooms, too.

All the players know about Randy Moss getting a $19-million signing bonus. We know that NFL contracts, unlike those in other team sports, aren't guaranteed, and that's why signing bonuses are so important. You may never get the money you're signed up for in the third or fourth year of your deal, so you can only count on what you get up front. Players are very aware of who the highest-paid person is at our own position, and we gossip about contracts. At times, we feel envy, anger, and jealousy. When someone like Ray Lewis ($19-million bonus) or Simeon Rice ($20 million) gets a new deal during the off-season, we can't help but think about our own situations.

In 2002, I'd caught one hundred passes for 1,300 yards and thirteen TDs. A prominent coach of a successful NFL team mentioned these numbers to a friend of mine in the off-season.

"You tell Terrell Owens and his agent," he said, "that I would personally get on my knees and suck their (*bleeps*) to get him down here."

Now, that's what I call tampering!

After the 2003 season, the former great tight end of the Cleveland Browns, Ozzie Newsome, now an executive with the Baltimore Ravens, approached me at the Michael Jordan celebrity golf tournament and kept asking me, "Can I trust you? Can I trust you?" At first, I thought he was talking about meeting a woman. It took me a while to figure out that he meant could he trust me not to sign with another team if I eventually became a free agent without talking to the Ravens.

David and I liked hearing that other teams were interested in me, but we wanted to see if we could work something out with the 49ers. I had many friends and contacts in the region and had bought a home south of San Francisco. I still felt a passion for the organization after seven years in the league. It was stronger than ever before, but the clock was now ticking each time I put on pads. Every athlete knows that he's one hit away from being out of the game forever. No matter how many muscles I'd developed or how good a shape I stayed in year-round, I can't control what happens to me on the field. All I can do is have faith and keep working hard; the rest is in God's hands, and God has been exceptionally good to me. But you never know what's coming next in the NFL. That's the strange thing about the ball we use in this game. It's not round like a baseball or a basketball or a golf ball or a soccer ball or a tennis ball. It's not flat like a hockey puck but oval-shaped, which means that you can't ever predict which way it's going to bounce.

In early June 2003, about six weeks before training camp started, David flew to San Francisco to sit down with Terry Donahue, John McVay, John York, Dominic Corsell, and Dennis Erickson. At the first meeting, the organization triple-teamed him with Donahue, McVay, and Corsell. They made it clear to him that they wanted to re-sign me, and he made it clear that we were interested in staying with the Niners. David said that he was seeking market value for me, but we wanted to be cap-friendly. We could structure a deal that would keep me on the team and keep the franchise under the salary cap. We could make it work. The talks were going well until they brought up with David a couple of fines that I'd gotten over the past few years, for being late to a practice and having a uniform violation. David was surprised by this.

"It was nitpicky crap," he told me on the phone after the meeting. "They didn't mention any contract numbers but wanted to focus on this other stuff. I humored them about the fines. I told them that they live in the worst traffic area in the United States and that people are going to be late once in a while."

Despite the fine issue, David thought the meeting went well and the negotiations were about to get started. We wanted the deal done before the season started, so I could just focus on football. At the end of their meetings, Donahue said he would be in touch soon, but he didn't call. Two days before training camp began, in mid-July, David phoned Corsell, who again said that Donahue would be in touch. He never called. During training camp, he announced in the press that the Niners wouldn't do anything with my contract until after the season. Several months later, in December, David called Donahue and heard the same thing: there was no rush to get this done; they would get around to it once the season was over.

This situation was in the background throughout my 2003 football year, and it affected me. I'd like to be able to say that it didn't, but that would be a lie. Since 1996, I'd given everything I had to the 49ers, and in the winter of 2003, I'd done whatever I could to make myself healthier and stronger for the upcoming season. I was bothered that Donahue never called David back and that they let all this dangle in the wind during the summer, the fall, and on into the winter of 2004. I don't know that all this impacted my play in 2003, but it affected my mind and my emotions, and it set the backdrop for what was to come. All I wanted to focus on was winning football games and getting back to the playoffs but every time I turned around, there was another distraction, another eruption. The truth is that I was stung by the Niners not making any effort to re-sign me in 2003. Maybe being TO, living and playing football and celebrating the way I wanted to instead of playing the PC game the way Jerry Rice had played it, was starting to hurt me after all. Maybe I'd had a bigger effect on the 49ers and the NFL than I'd realized.

And maybe it was going to financially damage me—and my family. I didn't have fewer responsibilities or worries because of my success but a lot more. My grandmother was in assisted living and needed all the care she could get, and I was paying for it. My siblings were in college, and I was paying for that, too. My younger sister, Sharmaine, had just had a baby, and my mom was spending her days taking care of the infant. Life had gotten larger, more complicated in all directions, and more expensive, and I was the financial foundation of everything.

One Sunday morning a few years ago, I was visiting my mother's home in Alex City, and Terique was there with me. It was Father's Day, and my son and I were spending it together with my mom and some relatives. Everyone else was still asleep when my mom came into my room and handed me an envelope. Inside was a Father's Day card, signed by her. I looked at it and read the words, not quite understanding, so I read it again. On the card, she thanked me for all the things I'd been able to do for her and for everybody in our family.

We looked at each other and started crying.

"You're like the father I never had," she told me. "You're the provider I never knew. You've given me so many things that I could never have given myself, and you've made my dreams come true. I just want to thank you for that."

There wasn't anything I could say. This made everything I'd ever done to achieve athletic success more than worthwhile. I just wanted to make more dreams come true, for her and many other people. I was determined to have a good year in 2003 for the team's sake, for my own sake, and for my family. No upcoming season had ever held such high expectations, and I'd never worked harder to get ready to play football. Looking back now, I think that was a part of the problem. My expectations got higher and my desires got deeper every time I drove to the doctor's office and got another round of shots. I wanted all this to count for something important.

In 2003, the three themes of my life—faith, family, and football—were about to come together in a whole new way. Everything in my career as a player and my life as a man would be revealed this season, for better and for worse.

XXVIII

AS WE APPROACHED opening day, I wasn't yet 100 percent, and I told that to Coach Erickson with two games left in the preseason. I still had a throbbing pain in my groin, and I couldn't move without feeling it. Erickson was very understanding and let me sit out those final two exhibition games, and I really appreciated this. Since our chance meeting on that plane the previous February, we hadn't had much opportunity to talk, but on one occasion he'd told me that in 2003, we were going to try to throw the ball downfield more, which was exactly what I wanted to hear. Under Mooch, there had been issues about whether or not Jeff Garcia could throw deep balls and do it with accuracy, but Erickson seemed committed to the longer passing game. I was anxious for the chance to show my speed and stretch opposing defenses. In early 2003, Erickson's coaching philosophy was another reason to feel optimistic.

The season started great. In the opener, we beat Chicago 49 to 7 in front of 67,000 people in Candlestick Park, the Niners' largest margin of victory since 1989. In the last six minutes of the first half, we scored 23 points, and this time, despite our big lead, we didn't let up on the Bears. Our defense successfully blitzed throughout the day—something else Erickson had promised to do—and Chicago's quarterback, Kordell Stewart, looked totally lost. The best moment of the game came when our defensive back, Ahmed Plummer, intercepted Stewart in our territory and returned the ball 68 yards for a touchdown. As he blew past our sideline, the white-haired Erickson ran right along next to him, jumping in the air and pumping his fists. The hometown crowd was completely with him; this was the kind of coach we'd wanted and the fire we needed to kickstart the season.

Our running backs, Garrison Hearst and Kevan Barlow, looked solid, kicker Jeff Chandler made five field goals, Jeff Garcia passed for 229 yards and two touchdowns, and all of our top receivers—Tai Streets, Cedrick Wilson, and myself—got into the action. I caught seven balls for 112 yards and had nothing to complain about. Erickson had even used some innovative formations with five wide receivers or with two tight ends, and everything we threw at the Bears worked. The good feeling I'd had about the 49ers throughout the preseason seemed accurate. This was the Bears' worst loss since 1977, and while they weren't much of a team, it was still an impressive win for us. I couldn't wait to feel better and get back on the field the next week against the strong Saint Louis Rams. They'd played in two of the past four Super Bowls (winning one of them), and a road win would send the message that we were on our way.

By the time we got to Saint Louis, I was virtually 100 percent and felt confident for both myself and the Niners. We took a 7-to-0 lead, but on the first pass Jeff threw to me, I was laid out by a defensive back and knocked cold to the turf. I don't know how long I lay there. I don't even remember the hit. People watching all this on TV later told me that the announcers thought I was out for the game and maybe seriously hurt. When I could stand, they walked me over to the sidelines and asked me the usual questions about what day it was and what city we were playing in. I answered them correctly, and when the cobwebs had cleared a few minutes later, I had only a mild concussion. For the next series of downs, I regrouped on the sidelines while riding a stationary bicycle. As I was getting ready to go back onto the field, Jeff got knocked down with his own mild concussion and had to sit out several plays. Our offense stalled, and by the time we were both back on the field, the Rams had tied it 7 to 7.

In the second quarter, our field-goal kicker, Jeff Chandler, missed a short field goal, wide right. He'd come in this year to replace Jose Cortez, and so far he'd been good. His miss didn't seem that important—it was early in the game, and we were moving the ball with Jeff and me back in the flow of the offense. We'd connected on a couple of passes after Saint Louis put a young safety on me in single coverage. I was not only taller than he was but quicker and more experienced. I was consistently getting open and knew I could score on him if Jeff could get me the ball. But he wasn't doing that, and I was getting frustrated. As the game wore on, the TV commentators began focusing more and more on my situation and why I wasn't being thrown to. Fox analyst Cris Collinsworth now sang a different song: he kept saying that TO had a clear mismatch in the secondary, but the 49ers weren't getting him the ball. As one of the top receivers on the Cincinnati Bengals when they were a Super Bowl contender, Collinsworth knew something about pass coverage; what he and his nationwide audience saw over and over again wasn't obvious to the 49ers, because Jeff and I weren't connecting on the field.

For me, the hardest thing about football has never been the contact or running over the middle or the notion that you can get hurt on any down. It's that you're only one small part of the game, one of fifty-three players on a roster. Unless you're a running back carrying the ball thirty times an afternoon or a quarterback who touches the ball on every down, you're cut off from a lot of the action. Your fate on the field is often not in your own hands. There are about 120 downs per game in football, and your offense plays only half of these. That leaves 60 plays, and some of these involve special teams. I might get thrown the ball ten times in a game, and not every throw is going to be perfect. Or I might not be open on every pass. Or I might drop a catchable ball, which happened in the second quarter in Saint Louis and left me feeling terrible. If you make a mistake in football as a receiver, it's very tough to make up for it right away, unless the quarterback comes right back to you. You live with your failures, and millions of people see them either in person or on TV. You ache to put the bad plays behind you, and that's what I was going through in Saint Louis, but without the ball, there was nothing I could do. Whether or not I should have, I was getting angry with Jeff but trying not to show it.

And that's the problem with football and why I've always wanted to play pro hoops. In every other team sport, you have a much clearer sense of what you can do to help your side win. In baseball, everybody gets about four at-bats in a game, and you have to make the most of it. In hockey, if you're not much of a scorer, you can play fierce defense and check your opponents with hits along the boards or pass the puck to your teammates. There's always something to do on the ice. The same is true in basketball, where you should never just stand around on the court but body people under the boards, block shots, get in position for rebounds, use your shoulders and legs and butt to get people out of the lane, throw outlet passes to teammates, tip balls away from opponents, dive on the floor and try to make steals, run the court and get back on defense—and shoot the ball or get a tip-in or a dunk. The game moves back and forth quickly, so you get the chance to do all these things all the time. In football, you run the route they tell you to run, time and time again, and on most plays, you never get close to the action. You can't improvise until you have the ball in your hands. Maybe I should have played an individual sport like golf or tennis, where I could have been more in control of the final score, but I was never exposed to those games as a child.

I play pro football because God gave me the gifts to do it at a high level, and I'm very grateful for that. I do it because I can support my family and myself in a comfortable way, and I'm also grateful for that. But the game and the people who run it frustrate me and always have. It's too controlled and repetitive, way too much like being in the military. Everything in the league is designed to make you be like everyone else, and that rubs me the wrong way. These feelings had been building up in me for a long time before the 2003 season started, and I was a lot more upset about this than I realized. My halftime speech in the 2003 playoff game against the Giants was a breakout moment for me; it had let me feel that I could express more of myself to the team, and this would help us win. I guess I'd always wanted to be more of a leader, and now I felt that I was coming into my own.

I felt that I'd earned the right to get the ball more, especially when I was consistently beating my man and getting open.

Late in the second quarter, we drove deep into Rams territory, but then Jeff threw an interception. A defensive back took off with the ball and ran 50 yards toward our goal line before I was able to catch up with him and make the tackle (this was one time when I could switch over and play defense; I loved running this guy down from behind and preventing them from scoring). The Rams fumbled, and we got the ball back without giving up any points. In the third quarter, Saint Louis scored another touchdown to go ahead 14 to 10, but we came back on a Kevan Barlow run, and with sixteen minutes left in the game, we were up 17 to 14. On offense, I'd disappeared from the game. It had never been my way to talk in the huddle or to demand that Jeff throw to me, so I kept still and kept running my routes. With thirteen minutes left in the fourth quarter, the Rams scored again and took a 21-to-17 lead. Our offense had been ineffective the entire second half, and now we couldn't even make a first down. The Rams got the ball back, and after a terrible pass interference call against us, they kicked a field goal to make it 24 to 17.

With four minutes on the clock, starting from our own 15-yard line, desperation time had come to the 49ers. A field goal wouldn't get us where we needed to be. We had to put together a long drive fast and get seven points. It was the same position we'd been in many times before, so Jeff did what he had to do: he finally started looking for number 81, who'd been open all day long. I'd caught only four balls in the game, but after Garrison Hearst broke a 40-yard gain to the Rams' 13, Jeff dropped back and scanned the field, spotting me in the end zone. He fired, and I grabbed it for my first touchdown of the season. I did a little dance but was in no mood to celebrate—yet. With nineteen seconds on the clock, we tied the game with the extra point and had the chance to win if we could pull off an on-side kick and get the ball back into Jeff's hands. Mooch wouldn't have tried a gamble like this, which can always backfire and hand the other team the ball past midfield with enough time left for a long pass and a field-goal attempt. Mooch would have settled for a tie and then tried to win in overtime, but Erickson told us to go for it and to get out of Saint Louis with the victory right now. This was what everybody wanted to hear.

The on-side kick worked perfectly, and receiver Arnaz Battle recovered it at midfield with thirteen seconds to go. We had a time-out left, and one complete pass could take us far enough into Rams territory to give Jeff Chandler the opportunity to kick the game-winning field goal and erase the memory of the one he'd missed in the second quarter. Despite all the things that had gone wrong this afternoon, we could still get out of Saint Louis with a 2-to-0 start. Nine seconds remained as Jeff threw a 25-yard pass over the middle to Cedrick Wilson, who needed to get down immediately and call time-out. But Cedrick either forgot how much time was on the clock or thought he had to gain more yards to put Chandler in field-goal range. By the time he hit the ground and the play was over, regulation had ended.

Our sideline had been pumped with the feeling that we were going to win this heart-stopping game and send a message to the league about our new season and our new coach. Dennis Erickson had been as passionately involved in every play this day as he was a week earlier. Everyone was stoked for this victory, but Cedrick's failure to call a time-out sent another kind of message, the kind that can change an entire game in an instant: maybe this wasn't the Niners' day after all. Maybe we'd blown our best chance to win, through a tiny mental mistake. A minute later, we lost the coin toss for overtime, and then the Rams' return man, Arlen Harris, ran the kickoff back 46 yards to their 48. We also committed a face-mask violation on this play, which moved the ball another 15 yards closer to our end zone. By the time our defense took the field, Saint Louis was lined up on our 38-yard line.

Rams quarterback Marc Bulger hit Marshall Faulk on a screen pass for 22 yards, all the way down to our 10-yard line. Moments later, Jeff Wilkins kicked a field goal, and the game was over, Rams 27, 49ers 24. The field goal that Chandler had missed in the second quarter had come back to haunt us, as these plays often do, and Cedrick Wilson was so upset about not calling a time-out that he could barely speak, even to his teammates. Our locker room was deflated, because we all knew we should have won. It was a very long plane ride back to San Francisco, but we were still 1 and 1 on the season.

XXIX

THE NEXT WEEK, we played Cleveland at home, and this game carried a special edge. The new Browns franchise was only four years old, and the people running it were Dwight Clark and Carmen Policy. Clark had risen to fame as a Niners receiver, and for eight years Policy was the 49ers' president. Both men symbolized the glory days in San Francisco, and both reminded me of the Super Bowl trophies on display at Niners headquarters. I'd been told many stories by players like William Floyd about how 49ers owner Eddie DeBartolo had taken the whole team out for huge parties after Super Bowl wins, with good vibes flowing everywhere. Floyd gave me a vivid picture of what it was like to be a champ—what it felt like to relax finally and really celebrate after achieving your ultimate goal. I'd never known that feeling of relaxation, but Floyd fueled my desire to have this experience. When DeBartolo was in charge and winning, the Niners were flush with money, and the small things were taken care of by the team. Now we were expected to pay for soft drinks in the players' lounge. It was a symbol of what happens to a franchise that's going downhill.

Any NFL win is sweet, but beating Clark and Policy on this sunny afternoon at Candlestick Park would feel especially good for our whole organization. At the kickoff, we were favored by 7 points, and most football people had seen our loss to Saint Louis as kind of a fluke, a game we let slip away. We started off strongly again, driving the ball down to the Browns' 1, but we couldn't get into the end zone after two tries. Jeff took a bad hit trying to run the ball for a TD, causing everybody on the team and throughout the stadium to cringe and wonder why the hell he hadn't handed off to Garrison Hearst or Kevan Barlow. No one on the Niners had ever gotten used to seeing Jeff run the ball—or get smashed head-on by linebackers. At 195 pounds, he was the lightest quarterback in the league, he'd never been the fastest or most mobile signal caller in the NFL, and he was thirty-three years old. He'd already had serious back problems and more injuries than you could count. It took a mile of tape just to get him ready to play, and he always seemed to be limping, even in the locker room. Everyone on our side of the ball held his breath every time Jeff tried to run, and no matter how many times he got banged up or thrown to the ground, he seemed eager to get up and run the ball again. Some things you just can't explain.

On the opening drive, I'd caught a 20-yard pass and felt certain that I'd be a bigger part of the game plan than I was in Saint Louis. Yet Jeff didn't throw to me in the end zone when we were on the verge of scoring. We had to settle for a field goal by our new kicker, Owen Pochman (Jeff Chandler had been cut after the last week's miss), and we took a 3-to-0 lead. Throughout the first half, Cleveland looked like one of the weakest teams in the NFL. Our defense was very fast and successfully blitzed their young quarterback, Kelly Holcomb, who was playing with injuries. They couldn't get anything going, and the game had the makings of a blowout. But our problem was the same as it had been the week before: we put together good drives, but couldn't finish them. With time running out in the half, I caught a 25-yard pass from Jeff, my best play of the young season. We took the ball inside the Browns' 20 but then stalled, and I didn't get any more looks in the end zone. The pattern was repeating itself, and I was getting frustrated again. Pochman kicked another field goal, to make it 6 to 0 at the intermission.

In the third quarter, we put together another long drive but once more settled for a field goal: 9 to 0. The Browns missed a field goal, and we got our fourth of the day, to go up 12 to 0 in the final quarter. We hadn't played very well on offense, especially in the red zone, and I wasn't getting the ball. My frustration was turning into anger, and I didn't know what to do with it. My job was to run routes and get open, and that's what I was doing, but Jeff wasn't getting the ball downfield. Still, our defense was brilliant in shutting them out and holding them to only 113 yards in the first three quarters; they could win the game for us. But sometimes defenders start to wear down, and your offense has to help them out. That hadn't happened because we couldn't move the ball over the goal line. With twelve minutes to go, Kelly Holcomb led them on a 75-yard drive that ended with a 2-yard touchdown toss to André Davis. All the opportunities we'd missed earlier to score TDs were staring back at us from the scoreboard: 12 to 7. Halfway through the fourth quarter, we needed several first downs to come away with at least a field goal and an 8-point cushion.

The week before, former wide receiver Cris Collinsworth had told the world that the 49ers weren't throwing to me enough. Now a retired Super Bowl–winning quarterback delivered the same message. Ex–New York Giant Phil Simms, working up in the broadcast booth for CBS, wondered why the Niners weren't using me more in critical situations. I was wondering the same thing, and down on the sideline, I raised the issue with offensive coordinator Greg Knapp. He had no answers, either. For years, I'd been called a selfish player because I thought I needed to be a bigger part of the offense. But I wasn't the only one who saw this or talked about it. It was all right for them to say it, but I was supposed to keep my mouth shut and keep running routes that led nowhere.

We weren't able to pick up a first down, and the Browns got the ball back. On their next drive, linebacker Julian Peterson picked off Holcomb, and our lead seemed secure. A couple of decent gains, and we could hold on for a 12-to-7 victory. The media like to call this "winning ugly," but you rarely hear that phrase from players or

coaches. We know how competitive every team is and the tiny difference between winning and losing a game. In college football's
ranking system, you get style points for the margin of victory; that
doesn't apply in pro football, where every win is beautiful. What's
ugly is what the coaches say to you on Monday or later in the week
after you've blown a lead in the fourth quarter against a team like
the Browns. You watch game film with them, and there's nothing
worse in football than sitting and viewing, over and over again, a film
where you know the outcome, and it's not good.

All it would take to avoid that scene was a couple of first downs.
We didn't need a long bomb against the Browns. We just needed to
eat some clock and move the chains—but we tried several long
passes, and all of them failed. It wasn't anybody's fault. They just
didn't work, and we had to kick the ball back to Cleveland. All I
could do now was watch from the sidelines as Holcomb drove his
team 91 yards, finishing off with an 11-yard pass to André Davis in
the end zone. Davis went up between four 49ers defenders and
somehow came down with the ball, his second score of the day.
Their extra point made it 13 to 12 with only twenty-nine seconds
left on the clock. Time ran out before we could mount a comeback.
I walked off the field listening to thousands of boos and catcalls
aimed at our sputtering offense. The fans had a right to be pissed.

I'd caught eight passes for 90 yards, but that didn't mean a thing
to me. I hadn't scored any touchdowns, no one on our team had, either, and we'd just lost our second straight game to a team that
should never have beaten us. This defeat was even worse than the
one in Saint Louis, because the Browns weren't much good. We'd
get another shot at the Rams later in the season, but Cleveland had
kicked us at home with two late drives, and our offense did nothing
when it mattered the most. Watching the film of all this the next
week was going to be about as ugly as it gets.

In the locker room after the game, I was upset because I'd been
a nonfactor at the end of the fourth quarter, but ever since Sharpie,
I'd made a point of not talking to the local media. Then a reporter

asked me a question, and my feelings were too raw to be ignored. I hadn't worked so hard in the off-season for us to be 1 and 2 after three games or to lose to the Cleveland Browns, so I looked right at the journalist and did what my grandmother had been doing her whole life: I said what was on my mind.

The next day the Associated Press printed this quote from me: "I don't know how many times we've been in the red zone and my number hasn't been called. I feel bad from an offensive standpoint because we're letting the defense down. They're playing their tails off, and we can't help them out."

Some people interpreted this to mean that I just wanted the ball so I could put up big numbers because my contract was coming up for renewal. I wasn't a team guy, they said again, but only in it for myself and the money.

I'd meant that I was very upset because we'd lost the game and I hadn't done enough to help us win, because the ball hadn't come my way when it really counted. With this one quote, the fuse was lit, and the keg was about to blow. The season I'd had such high hopes for was already spinning out of control. The tension between Jeff and me had been growing for years, and it was starting to erupt. I'm sure he felt that way, too. I'd tried to repress my feelings about all this, but it just wasn't possible anymore. I was tired of losing and tired of not speaking my piece. My grandmother was a bigger part of me than I'd realized. She'd told me to stand up to the truth, and I thought that was the right thing to do. But whoever said that free speech is free never played in the NFL.

XXX

THE MINNESOTA VIKINGS were 3 and 0 and looked like one of the most improved teams in the league. We were both NFC contenders, but the game wasn't billed so much as San Francisco versus Minnesota as it was Terrell Owens versus Randy Moss. The media were always looking for a hook, a way to promote the Sunday match-ups, and this was a natural. We'd both played college basketball and still loved that game. He and I had both learned our trade from masters: I'd had Jerry Rice beside me in the locker room, and he'd studied under Cris Carter. People were always comparing the two of us. Who was the better receiver? Who was the better overall player? Who was the better person? He'd been in jams with the law, and I hadn't, but we both knew how to steal the limelight and stir up controversy. Some people said he was faster and more agile than I was and could jump higher for footballs, but I was a more physical player who liked running with the ball after catching it and throwing blocks downfield. On ESPN's pregame show on Sunday morning, September 28—week four of the NFL season—the debate centered around TO and Randy Moss.

Steve Young co-hosted the program, and he had my back on this one. He said that he would take me over Moss, not because we'd been teammates in San Francisco but because I always showed up and played hard. Tom Jackson disagreed; he thought Randy had become the Man at our position. The tiebreaker in the argument went to the great ex-Cowboys receiver, Michael Irvin, who knew something about getting open and had three Super Bowl rings to prove it. He came down on my side, saying that I was "better on the slant." This meant that I didn't mind taking—or giving—big hits in the middle of the field, which certain unnamed receivers shy away from (he didn't want to insult Randy on national TV).

The game shaped up as a classic battle between two potential contenders and their star receivers. Despite being 3 and 0 and playing at home, Minnesota was favored by only a point, because their talented starting quarterback, Daunte Culpepper, had an injured back. His replacement was journeyman Gus Frerotte, who'd bounced from the Redskins to the Broncos to the Vikings without ever really establishing himself anywhere. He was your basic NFL second-stringer, now called upon to fill in for the multigifted Culpepper. On the morning of September 28, while the talking heads were debating me versus Randy on the nation's airwaves, nobody imagined that Frerotte was going to come out in the first quarter and throw like Joe Montana, Dan Marino, and John Elway all rolled into one. On the Vikings' first possession, he tossed a high ball to Moss, who leaped up and grabbed it for a touchdown. Then they ran the same play again. And then again, with Moss scoring on passes of 15, 35, and 59 yards.

Meanwhile, the 49ers were faced with a dilemma that had become very old: we couldn't make first downs. By the time we came out of our sleepwalk in the Metrodome, the Vikings were ahead 28 to 0. Things were so bad that even though this was Fox's featured game of the week nationally, at halftime they switched to another match-up. The final score was 35 to 7. The Vikings were 4 and 0, we were 1 and 3, and our season looked dead.

I'd stared out at the field for most of the game, feeling shock and denial: this wasn't really happening, we couldn't be this awful, and they couldn't be this good. I could already see tomorrow's headlines: "Vikes Slaughter Niners! Moss Crushes Owens!" As the game wore on, my shock gradually turned into the same anger that I'd been feeling the week before against Cleveland, only now it was stronger. I was angry that we were getting our butts whipped and letting down our fans. Angry that Randy was playing so much better than I was. Angry that his quarterback, a bench warmer for much of his career, kept getting him the ball and mine didn't. Angry that all the hopes and dreams I'd put into this season were collapsing right in front of me.

In the third quarter, something snapped, and I lost it after the Niners were stopped on a fourth-and-1 running play on the Minnesota 31-yard line. Trailing by five touchdowns, I thought we needed to throw the ball, and I went off on everyone, pacing the sidelines and screaming at offensive coordinator Greg Knapp. I don't even remember what I said. The week before against Cleveland, I'd had words with Greg when I felt I should be playing a bigger role in our passing game, but now everything came out. Greg was sitting on a bench watching me pace; he looked up at me as if I were crazy. In that moment, maybe I was. I wasn't venting about just this game or about the team's play calling that afternoon. It was much more than that.

I lost it because I'd spent a decade training to become a champion, and now my team was falling apart—again. I lost it because I'm a deeply competitive person, and I think that comes from watching my mother and grandmother struggle when I was small. They didn't have the opportunities I've had, and I saw what they went through day after day. I saw what it took just for them to survive. That stayed with me and made me hungry in ways that some people can't ever understand. That hunger has never gone away. Money doesn't make it disappear. Neither does becoming famous. As I've gotten older, it's gotten deeper. Because God has blessed me with athletic ability, I want to make the most of it before I'm too old to compete. I want to maximize my potential on the football field to help my team win, and sometimes the frustration and the anger get the better of me.

I melted down because I'm not a slick or polished person, and I don't know how to be politically correct. As a child, I was expected to speak the truth, so that's what I do. I try to express it as best I can, and sometimes it's not pretty, and sometimes it's downright ugly. I lost it because we're told by our coaches every day to be as aggressive as possible, but when the team screws up and we lose, we're supposed to sit there and be quiet and polite and not say anything. And not feel anything. Not show any emotion. Not show any hurt.

I was hurting, and the team was hurting, and I decided to do something about it. Of course, the cameras were on me when I cut loose, as they had been constantly for the past several years. They always follow me on the sidelines, and this time they captured something real: I can't be strong and in control all the time. I can't be what everyone tells you that you have to be, whenever you become a public figure. I can't always give people what they want, the way Jerry Rice told me to when I was coming up. I can't pretend to be Jerry Rice. I'm a different human being with different flaws, and sometimes I can't hide them, especially when I care about something and that caring fills me with pain. There's a reason I cry when I sit with my grandmother and watch her go through the horrors of Alzheimer's. There's a reason I cried when my mother gave me a Father's Day card. There's a reason I screamed at Greg Knapp. I went off because I wanted something more for myself and for the team. If that's selfish, so be it. I went off because no matter how much I pray, I still have my troubles and imperfections, and I'm still striving to improve myself.

God is not finished with me.

We stumble, and we fall, Coach Willie Martin told me back when I played for him at Benjamin Russell High in Alex City, but we have to get up and go on. There's nothing wrong with stumbling, but if you can't stand up after it and move forward, you've got a real problem. Against the Vikings, the stumbling and falling were just starting, and things were going to get worse before they got better. All across America, sports commentators were lining up and getting ready to lay into me. Most of them had never been in the NFL or

tried to rehab from a groin injury or attempted to cope, every working day, with an inner fire that seemed to have a life of its own.
They'd never lived with my moodiness or intensity. They had no idea
what it was like to be inside my skin, but none of that mattered.
They weren't players but talkers. Their job was to bash, and they
were good at it, and the bashing would go on for days and weeks, and
in some places it would last through the rest of the season.

When I hit the locker room in Minnesota after our 35-to-7 loss, my
anger hadn't subsided. Reporters were sticking their pens or micro-
phones in my face and asking for a quote or a story. They wanted to
know what I thought and felt about that afternoon's performance, so
I gave them just a little of who I am and what really goes through my
mind. I said that our team had "no heart," and I didn't understand
why I wasn't getting the ball more. People say they want the truth,
but it's almost never that simple.

In the second half, Coach Erickson had replaced Jeff Garcia with
Tim Rattay, our backup quarterback, who was known as a good
pocket passer with a live arm. By the time he came into the game, it
was over, but Rat had played pretty well in bad circumstances. I'd had
my eye on him for some time, because I thought he could get the ball
to me downfield. In the locker room, I was asked if the Niners should
replace Garcia with Tim, and I didn't say they should. But I did say
that Rat had done a good job against the Vikings and that making
quarterback decisions was not my role on the team. I wasn't paid to
decide who started for San Francisco at this position or any other. I
was paid to catch the football and run with it, and today I'd had five
catches for just 55 yards and no TDs. Our team was 1 and 3, and
some reporters felt that it was time to question who should be in the
starting QB role. Or maybe they were just baiting me with this question, and this time I'd taken the bait. Either way, I'd just lit my second
fire of the afternoon, and this one was flaming out of control.

When Jeff heard about my comments regarding Tim, he was enraged, and he told Thomas George of the *New York Times,* "I'm really through with answering questions about TO and his frustration and his situations on the sidelines."

For years, I'd repressed most of my feelings about Jeff. I thought he played his heart and guts out for the Niners, but he was injury-prone and seemed too quick to tuck the ball under his arm and run with it, which was dangerous for a guy his size. I didn't think that was the way to win football games or to keep him healthy and in the game. When he and I clicked, we were a great pair, but this year, we weren't clicking, and that was obvious to anyone watching us play. He probably thought that I expected too much from him and from the offense and that I was dogging him in public. I was, because I didn't know what else to do. Many NFL teams have issues like this but try to keep them hidden; I'd exposed this one, and now there was hell to pay. I'd spoken the truth as I saw it without trying to put anyone down, but throughout our locker room, feelings were raw after this loss, and nobody was in a forgiving mood.

The next day, we gathered at the 49ers practice facility, where we'd come to watch film of the Vikings game. You can imagine how much fun that was. Things don't get better the second or third time you view a football disaster—they just keep getting worse. Receivers and quarterbacks watch film together, along with their coaches. Throughout the film session, Jeff and I iced each other. He didn't speak a word, and I didn't, either. We were both fuming, and everyone knew enough to give us a lot of space.

Later that day, Coach Erickson met with me privately and reprimanded me for my behavior on Sunday. He told me very directly that he wouldn't tolerate any more of my sideline outbursts, and they had to stop. I listened and didn't argue with him. I wanted to stop, too. I was tired of the whole thing and knew that I couldn't keep repeating these blowups. Something had to give, but athletes are very proud people, and my pride flared up whenever I saw Jeff walking around the training facility. By Tuesday, he and I still weren't speaking when we ran into each other at 49ers headquarters.

After my comments about Rat to the reporters on Sunday, Jeff had told the media that there was a "sickness" on the Niners, and he didn't want it to spread. I didn't have to guess what he was talking about. He was calling me a "sickness," and that was harsher than I'd been expecting.

When we saw each other on Tuesday, I confronted him about this remark, and he didn't know what to say. He stumbled and fumbled for words, but what came across was pure anger. He was hot because he felt that I hadn't backed him enough after the loss to Minnesota, and he was sure that I wanted the coaches to replace him with Tim. I'd never said that to the media or the coaching staff, and I never would. I'd told them only that Rat had played well, and I stand by that comment.

Neither Jeff nor I backed down. We had words—I wasn't going to let him get away with calling me a "sickness"—and then we went our separate ways. It was heated but never got close to being physical.

In the past year, ESPN created and aired a show called *Playmakers,* about life inside a fictional NFL team. I'd watched it a few times, but it really got under my skin. It showed players being late for games and using cocaine when they were playing and having fist-fights in the locker room over women. Basically, the show was nonsense and about as close to real life in the NFL as to life on Mars. On the other hand, there is real tension on football teams, but it's more interesting than what ESPN was selling. Football players and coaches are extremely driven people (the better the coach, the more the control freak). Practicing and playing the game is our job, our career, our livelihood. Success is only defined by winning. About 99 percent of the struggles we go through revolve around that, not around drugs or women or other things. There's no one right way to play or win games, so people are going to disagree over the big and little things that take place on the field. Sometimes, if you do exactly what the coaches tell you to do, everything works out perfectly. Other times, you have to improvise to make things happen. You have to use your God-given instincts.

We all remember the great play John Elway made in 1998 in Super Bowl XXXII, when he took off running with the ball in the fourth quarter and banged headlong into three Green Bay Packers, making a critical first down near the Packers' goal line. Elway was in his late thirties, he wasn't nearly as fast or agile as he used to be, and he could have been severely injured on this play. It came to be known as "the helicopter," because when he collided with those three opponents, they spun him up into the air like a propeller. But when he came down on the field in San Diego, he'd moved the chains closer to the Pack's end zone and sent the message that nothing was going to stop him—or the Broncos—from winning this Super Bowl. It was the signature moment of Elway's career, and nobody had ever drawn up a play that looks like that. He brought it off because he was a great football player who knew what to do when the opportunity presented itself.

All players basically want the same thing—a Super Bowl ring—and anything that gets in the way of achieving that can look like your enemy. Jeff Garcia wants to win football games as much as I do, but we come from different worlds. He's from the Bay Area, went to San Jose State, and has always been seen as a local hero. The Niners franchise and the local press always have treated him well because he's local and because he's Hispanic and they want to appeal to that part of the Northern California population. There's nothing wrong with that, but Jeff and I have different ways of seeing things. That's the real conflict, the deeper issue, and the problem that needed to be worked through. We're different people, and in today's media, that is usually presented as being some kind of mortal sin. It isn't. It's just reality, just another challenge in life. We're not supposed to be the same. We're supposed to be different, but when the heat is on, those differences can drive you crazy.

After Jeff and I went at it that Tuesday, nothing was resolved. We didn't speak the rest of the week, but a lot of other people were doing a whole lot of talking about what a terrible person I am and how bad I am for my team. It didn't matter that just a few weeks earlier, another Bay Area pro football star, Raiders quarterback Rich Gannon, had gone off at his coaches on the sideline after his team got off to a miserable start in 2003. They left Gannon alone, maybe because he's a quarterback, and white, but it was open season on TO. The only positive thing I heard on the airwaves that week came from Tony Gonzalez, the great tight end for the Kansas City Chiefs, who told nationwide talk-show host Jim Rome that in 2002 I'd been the best receiver in the league. I really appreciated hearing this from a player of Tony's caliber, because he knows what it takes to make it in the NFL.

One off-field development took a little media pressure off me that week. The day of the meltdown in Minnesota, September 28, conservative talk radio star Rush Limbaugh had said on ESPN's pregame show that the liberal media had been too easy on Philadelphia quarterback Donovan McNabb because he was black and the white press wanted him to succeed. In politics, you can talk BS all day long, and no one might notice, but in the sports world, if you don't know your subject matter, it becomes obvious very fast. (Remember Dennis Miller's short stint on *Monday Night Football*?) According to Limbaugh, the largely white media was soft on black athletes. The interesting thing about sports, compared with some other fields (like gabbing on a talk show), is that you can actually measure at least a portion of what an athlete contributes to his team. In the past two years, Donovan McNabb had led the Eagles to a couple of NFC championship games. In the 2001–02 seasons, he'd accounted, through his running and passing, for 70 percent of the Eagles' offense and had clearly been the most important player on a very successful franchise. Anyone with any knowledge of football understood that. And anyone who knew anything about the sports media in Philly knew that they were the toughest bunch around. They didn't care what color you were or what you'd done for them in the past; they'd kick you whenever they felt like it.

Two days after Limbaugh said these things on ESPN, he resigned from his TV gig and announced that he was addicted to painkillers and going into rehab (he was under criminal investigation for this habit). Maybe the drugs had clouded his judgment. Or maybe he just didn't know anything about football and had no concept of other people's reality. While he was telling the world that the white liberal media was showing favorable treatment to black athletes, I was being blasted from coast to coast by a series of white media commentators from Jim Rome to Joe Buck on Fox-TV to Mike Ditka, Cris Collinsworth, Boomer Esiason, Chris Mortensen, Sean Salisbury, and many others. They were taking their best shots at me around the clock. They were ripping and tearing at what was left of my reputation. If you were only listening to the supposedly liberal media that week, you'd have thought that this was the only point of view out there and that everybody in America was against TO for blowing up because he was tired of losing. But every pancake, somebody once said, has two sides. And behind the scenes, another story was unfolding. It always does, even if people don't know much about it.

During the week after the meltdown, I got three calls from three of the greatest athletes I know: Deion Sanders, Michael Irvin, and Michael Jordan, who just happen to be black. They all told me the same thing. They understood what I was going through because their own competitive spirit had at times caused them to explode. They couldn't always be nice and polite, because they hated getting beaten and they wanted to be the best in the world at what they did. The thing that made them champions was the same thing that caused them to blow up once in a while. They all had to learn to live with this inner demon, and that was never an easy thing to do. Michael Irvin and Deion were very supportive, but nobody understands the big game like Michael Jordan, and his call was the most important to me. When I was a kid, his picture hung on my wall, and I looked at it every morning when I woke up and every night before I fell asleep. I studied how he went to the hoop with his tongue hanging out and imitated his moves on the basketball court. I tried to dunk the way he dunked. I wear his number 23 at my home in Atlanta when I go into my gym to shoot baskets. He's still my inspiration for pushing myself to improve at sports.

It was worth every bit of grief I was getting from the white mainstream media to get a call from MJ when I needed it the most. He told me that he'd stood where I was standing now and that I had to be strong, stronger than ever before. He said that it's all right to hurt in your guts after losing, but you can't let reporters see you ache and sweat. When they see you sweat, they know you've lost your cool and you're vulnerable, and then they go on the attack. Losing your cool for an athlete is like blood in the water to the press. It's okay to blow up, but only behind closed doors. Michael told me that I shouldn't say certain things myself but get other people to say them for me. Let them take the heat for what needs to be said about the team, while I stay in the background. This was hard for me to hear because it had never been my way. But I listened and decided to try to follow his advice.

As I said earlier, neither God (nor MJ) is done with me.

And one other thing on this subject. Hey, Rush, if you manage to beat this drug rap, I've got a job for you. If you run into any of those white liberal media types, send them my way. I've got some stories to tell them.

XXXI

WHEN YOU'RE IN THE TRENCHES, you naturally turn to the people you know and love best. So that's what I did in the first week of October 2003, after the troubles in Minnesota. I flew my mother in from Alabama and brought my son over from his mom's house, not far from where I live in Northern California. They both stayed with me that week. My mother watched some of the TV coverage about me—they were running polls to see if the Niners should get rid of TO—and she didn't like it one bit. She also didn't like hearing Jeff Garcia talk about a "sickness" on the 49ers, but we'd been through some of this before and knew we had to ride this storm through. My mother and I don't talk a lot, but we tend to know what the other is thinking and feeling. She knew I was hurting inside, and I knew that I needed to draw on her strength, the same strength that she'd shown to our family when I was small. She'd been the rock back then and still was. I was now there for her financially, and she was there for me emotionally, when I needed my family the most. During that week, I prayed a lot with her and by myself.

After I became a well-known football player and started to get media attention, reporters always asked me the same questions: Why did I act the way I did? Who was I, really? The answers are hard to express, because they're all about faith. I had the feeling that whenever I tried to address these questions honestly or deeply, most people stopped listening. But I'm going to try once again, right now, because they were the most important part of the 2003 season, when I thought everything was going to be so good for the 49ers and everything went the other direction.

I've tried to walk the walk my mother has walked with God and to hold fast to my faith, especially when things were at their worst. I've never stopped believing, never stopped praying, never quit trying to get closer to God. I give thanks not just for what goes right in my life but also for what has gone wrong, because I know there's a reason for these things. I know that if we don't give up, they can lead to something better.

Throughout the 1999 season, Saint Louis quarterback Kurt Warner had been the feel-good story of the year in leading the Rams to their first Super Bowl championship. Two years later, the media approached him after the Rams had just lost to New England in the 2002 Super Bowl. The journalists looked baffled when Warner plopped a Bible down next to him as he met the press after the game. He was clearly bummed. They say there's nothing worse in the NFL than losing the Super Bowl (I can't yet imagine the feeling), and he was making a simple point: it was his faith that was going to get him through this, because that was the foundation of his life. This produced an eye roll from all the reporters present. My secrets are the same as Kurt's: the only things that have ever pulled me through my difficulties on the football field—or elsewhere—are faith and family. In the fall of 2003, I was leaning on them once again.

Ever since the blowup in Minnesota, I'd been asking the Lord to show me if I'd done something wrong and how to make it right. I didn't have the answers, but God did. If I needed to humble myself in this situation in order to get past it, then that's what I would do. If I needed to apologize, then put it in my heart to do that. Give me the opportunity, and I would make the best of it. I asked God to make me stronger than before, for myself and my family and my football team, because this was crunch time.

*   *   *

While I was going through all this turmoil, Bill Walsh called me into his office to talk. I was really concerned about what he was going to say. Of all the people connected to the 49ers, he's the one I had the most respect for, despite his run-in with David and me over the Dallas star incident. With his gray hair and solid jaw, he just looks as if he has something important to tell you. Twenty years earlier, he'd built the team into a three-time Super Bowl champion, putting together maybe the best NFL offense ever, and he knew as much about football as anyone. He also knew about personalities and human feelings, and he didn't waste words the way some coaches do. Like my grandmother, if he had something to say, he'd say it and move on. When he got upset with you, you knew it, so I was worried about what he would say now.

I went into his office and sat down, and he began telling me that he needed to have another back operation. He'd had problems in that part of his body and was going through a lot of pain. I understood being injured and wanting to heal, so I wished him the best with the operation. After a while, he started talking about my receiving techniques and my recent game performances. He said that I'd been pressing too hard and was trying to do too much on the field. I'd been taking my eyes off the ball at the last second, just before it arrived in my hands, and that's why I'd dropped a couple of passes. I needed to concentrate more on catching the ball before turning upfield and running with it. When he finished speaking about this, he thanked me for coming in and said he hoped I did well in the upcoming games. The troubles between me and Greg Knapp and me and Jeff never came up. I wanted to tell Bill that I hoped to come back to the 49ers and be a member of this team in the future. I wanted to sign a new contract with the franchise and finish my career in the Bay Area, but this wasn't the right time or place to bring that up.

I walked out of his office, grateful to him for not lecturing me about what had happened against the Vikings. I didn't need that at this point. I needed to hear that he had confidence in me and in our team to turn things around, and that's what he conveyed in the meeting. Sometimes, what you don't say is more important than what you say.

But I still had concerns. I wondered if the 49ers had already decided that they weren't going to renew my contract after this season, so there was no point in Bill making a stink about the recent controversy. Is that why Terry Donahue hadn't returned David's calls about starting the negotiations? Were we just acting out our roles together before moving down different roads? If that was the case, I was going to play just as hard for the organization as I had in the past. I still wanted to live up to my potential and to the tradition that Bill Walsh had established in the Bay Area. He was a great football man and knew how to handle me a lot better than some other people ever did.

The week wore on, with a backdrop of constant media criticism and an icy atmosphere in the locker room. Instead of talking about our upcoming game against the Detroit Lions—and their new head coach, Steve Mariucci—everyone was talking about the rift between TO and Jeff Garcia. Sometimes all this got me down, but whenever it did, I wouldn't think about football but go home and look across the room at my mother and think about her raising four kids in Alex City on very little money with nobody to turn to for help. She'd found a way to get through that and make everything work for us, and if she could do that, then what I was facing was pretty small. And I'd remember things that my grandmother had told me when I was a child.

"They talked bad about Jesus," she'd said a long time ago, "so they're going to talk bad about you. You might as well get used to it."

God was answering my prayers, as usual. While I was being criticized on the airwaves as a football player and as a human being from coast to coast, I took the time to realize that I was also surrounded by the love of my family and friends. Throughout the turmoil of the 2003 season, I flew my three best friends—Coop, Pablo, and Shaw—in to stay with me. I needed their strength and trust more than ever.

I understood that my life went a little deeper than hearing myself torn apart on ESPN or talk radio. My connections to what was truly important were a lot bigger than the sports world that enjoys building people up and then taking them down because they're not perfect. Sometimes, the best thing that comes out of pain is the knowledge of what you really care about and who you really are. Sometimes, it takes all that to make you know what's in your soul. The only thing I could think about that week was how much my family and faith meant to me and how many blessings we'd already had. Maybe there were more to come.

On Saturday afternoons before home games, the Niners go to a hotel near the San Francisco airport to spend the night. The organization wants us to be away from our own houses and our families and all together as a team. Not much happened that night; I hung around my room and went to bed earlier than usual. I slept well, and the next morning I had a breakfast meeting in the hotel. I was in there with my trainer, Melvyn Williams, talking about some of my ongoing physical issues, when Jeff walked in alone. I wasn't expecting him. He and I stared at each other across the room, but neither of us said anything. He'd stopped walking, and I was frozen in my chair. I could instantly feel the tension building in the room, and my stomach muscles had tightened.

He started walking toward me. A part of you always wants to avoid these things, but the better part of you knows you shouldn't and can't. Sooner or later, you've got to face reality.

I didn't move and watched him come closer. I couldn't tell if he was angry or not, and my pulse had started to race.

He stood over me, and I looked up. In that moment of silence, anything seemed possible. I had no idea what he was going to do.

He said that he was tired of the fighting and wanted to put this conflict behind us and move on.

It felt as if something had lifted from my chest, something heavy and hard.

I stood up next to him, reached out, and we shook hands. He had tears in his eyes, and I had tears in mine, and they were flowing down our cheeks. For a few moments, neither of us could talk.

The trainer excused himself from the table and left.

When we were alone, Jeff and I apologized to each other for the things we'd said. We were both sorry for the pain we'd caused and the distractions to the team, and we both promised to do better.

I gave him a lot of credit for walking over and doing what he did. And he gave me credit for being receptive.

The air between us was suddenly clear. We hadn't wanted to go into that day's game against Detroit and Mooch feeling the way we had the past week. It would have been bad for us and bad for the team (and we sure didn't want to do anything to help our old coach win). At the right time, the right thing had happened, and we were getting another chance to go forward.

Jeff left the breakfast area, and as he was walking away, I closed my eyes and lowered my head and said, "Thank you, Jesus."

As Melvyn and I stood there together he said, "T, you've got a big heart."

It was one of the most meaningful things I'd heard in some time. This was the same thing my mother had told me a couple of years before, when I'd given my autograph to the small boy in the restaurant in Alex City who'd repeatedly called me a "nigger," A lot of people don't believe this about me, and there isn't anything I can do to change their minds. But when somebody does recognize this it's a great feeling.

The awful stuff was behind us, at least for a while, and it was time to put on the pads.

XXXII

WHILE I WAS going through all this with Jeff that Sunday morning, my mother and my son, along with some other friends and relatives, were preparing to ride up to Candlestick Park from my home below San Francisco. Back when I was in high school, my mom couldn't see me play very often because she was working at the Russell Mill and wouldn't take time off. When I was in college, she had to race up to Chattanooga on Saturday mornings in a used Malibu, with three kids in the car, so she could be there for opening kickoff. A lot of times, she was too busy to get to these games. Years ago, I'd made a promise to myself that if I ever had a career in the NFL, things were going to be different for me and for her, and now they were. At about eleven A.M. October 5, a black stretch limousine came to my address and picked up her and Terique. With five other people in the limo, they rode north to the game in style, with a fully stocked bar, lights twinkling overhead in the ceiling, and a great sound system pounding out the music. My mother was dressed in her black Sunday best, and the limo was rocking. She makes her own clothes, and I was never prouder of having her as my mom than a couple of years ago when I took her to the ESPY awards and we walked down the red carpet together as we were leaving the event.

Someone in the crowd yelled out to her, "I love your dress!"

Without missing a beat, she turned around and shouted back, "I made it myself!"

On their way to Candlestick, the crowd in the limo picked up a huge pan of fried chicken, cookies, and some other excellent food. The week had been hell on everyone in my family, but today they let the good times roll. After eating lunch, they walked into the stadium and found their seats at about the 50-yard line.

When I ran out onto the field to play the Lions, I had a very bittersweet feeling. Part of it came from seeing Mooch on the other sideline and knowing how quickly everything could change in the NFL. Part of it was sensing that I might not be playing there much longer, either. It was a perfect football day—about seventy degrees and sunny, with a little wind starting to kick up and blow pieces of paper into the sky. I looked at the stands and saw thousands of jerseys with number 81 on them, worn mostly by younger fans, both white and minority. Some of them had tattoos on their arms, stocking caps on their heads, jewelry on their faces, and plenty of fire for the 49ers. They didn't look like the older 49ers fans, but they cared deeply about their football team. They were a new generation of football fanatics, just as I was a new-generation player. They liked hip-hop music, the same way I did, which was why I was building a hip-hop studio down in Atlanta, called "Dirty South" (that's the name Atlanta goes by in the African-American community). That's why I had hip-hop star 50 Cent sing on my Web site, because my fans knew all about him. We didn't want to do things the same old way, the way that had worked forty or fifty years earlier, and we didn't want to repeat the past. We wanted our own style and to express our own passion for life and for football in our own way.

This generation gap has been going on forever in pro sports. Running back Ricky Watters talks about when he first showed up at the Niners facility, in the early '90s, and the team was loaded with all those big-name stars. George Seifert was trying to win an unprecedented third straight Super Bowl title, but he felt the team needed an infusion of youth and attitude, including the versatile talents of this

Watters kid from Notre Dame. No problem there, until Ricky showed up in combat boots and carrying a boom box. He freaked out even some of the cooler veterans. Celebrations in sports have evolved, just like trends for young people that now include tattooing and body piercing. What wasn't acceptable decades ago becomes normal after a while. Change happens. Why people are so afraid of it and feel so threatened by it is the mystery.

Back in the day, adults thought rock 'n' roll came straight from the devil. Later, it symbolized hippies and a peace-loving generation. Fast-forward to 2003, and even white suburban families are watching their children listen to rap stars or get large tattoos. Young people look for new methods of self-expression. Some may be in it for shock value and others just because it's cool. Sports are the same way. I reached a point in San Francisco where I didn't want to be anybody else but myself. That bothers a lot of people who are living in the past, but it didn't bother the thousands of young fans who came to the games every Sunday dressed in my jersey. I'd gambled on making a connection out there in the new football generation, and I'd made it. It helped, of course, that I could play and had been selected to three straight Pro Bowls, but these kids were looking for someone to identify with, and we'd found each other.

Long gone is the era when chivalry and being repressed were important in athletics. Guys still help players up after laying a nasty hit on them, but that was once the norm. There used to be a little trash-talking on the field, but now it goes on nonstop. On almost every down, players call you every name you can think of and don't stop until they've burned your mother. That old saying, "Act like you've been there before," in terms of getting to the end zone is dead, too. The NFL once had a Billy "White Shoes" Johnson or Deion dancing down the sideline, but that was it. Now it's a different world, and everyone blames me for the change. I can handle that. I don't mind being known as the man who was willing to celebrate because he felt like it and he wanted his mother to see him having fun after scoring a touchdown.

The old media guys, the people who love to blast me, don't understand this and never will. Some of them once played football, so they think they own the game, but they don't. The people up in the stands know better, and they have my back on all this. They convey their feelings to me by wearing my jersey and calling out my name whenever I get close to them on the sidelines or the field. They're more like me than like the older generation, and we're all about change and creating something new. The NBA seems to get this idea, but the NFL never has. It's afraid of losing its grip on its game, so it holds on too tight. The owners own the teams, but they don't own the game. They're just renting it for a while—and neither they nor the media get to define how I play football or how much I get to enjoy myself on the field. I believe that the people who pay for their tickets and come to the games and wear players' jerseys and drink a few beers and celebrate like mad when we score don't really give a damn about what the talking heads have to say. They know that opinions are worth about as much as they weigh and that rings are what count. These fans want to win football games and championships as much as I do, and they're the guts of our support system in the NFL. The rest is hot air.

As I stood on the field during warm-ups that afternoon, I felt that my years as a Niners wide receiver may have been coming to a close. Media people were talking about this from coast to coast; it was time, many were saying, for me to go. I really didn't want it to be that way, especially when I looked up at all those jerseys, but you don't always have control over where life is taking you. If this was the end, I wanted to go out strong.

On the game's opening series, we drove deep into Lions territory. Jeff's first pass of the day was to me but low and out of reach. He came right back to me, which is what I always wanted him to do after an incompletion, and I grabbed the ball over the middle for a 15-yard gain that took us to the Detroit 5. The crowd was on its feet and screaming very loudly, calling out my name from all sides. The sound of "TO! TO! TO!" rolled over me and let me know that, at least for today, I was still one of them. This was the way the 49ers used to start games, back when Bill Walsh scripted the first fifteen or twenty plays, and they usually led to a couple of touchdowns. This was what the fans had been waiting for and hadn't seen in the loss to Cleveland: get TO the ball, and let's see what he can do with it. All the arguing and talking had finally stopped, and now it was just about playing football.

On the next play, I ran a slant into the secondary, but after six or seven steps, I lost my footing and fell down. Jeff dropped back in the pocket and looked for a receiver, glancing left and right but not finding anyone open. I jumped up waving my hand, and he fired the ball my way. I grabbed it and carried it in for the score. Jeff came running toward me as fast as he could, opening his arms and leaping into the air like a child who'd just made his first touchdown. I opened my arms to him, and we stood there together in the autumn sunlight in the end zone, face to face, with the wind blowing all around us and the scraps of paper twirling in the sky, and for a couple of moments, everything was perfect. He put his hands on the sides of my helmet, and I put my arms around his back, and we had our own celebration near the goal post. The other players joined us, and the crowd gave us everything it had. They knew all about the conflict that had been in the locker room during the past week, and they gave it up for us now. It was almost enough to bring back the tears, and it looked as if the past really was being put to rest. This was what sports had always been about for me: working hard to win and then enjoying the moment when it came. I wished it could have lasted longer. We made the extra point and then shut down the Lions offense. After kicking a field goal and scoring another touchdown, we went up 17 to 0.

Detroit began a comeback, and it was 17 to 10 at halftime. In the third quarter, Jeff ran for a touchdown to make it 24 to 10, but the Lions' good young quarterback, Joey Harrington, wasn't finished. Late in the game, he led them on another scoring drive to pull to within 7, but time ran out. The final score was 24 to 17, and I'd caught five balls for 73 yards and a touchdown. More important, we'd gotten a victory that we absolutely needed and had beaten Mooch on his return to Candlestick. We were ranked sixth overall in offense in the NFL, second in defense, and first in sacks. We were 2 and 3 but had almost played well enough to be 4 and 1. If we could put together a couple more wins, we'd have the momentum back that had been there against the Bears in the opener.

In the movies, and especially in movies about sports, there's usually a turning point where everything bad starts moving in the right direction and the team you're watching goes on to win the big game or the title. Real life and real sports are much more complicated and stickier. Nothing is ever predictable on a football field, and there is no script. Games are often decided by one or two moments that as a player you're standing and watching from the sidelines. The margin between celebrating a win and feeling like hell can be measured in fractions of inches and microseconds. One pass sliding off your fingertips or one fumble at the wrong time can be the difference between making the playoffs and looking at a whole season as a failure. A lot of sports stories are about how a team learned a hard lesson and then all pulled together to win a championship. Take it from me, that's a very rare thing. The much more common story in athletics, at every level, is about losing and then trying to come to terms with that when it eats away at your insides throughout the year and all during the off-season. You want one more opportunity to get it right and one more shot at glory.

For almost all of the 1,700 or so players in the National Football League, that moment never comes, and they never know what it feels like to be a Super Bowl champion. That's what life is really like in the NFL and why tempers flare and people scream and coaches get fired and tears sometimes fall. Losing is never easy and never fun, but it's a lot more real than what goes on during those episodes of *Playmakers*. And it's what pushes us to keep trying harder—sometimes too hard.

XXXIII

NEXT WE TRAVELED to Seattle for a Sunday-night match-up against the Seahawks. This game was even more loaded with hype than the one we'd just played against Mooch. It was being shown nationwide in prime time, the first chance this year for the Niners to play after dark and my first time back to the scene of Sharpie. Everyone in the media said it was payback time for TO, and the Seahawks were going to get even with me for signing a football in their end zone. In the pregame promo on ESPN, Seattle's talented running back, Shaun Alexander, looked straight into the camera, addressed me, and said this about Sharpie: "That never happened."

Commentator Joe Theismann told his ESPN audience, "Terrell, if you go over the middle, keep your head on a swivel."

Going to Seattle was also a homecoming for Dennis Erickson. After winning two college titles at the University of Miami, he'd been hired by the Seahawks in the mid-'90s and coached them for four years. His record was 31 and 33, and they unceremoniously bounced him out of town. In the week leading up to the game, he'd played down his feelings about this, as he did about most things, but he was quietly very hungry for a win against the Seahawks. We all were. This was billed on TV as the "Battle for the West," because Seattle was leading the Western division of the NFC, but we weren't far behind.

It was a pivotal game, and with the recent victory against the Lions, we felt confident going into their stadium.

That attitude showed on our opening drive, when we took the ball down to their 20, after Jeff threw a long completion to Tai Streets and a 15-yard penalty was tacked onto this gain for a personal foul. But our offense stalled in the red zone, as it had so many other times that season, and we had to settle for a field-goal try, which failed. Our kicking game was unbelievably inconsistent, and the end result of the drive was nothing. The momentum we'd had minutes earlier was gone.

The Seahawks scored a touchdown and then added a field goal. We were down 10 to 0 before I even got a ball thrown to me, and I was having trouble understanding why. In the past four years, I'd caught 46 of Jeff's 101 TD passes, but when the Niners moved inside the opponents' 20 this season, I seemed to disappear. When you don't get thrown the ball, you tend to start pressing more on the field, which takes you out of the flow of your game. You plan too much, think too much, and worry too much instead of running on instinct. The further behind we fell, the more I wanted to touch the ball and do something with it.

All that hype about me and Sharpie and payback looked pretty meaningless now, but in the second quarter, I finally caught a pass, and the crowd let me have it. Boos came down from every corner of the stands, which was fine with me as long as I could help move the chains and mount a comeback. I wasn't having a good night—it was windy on the field, and I'd dropped a couple of balls. Sometimes, no matter how much you want to win, you don't play your best. I was doing what Bill Walsh had told me not to do a week or so earlier: trying too hard and not getting the ball firmly in my hands before turning upfield and running with it. I felt bad about this and just wanted Jeff to keep throwing my way.

I wasn't the only one having a tough night. Our offensive line, which had been hit with several injuries, was having trouble pass blocking and giving Jeff enough time to find his receivers. He got sacked three times in the first half. One reason I'd blown up in Minnesota was that I didn't think that our linemen were giving Jeff enough protection in the pocket, and I'd taken a lot of heat for saying that. The talking heads had called me out for making this criticism, but this evening, the ESPN crew in the broadcast booth was saying exactly the same thing to football fans nationwide.

"They're not blocking anybody," Paul Maguire told the TV audience.

"The left side [of San Francisco's line] isn't," Joe Theismann echoed.

As former football players, they understood the problem. Everything in our West Coast offense depends on precise timing, and that's what we constantly practice during the week. If the line doesn't give Jeff a few seconds to set up in the pocket and if the receivers don't have enough time to finish off our routes, the system breaks down. Not to mention that if Jeff gets sacked, he has a very good chance of getting reinjured. And if he tries to run downfield, he's a target for abuse by linebackers and safeties. It was happening all over again against Seattle.

With the half running down, the Seahawks were up 17 to 0, and our offense had done nothing. We had only four first downs, but then I caught a pass for 8 yards, and Garrison Hearst made a good run to take us within field-goal range. Pochman converted this kick, and we went into the half trailing 17 to 3. It had been ugly, but not so ugly that we couldn't come back in the final thirty minutes. As we ran off the field and into the locker room, everyone on the Niners knew that our season could be riding on the second half.

In the third quarter, our sense of desperation turned things around. The offensive line started blocking, and the timing that we couldn't find in the first half was back. Garrison ran for a touchdown to close the gap to 17 to 10, and on Seattle's next possession, our defense intercepted Seattle QB Matt Hasselbeck on their 35-yard line. With Jeff under center, I ran into the left flat, caught a pass, broke two tackles, and carried the ball down to the Seahawks' 2, my best play in weeks.

With goal to go, Jeff ran a bootleg to the right and turned toward the end zone, crashing into linebacker Randall Godfrey but squeezing in for the score. Everyone gathered around Jeff to see if he was all right (he was), and our sideline was electric as we set up for the extra point to tie the game. This was our best comeback since beating the Giants in last year's playoffs. The celebration lasted about thirty seconds, until our holder, Bill LaFleur, mishandled the ball and Owen Pochman missed the kick wide right. Dennis Erickson's face showed total disbelief and total disgust, and he wasn't the only one feeling that way. We trailed 17 to 16, with a quarter left to play.

We quickly got the ball back and put together another drive that stalled in Seahawks territory. With twelve minutes on the clock, Pochman hit a field goal from 33 yards, and we took the lead, 19 to 17. We'd scored 19 straight points, but Seattle wasn't finished, making a couple of first downs before hitting its own field goal from 37 yards, to go up 20 to 19. Just over three minutes remained for us to move the ball into field-goal range. I'd had a tough night, but other players were stepping up to help out. Since I was being double- and triple-teamed, Jeff needed to find other receivers who were open. With a little more than two minutes left, he hit Cedrick Wilson with a first-down pass at midfield. Another 20 yards or so would get Pochman close enough for a chance to give us the win. If we pulled out this road game, after playing so miserably in the opening half, it would help shake off the losses to Saint Louis and Cleveland and even our record at 3 and 3.

On the first play after the two-minute warning, Garrison took the ball off tackle, and as he crossed the line of scrimmage, Seattle linebacker Chad Brown reached out for him, just trying to slow him down. Brown's fingers wrapped around the ball, and he stripped it from Garrison's hands. There was a huge pile in the middle of the field, with legs and hands and elbows flying everywhere. Players were screaming they had the ball, but you couldn't really see anything. After the referees got down on their knees to untangle the players, they ruled that Seahawks safety Ken Hamlin had recovered the ball.

The game was suddenly over—our comeback had counted for nothing. The missed extra point had cost us badly, and this was our fourth defeat in six games, this time to the team leading our division.

The next day, Skip Bayless, a columnist for the *San Jose Mercury News,* blamed the loss on me because I'd dropped a couple of passes. In the past, he'd been fairly supportive of me, but now he went off on me not just in the paper but during the following week, when he was sitting in as the host on Jim Rome's national radio show. He told listeners from California to New York that I'd gotten soft and gone Hollywood on the Niners. He labeled me "Terrible" Owens, adding that I should be benched.

"This time," he wrote about the Seattle game, "this team nearly sucked it up and won in spite of Terrible Owens. . . . The other 49ers had the guts to turn a rout into a battle on the night King Sharpie ran out of ink. . . . 'The Playmaker' again became the Mistake Maker. Owens has dropped more this season than a gumball machine."

I wonder if Bayless has ever had a shot in the groin to ease the pain of torn muscles. I wonder if he's had forty or fifty of them. I wonder if he's ever lain in bed and cried because his feet hurt so much that he didn't want to get up and walk to the bathroom. I wonder if he's ever felt bad inside because he wrote something that was angry and hurtful toward another person. Wonder if he's ever let anyone down or made a mistake in his life. Probably not.

The season I'd worked so hard for had turned into this.

XXXIV

THE NINERS WERE 2 and 4, and just about everyone had written off the 2003 campaign as a bust. I still felt the sting of the Seattle loss two days later when I drove out to the 49ers Academy in Palo Alto. We had kicked off the Sharpie Metallic Autographs for Education Program in Atlanta and were now taking it around the country. I loved giving the pens to the kids at the academy, because they seemed to appreciate everything you did for them. Just interacting with these youngsters and seeing the looks on their faces when you gave them a gift lifted my mood. There was more to life, at least on this Tuesday in Palo Alto, than winning or losing football games. I was also doing media promotion that day for Autographs for Education, and ESPN radio had asked to interview me. The Dan Patrick show set up a time for this, and I agreed to do it, but I wanted to stay focused on the charity work I was doing with Sharpie and stay off the subject of football. We'd tried to make this clear before I hit the ESPN airwaves, and we thought we had an agreement with them, but agreements are easy for some people to break.

I'll admit it: I was having a tough week, a tough season. I still didn't feel 100 percent and wasn't playing as well as I wanted to. Neither was the team. I needed to get away from all the stress this was creating, but Dan Patrick had other things in mind. On the air, he jumped on me for criticizing Jeff Garcia and for yelling at my offensive coordinator, Greg Knapp. He was under the impression that I'd never apologized to Knapp for my sideline rant in Minnesota, but he was wrong; I'd gone to Greg and told him I was sorry, and he'd accepted my words, and we were cool. That was in the past, where it belonged. I didn't want to talk about it on the radio and to dredge it up again, especially with someone who had his facts twisted, but Patrick was unstoppable. Before I knew what was happening, he was all over me about my behavior and the 49ers' troubles. This was everything I'd wanted to avoid.

His attack on me was so blunt and forceful that I couldn't even think of a comeback. It hit me for the first time how much some people out there really disliked me and how much damage had been done. Instead of trying to fight back or defend myself, I told him that I had to go, and I got off the phone. That really burned him, and he lit into me again—after I was no longer there to make a response. Let's give it up for Dan Patrick, another one of those white liberal media types who is way too easy on black athletes. Add him to your list, Rush, right near the top.

David Joseph was listening to this show live, and so were members of the Niners, and all of them were shocked. Kirk Reynolds, a public relations man with the team, called ESPN to lodge his complaint. David phoned Patrick's producer to say how upset he was with my treatment. He pointed out that Patrick had been rude, mean, condescending, and bitter. I hope he didn't leave out arrogant, shallow, and smug.

Then David called me and tried to calm me down, because I was still shaken. I was so upset by this confrontation that I was crying on the phone and couldn't even talk to my agent. I hung up on him, too, because I just needed to get away from everything and everybody. But this ESPN encounter, like everything else that was going on during that crazy season, was also a blessing. Sometimes, you need a jerk like this to show you just how stressed out you really are and how much you need to back off and take care of yourself. You need to put your life in perspective and realize that you're never going to make people like this happy. I was through talking with the media for a while, maybe even for the rest of the season.

Somewhere along the way in sports reporting and entertainment, it had become all right to be vicious to guests on the radio, but that can't be good for any of us. If they hate me, let them be filled with hate, but I want no part of it.

Our next game was at home against the defending champion Tampa Bay Bucs, whom many experts had picked to repeat as Super Bowl winners. With a good offense and a great defense, they came into Candlestick Park as the favorites to end our 2003 football hopes once and for all. For this game, Dennis Erickson put in a few new offensive wrinkles, focusing on the running game first and the passing game second. Maybe Bill Walsh had told him what he'd told me: we were putting too much pressure on our receivers to make things happen, not to mention that Jeff wasn't always getting the protection he needed from the offensive line to make the passing game work. One more hit on Jeff, and he might not get up next time.

Whoever came up with this game plan against the Bucs understood football strategy. Garrison Hearst and Kevan Barlow came out running the ball hard, causing Tampa Bay to focus on our two backs and opening up the secondary for the Niners pass catchers. In the second quarter, Jeff hit me with a 5-yard toss near the 49ers sideline. This time, I got my hands on the ball first before turning upfield and doing what I've always enjoyed the most on a football field: running through or around defenders. I went 40 yards straight down the sideline before cutting back toward the middle, dodging tacklers, and zig-zagging toward the end zone. Nobody could stop me. After crossing the goal line with a 75-yard score, I pretended to run into the goal post and fall down. It wasn't much of a celebration, but I didn't care. I'd had so many things to think about lately that I hadn't devoted time to doing anything new in the end zone. Maybe my days of creative celebrations were coming to an end. All that mattered was that I'd helped the 49ers by finding my old form and getting the taste of the Seattle loss out of my mouth.

The pattern the Niners had relied on during the past few years surfaced in this game: when I played well, the team usually won. Against the Bucs, I caught six passes for 152 yards, and we beat the defending champs, 24 to 7. Afterward, Tampa Bay coach Jon Gruden was asked about my 75-yard TD catch.

"I don't care what anyone says about him," he said. "He's as good as anyone in the league."

Gruden's comment meant a lot more to me, coming from a Super Bowl–winning coach, than any label the talk shows stuck on me, and it gave me a jolt of hope. Maybe our season wasn't dead yet.

A week later, we traveled to Arizona to play the Cardinals, one of the worst teams in the league. Seattle was still leading our division but had lost earlier in the day, so a win this afternoon would put us right back into the NFC West race. Everyone on the Niners understood that, but you still have to make plays, and we fell back into our old inconsistency on offense. In the fourth quarter, we trailed the Cardinals 13 to 6 with eight minutes to go. Owen Pochman had missed another extra point, and I'd only caught two balls for 17 yards, once again vanishing from the 49ers offensive scheme. But it was crunch time now, and the team needed a spark, so they turned to me. I don't know why we had to become desperate before they called my number, but I was getting resigned to the situation. As much as coaches try to make everything in football logical and rational during those endless team meetings, some things make no sense at all.

I suddenly caught three passes, and we drove down inside the Arizona 5. Jeff had been taken out earlier for an ankle injury, but with time running out, he came back onto the field. He was our leading rusher today (talk about making no sense), and with the ball on the Cardinals' 3, he tried to run again. It was enough to make the toughest football fan in America wince and lower his eyes. Here's thirty-three-year-old Jeff Garcia, a battered quarterback limping in pain, attempting to run over Cardinals linemen instead of handing off to Hearst or Barlow. Is that rational? Is that reasonable? Is that intelligent football? As Jeff approached the goal line with the ball tucked under his arm, he was met by the huge Justin Lucas. Jeff crumpled up like a wad of paper, and the ball flew into the air. Niners offensive lineman Kwame Harris grabbed it and carried it into the end zone—one of the luckiest plays anybody had ever seen. After Pochman kicked the extra point, the score was tied at 13. Forget being rational. A miracle had arrived at the best possible time.

After the Cardinals' offense stalled, we got the ball back, and Jeff again looked for me. I caught a pass for 16 yards, and we drove the ball down inside the Cardinals' 20. The final seconds were running down as Pochman lined up for a 35-yard field goal that would give us the victory and even our record at 4 and 4. A field goal now would redeem Pochman's earlier missed extra point and bring us within striking distance of Seattle. The snap was good, and so was the placement, but Owen hooked the kick, and the ball fell wide of the goal post. On the sideline, Dennis Erickson looked too stunned to speak. The disbelief that I'd first seen on his face after the loss to Saint Louis was getting deeper. He and everyone else on the team knew that Pochman, who'd missed seven field goals in the past four games, had just ended his career with the 49ers.

But first he had to kick off to Arizona in overtime, and he knocked the ball out of bounds. This is, if you'll pardon the pun, one of the "Cardinal" sins in football. Arizona was now given the ball on their 40-yard line, about 25 yards away from a field-goal try that could end the game. In eight years in the NFL, I'd seen a lot of good things, a lot of bad things, and a lot of weird things, but I'd never seen anything like this one. We'd already lost three games by three points or less, and if it hadn't been so painful to watch, it might have been funny.

The Cardinals drove to our 40, with a third down and 2 yards to go. A stop here, and we'd get the ball back with a chance to win. We did stop them—but our secondary committed a pass interference penalty on the play that moved Arizona within field-goal range, at our 22. As the offense stood together and stared out hopelessly from the sidelines, Cardinal placekicker Tim Duncan hit a 39-yarder, and the game was over, 16 to 13. The missed extra point had come back to kill us; we'd lost again by three points or less.

On Monday, Owen Pochman was replaced by Todd Peterson, the 49ers' fourth placekicker in the past fifteen games.

Jeff had gotten so banged up running the ball in Arizona that he couldn't start the next week against Saint Louis. I'd been heavily criticized after our loss to the Vikings for telling the press that our backup quarterback, Tim Rattay, had played well in the disaster in Minnesota. Now Rat was getting another chance, against the Rams.

He wasn't the only one looking for an opportunity to make good. Back in September, receiver Cedrick Wilson had possibly cost us the game at Saint Louis by failing to get down at the end of regulation and giving us a shot at a game-winning field goal. In the rematch with the Rams on November 2, he made up for that miscue by taking the opening kickoff and running 95 yards for a touchdown. Then Tim came off the bench and played brilliantly, throwing for 236 yards and three TDs: one to me, one to Tai Streets, and a great throw to rookie Brandon Lloyd, who stretched out in the end zone and made a fantastic grab. We won easily, 30 to 10, only our second victory against the Rams since 1999.

Because of the way Rat had played that afternoon, Coach Erickson was asked if there was a quarterback controversy on the Niners. Tim had not only looked relaxed and in command on the field but put up excellent numbers and was voted by ESPN as the NFL's "Stud of the Week." A few weeks earlier, I'd made the mistake, as I had so many times in the past, of saying something first and taking the heat for it, but I wasn't the only one now who'd noticed that Rat looked terrific quarterbacking the 49ers. Erickson immediately denied that there was any sort of controversy on the team. Jeff Garcia was his starting quarterback, and that was that, as long as he was healthy enough to play. But who got to make the final decision about his health, Jeff or the Niners doctors or the coaching staff? We had a bye week coming up, before playing our next game on November 17 on *Monday Night Football,* at home against Pittsburgh.

Hadn't Rat earned another shot before getting benched?

XXXV

AFTER A WEEK OFF, our coaching staff decided to start Tim against the Steelers. I'd taken the down time to try to heal the pain that still burned in my groin. Muscles and tissues have their own timetables for feeling better, and this one wasn't going to be rushed. I couldn't ignore the injury, but I wasn't going to let it stop me from playing or use it as an excuse for my own difficulties on the field. More than halfway through the season, I had only forty-eight catches for four touchdowns, but I had seven games left to make up for this disappointment. Entering the stretch run, the Niners were 4 and 5, while both Saint Louis and Seattle were 6 and 3. We weren't eliminated from the playoffs, but we couldn't blow any more chances to catch these two and win the NFC West or grab a wild-card spot. This game against Pittsburgh, like every other one remaining on the schedule, was critical. Along with the national audience and 67,000 fans in the stands, I was very interested to see how Tim, a four-year veteran backup, would perform as a starter in prime time. Nobody knew what to expect, but I had a good feeling about it.

Rat and I had some things in common, so I understood his mindset. Like me, he'd come out of a small-time college program and had struggled just to make the team. After high school, he'd played quarterback for the Scottsdale Community College Fighting Artichokes in suburban Phoenix. The school wasn't big on sports and had given the team this mascot in the hope that they'd be so bad they'd eventually quit playing football. Tim had real aspirations to play pro football and left the Artichokes, transferring east to Louisiana Tech, where the competition was much better. Louisiana Tech had produced only one big-name player, but it was quite a name: quarterback Terry Bradshaw, who'd led the Steelers to four Super Bowl victories in the 1970s. At Tech, Tim had erupted as a talent, throwing for more than 12,000 yards and becoming the second-leading passer in NCAA history, but many experts felt that he'd never make it in the NFL.

He was too light and too slow, they said. He wasn't tough enough and had come from a lousy football college. He could only pass out of the pocket and wasn't mobile, like the new wave of quarterbacks who were lighting up the league: Michael Vick, Steve McNair, and Donovan McNabb. Rat didn't let any of these opinions discourage him. He was a born gym rat and had constantly studied the Niners system while sitting on the bench behind Jeff, working very hard to improve his game. When called upon to play, he'd usually done well, but nobody really was certain how good he could be. Now he was finally getting a chance to perform in front of the nation, on *Monday Night Football*. From watching him at practice and in games, I knew he was good at throwing the ball downfield and letting his receivers run after it, which was what I'd been asking for ever since coming to San Francisco.

The Niners-Steelers match-up got a lot of pregame hype because it was my first appearance on *MNF* since Sharpie, and people were asking what I might do next. I wasn't thinking about that but about getting the team off fast. Whenever a backup QB is starting, it's a special feeling. You want to do something to help him relax and get into the flow of the game. This attitude heightens your concentration, because you know he might have the jitters and needs your help. It was a rallying point for the team, which was good. We'd been unfocused through much of the season and couldn't afford any more of that.

On ESPN's pregame show, all the talk was about the quarterback controversy brewing in San Francisco. All three commentators— Tom Jackson, Ron Jaworski, and Michael Irvin—said that Tim had looked great versus Saint Louis, and if he played as well against the Steelers, the 49ers would have to make a tough decision about benching either Rattay or Garcia in the weeks ahead. The Steelers were going to blitz a lot that night, and that would test Tim even more. Would he step forward and begin to establish himself as an NFL starter, or would he wilt under this kind of pressure? They all agreed he had potential, but only Irvin reminded everyone that way back in September, TO had told the world that Rattay deserved more of a chance to show off his talents. A lot of people who'd called me out for saying this, Michael said on the air, were now singing Tim's praises. I'd just said it first.

The pregame hype was fed by the fact that the Niners were retiring Ronnie Lott's number. No one, not even Joe Montana or Jerry Rice, had represented the 49ers' pride and success of the '80s and early '90s more than number 42. A quarter-century earlier, when Bill Walsh took over as head coach of San Francisco, the biggest flaw he'd seen on the team was its pass coverage. He liked to say that when he first watched game film of the Niners' opponents catching touchdowns, the 49ers defensive backs weren't even in the picture. His number 1 pick in his initial draft was Lott, who came in not just with the desire to hit people hard but with the attitude that losing was unacceptable (the Niners had been losers for longer than most people could remember).

Ronnie played cornerback first and then free safety and then strong safety; before long, the Niners had the best secondary in the league and were on their way to a series of titles. If Montana was the heart of the offense, Lott was the soul of the defense. He went to ten Pro Bowls before entering the Hall of Fame, and he carried, as they say in the NFL, a lot of wood in his knapsack. He'd crack you so hard that if you were lucky enough to get up off the ground, you'd think twice about going back to the huddle. He played for one thing above all, he always told people, and that was respect. Everybody who ever played for or against Lott gave him his props, and a whole lot of receivers out there were glad when he retired. He stood for everything the franchise had once achieved—and hoped to achieve again.

It was fifty-five degrees in San Francisco that evening, with no swirling winds and no moisture, a night made for football. Playing in prime time, whether on Sunday night or Monday night, had always jacked me up the most, and I couldn't wait to touch the field. ABC's lead-in for the game was all about me. The hot young actress Jennifer Garner, who stars on that network's hit show *Alias,* talked about my feats while the cameras gave the audience replays of Dallas, Sharpie, and the pom-pom celebration. At the end of this feature, she looked straight into the lens and said, "Without men like Terrell Owens, it's just a game."

I didn't force anyone to use me for this promo. I didn't ask anybody at ABC to do this, and that's the funny thing about my life in football. When I do something new, I always take a ton of heat at first. People get angry, they blow up at me, they vent. They call me names and make me the target of their feelings, but then time passes, and they start to see things in a different light. They realize that what I did entertained them, or at least stimulated them and stayed in their memory, and maybe it wasn't such a bad thing after all. Maybe it wasn't threatening professional sports and the American way of life as much as they thought it was. Maybe it was *fun.*

Near the start of this broadcast, when it was time for me to tell the audience which college I'd gone to, I had some fun again. Everyone else on the Niners and the Steelers said they'd gone to Notre Dame or the University of Michigan or whatever, but I said that I was "from another planet." That could be accurate because I've had this feeling of being different my whole life, and I can't explain it or change it now. When we finally learn and accept that everybody *is* different from everybody else, and that's a true strength and not a weakness, we'll have made a great leap forward.

* * *

The Niners received the kickoff, and on our opening series I caught a pass for a first down, but I was so crunked that I lined up offside on the next play. In the broadcast booth, John Madden told the viewers that I must have been right about my college career, because any wide receiver who didn't line up onside *had* to be from another planet. We lined up again, and Tim dropped straight back to throw, looking like a classic NFL pocket quarterback. The Steelers cornerback, Chad Scott, had tried to bump me at the line of scrimmage, but I'd run through him, and he was now a step or two behind me. Tim unleashed a perfect throw over my right shoulder, leading me in full stride, and I grabbed it and headed for the end zone. Scott was never going to catch me, and I was alone at the goal line, so I stopped in front of it and spun around before scoring. The next morning, reporters described this move as a "pirouette."

In the end zone, I began to dance, and my teammates were all over me, and they were dancing, too. Everybody was in on this celebration. Someone in the crowd, who was wearing a number 81 jersey and a knit cap covered with Sharpies, yelled at me to sign the ball, but I ignored him. I was past that now. I just wanted to keep getting open and catching passes and beating the Steelers. Tim's TD strike was for 61 yards, and Pittsburgh's blitz wouldn't bother him much the rest of the evening. He'd started strong and would get stronger and more confident as the night went along. The whole Niners team was energized by his performance, and even the kicking game was working now. Todd Peterson would hit three field-goal attempts, while our defense completely shut down Tommy Maddox and the Steelers' attack. We went into halftime leading 10 to 0.

During the intermission, Ronnie Lott was honored on the field while surrounded by ex-49ers, including Joe Montana, Bill Walsh, and Eddie DeBartolo. The biggest moment came when Ronnie reached over and hugged former owner Eddie D., thanking him for bringing greatness to San Francisco football in the '80s and '90s. It was a heartfelt gesture, and Ronnie put into words what a lot of people, including myself, had felt for a long time. The franchise had never been the same since DeBartolo had left and taken his class act with him. Listening to Ronnie Lott and hearing the pride and passion in his voice made me think we could turn things around and win again. Ronnie stood for what sports are all about—pushing yourself to be the very best athlete possible and pushing your team to win. A lot of people in that stadium watched him grab Eddie DeBartolo and got choked up, and I was one of them.

In the third quarter, Pittsburgh scored a touchdown to make it 10 to 7, and it looked as if they might take over the game. Right then, according to people who were watching the broadcast, John Madden told everyone from coast to coast that it was time for Tim to start looking for me, the way he had in the first quarter, because the Niners needed to get me back into the action. With wide receivers, Madden explained, there was a very fine line between being selfish players and wanting to get the ball in your hands so you could do what you were paid to do. In his opinion, I fell on the side of the line that wanted to catch more passes and help my team win. That's all I'd been trying to say for the past few years, and now he'd said it for me to a nationwide audience. When I heard about these comments later on, they were sweet to my ears. Maybe Michael Jordan had been right back in early October, after the Minnesota meltdown, when he'd told me that it was time for me to keep still and let others do some talking for me.

Thank you, Mr. Madden, for getting the word out there on *Monday Night Football*. TO wants a ring more than anything else, and he wants to contribute to the team to make this happen. He can't do that unless he touches the ball and moves it down the field. End of story, but the game with Pittsburgh was just starting to heat up.

After the Steelers failed to score in the third quarter, we got the ball back, and Tim handed off to Kevan Barlow on a play called "94 whip." Kevan cut through the left side of the line and found an opening in the secondary. He veered to the right and took off. I'd set up on the right side of the field and run my route nearly all the way to the left sideline, but when I saw him moving toward the opposite sideline, I turned and sprinted in that direction. I crossed the field at top speed until I got in front of him—and in front of the two Steelers cornerbacks who were closing on him as he broke into the red zone. I took out one, Chad Scott, with my shoulder and just got a body part or two on the other man, Deshea Townsend. Kevan flew past them and over the goal line, completing a 78-yard run, the longest of his career. We had another great celebration in the end zone, and I was thrilled to be doing this with teammates instead of by myself.

Pittsburgh fumbled the kickoff, and we took over on their 28. On the next play, Tim dropped back, looked left, and threw a perfect toss to fullback Fred Beasley, who carried it in for the TD. In fourteen seconds, we'd scored 14 points, it was 24 to 7, and the rest of the night belonged to the Niners. Tim completed twenty-one of twenty-seven passes for 254 yards and two touchdowns, with no interceptions. His poise and his accuracy on both short and long balls were the talk of the football world. I grabbed eight of his throws for 155 yards and a TD of my own, my best effort of the season (we were 13 and 2 in the past fifteen games in which I'd gained 100 or more yards). The final score was 49ers 30 and Steelers 14, but the debate was just beginning.

Against a tough, blitzing Steelers defense, Rat had been about as good as anyone could be. He'd handled the pressure with total calm and a veteran's command of the offense. He was twenty-six and healthy, while Jeff was thirty-three and still injured. Who was going to lead us as we went on the road against Green Bay and then to Baltimore? What was best for the team, which had only a slim chance of making the playoffs unless we could put together a long winning streak?

Once again, I'll let others do the talking for me. Back when I'd blown up on the Minnesota sidelines at Greg Knapp and suggested to the press that maybe Tim could play a little football, one of my biggest critics had been Boomer Esiason, the former NFL quarter-back who now did *Monday Night Football* for CBS Radio. At the end of the Niners-Steelers game, when Boomer's partner Marv Albert asked him who should start against the Packers next week, Garcia or Rattay, Esiason responded with disbelief in his voice.

"You're gonna sit this guy down now, Marv?" he said.

XXXVI

IN FORTY-DEGREE WEATHER and a light mist, Tim Rattay started against Green Bay, but nothing went right for us. Our offensive line was injured again. Tim was sacked four times and knocked down five more. He had to hurry a lot of throws, completing only fourteen of thirty passes, and we could never find a rhythm on the field. The momentum we'd built against the Steelers had evaporated by the end of the first half. Our defense intercepted three Brett Favre passes, twice deep in Packers territory, but each time this happened, our offense stalled, and Todd Peterson missed a field goal. The defense couldn't stop the Packers' excellent young running back, Ahman Green, who had 154 yards and controlled the game. Late in the third quarter, we rallied when Tim hit me with a 24-yard TD pass to bring the Niners to within 7 points, but the Pack put up another field goal and won 20 to 10.

From week to week, we were a different football team, and there was no good explanation for this and no Hollywood script to rescue us from a 5-and-6 record. Following the Green Bay loss, the talking heads and local columnists immediately began calling for Jeff Garcia to replace Tim—and they got their wish. It wasn't what I wanted, but I didn't get to vote on the matter, and I didn't say anything in public about this coaching decision. Jeff came back to start the next game against Baltimore, and we lost 44 to 6 to the Ravens, their biggest margin of victory in franchise history. This wasn't just another bad road loss for the Niners but the bottom of the season.

Jeff had thrown four interceptions before being pulled in the final quarter, when the game was way out of reach. It felt as if the 49ers were drifting downward, without any leadership or direction, either on the field or off. We were 5 and 7, with only four games to go, and our playoff hopes were just about gone. Football people like to say that during the course of a season, teams either get better or they get worse. We weren't consistent enough to do anything that predictable—we got better one week and worse the next—but we were 0 and 6 on the road.

Four days after the Baltimore loss, *Mercury News* reporter Daniel Brown put this in the paper: "Terrell Owens stopped delivering his blunt and bombastic postgame reviews months ago. . . . It's a pity, actually, because, looking back on his comments, Owens seems irrefutably prescient. . . . He knocked the offensive line (an injury-ravaged unit that has turned out to be a season-long trouble spot). He hinted that the team might be better off with Tim Rattay at quarterback . . . (which sounded like blasphemy at the time but has become a mainstream debate). He questioned the play calling near the goal line, which remains a bugaboo. Even Owens's most blistering condemnation—'We have no heart'—no longer seems so outrageous."

Letting others speak for me was working out just fine.

Just when it looked as if our season had collapsed, we came home the next week and played brilliantly. On December 7, my thirtieth birthday, we crushed a very weak Arizona team, 50 to 14. Jeff had an outstanding game, running for two touchdowns and throwing for four more (two of them to me, a great birthday present). Despite this win, we remained a confused and confusing team, but we still had a shot at the playoffs. The following week, Jeff and the entire offense played well at Cincinnati, scoring five touchdowns, making thirty-one first downs, and gaining 502 yards, but somehow we managed to lose a thriller to the up-and-coming Bengals, 41 to 38, in a snowstorm. Jeff threw for two TDs (including a 58-yarder to me), he ran for one more, and Kevan Barlow carried the ball over the goal line twice, but he also fumbled twice in critical situations. Playoff teams know how to win tight games, but we'd failed to do that all season long. We were now 0 and 7 on the road, had lost all six games that were close in the fourth quarter, and had dropped five games by a total of 11 points. It was as if the good luck that the 49ers had known back in the '80s and '90s, when they were winning Super Bowls, had been used up, and the only thing left was the memory of winning tough games.

Our playoff chances died for good in Cincinnati in the snow. All I could do was stand on the sidelines and watch Bengals receiver Chad Johnson score a touchdown and then hold up a handwritten sign asking the NFL not to fine him for celebrating in this way. He was stealing a page from my book about how to act in the end zone, and I had to laugh at it. I hated losing to the Bengals, but I wasn't going to get upset at someone else who wanted to have a little fun after his team had turned its season around and won a big ball game. The problem wasn't that Johnson was carrying this sign but that we couldn't win a game on the road. Blaming him solved nothing.

It was time for me to try to let go of the tremendous disappointment the 2003 season had been and start focusing on the future, even though we still had two games left to play. But then things got a little worse. Against Philadelphia the next week, with two minutes remaining in the half and the Niners trailing 14 to 7, I caught a 20-yard pass from Jeff and was tackled awkwardly out of bounds, landing hard on my left shoulder. After taking me to the dressing room and examining me, the trainer told me that I couldn't play the rest of the game. The pain was deepening, but I didn't know if a bone was broken or not.

I watched the rest of the Eagles game from the sidelines, and then the team boarded a flight back to California. We sat on the runway in Philly for six hours because someone had threatened to blow up our airplane with a bomb. Those hours would have lasted forever no matter what, but during this time, the pain began to settle in, and I wondered if something was seriously wrong. The next day, I was examined by Niners doctor Michael Dillingham and learned that my collarbone was broken in two places. Dr. Dillingham recommended that I not have surgery to repair the breaks, but neither David nor I was comfortable with his opinion. Niners tight end Eric Johnson had broken his collarbone early in the season, and he'd never healed properly or gotten back onto the field. Months had passed, and he still wasn't well.

Dr. Dillingham said we could get a second opinion on my injury, which is a right established by the NFL's collective bargaining agreement with the NFLPA. In a memo issued only days after my injury, the NFL Players Association wrote, "You have the right to a second medical opinion and the right to have a surgeon of your choice perform your surgery. You also have the right to know of any adverse medical conditions. If the club is discouraging you from seeking a second medical opinion or selecting your own surgeon, call your regional director immediately. Your career depends on you receiving the best medical care, and your right to select the doctors who treat you is extremely important."

It was even more important right then, because I was most likely going to be a free agent at the end of the year. If I were damaged goods, my value in the football marketplace could tumble.

Dr. Dillingham told us that he would get us the name of a doctor for a second opinion. Several days later the pain had not subsided and David and I were getting worried. David began looking for another physician who could diagnose my injury and Derrick Deese and others recommended Dr. Art Ting. I went to see him on Monday, December 29, eight days after the Philly game. Dr. Ting had worked on many motocross injuries and knew a lot about broken collarbones. While Dr. Ting was examining me, David and another agent in his office, Jason Knight, were making a road trip through South Carolina to meet with a new football prospect. Dr. Ting told me that I needed surgery immediately, so I called David on his cell and relayed the message. He was so alarmed that he pulled into a truck stop and parked the car. Neither he nor Jason had a copy of the collective-bargaining agreement with them, and they wanted to review it to make sure we proceeded correctly. If I was going to have surgery that day, it was critical that we tell the 49ers first, in order for the operation to be covered by my health insurance. We wanted the team to sign off on the operation ahead of time to avoid any potential trouble later on.

All this was made more complicated because it was Monday afternoon, the team had just played its last game of the season, and we had to act immediately. With eighteen-wheelers groaning and humming in the background, David and Jason leaned out through their windows, opened up their cells, and began dialing. While Jason called a friend in New York State who did have the CBA on hand and David frantically phoned the 49ers, I waited in Dr. Ting's office. Jason's friend searched through the CBA and came to "Article XLIV: Players' Rights to Medical Care and Treatment." Under Section 3, it read, "A player will have the opportunity to obtain a second medical opinion. As a condition of the responsibility of the Club for the costs of medical services rendered by the physician furnishing the second opinion, the player must (a) consult with the Club physician in advance concerning the other physician; and (b) the Club physician must be furnished promptly with a report concerning the diagnosis, examination, and course of treatment recommended by the other physician."

In other words, David had to get Dr. Dillingham on the phone as soon as possible and tell him that I was in Dr. Ting's office and that Dr. Ting was ready to operate. At first, David was unable to reach Dr. Dillingham, so he left a message on his voice mail. Shortly thereafter 49ers executive John McVay called David and said that Dr. Ting's opinions on these matters shouldn't be trusted (Dr. Ting and Dr. Dillingham, we later found out, once had worked together and had not parted friends). Dr. Dillingham was reached soon thereafter and he suggested that we talk to his friend at USC, Dr. John Itamura. In the next forty minutes, David fielded about twenty calls from the Niners and the doctors. Finally, David was able to set up a conference call that involved Dr. Ting and Dr. Itamura, and they were able to look at my MRI together. Dr. Itamura agreed with Dr. Ting's diagnosis: I needed surgery. With that opinion in hand, Dr. Dillingham accepted these recommendations. He even decided to attend the operation, which involved putting a plate in my collarbone. When David asked me if it was all right if Dr. Dillingham was present during the surgery, I said yes, but he couldn't touch me.

My job now was to heal in the next six to seven weeks, and David's was to keep all this out of the papers. We didn't want any team that might want to sign me as a free agent to know that I'd broken my collarbone in two places or that I'd gone untreated for seven days. We didn't want them to know about how the Niners medical staff had handled the situation. Following my successful operation, the 49ers doctors decided on a new strategy for helping tight end Eric Johnson: they rebroke Eric's collarbone so they could perform surgery on it and make it heal much faster. Without my operation, I would likely have been like Eric and taken about eight to ten months to get well. This would not only have carried my injury into the 2004 football season but made me unfit during the free agency period, which began in March 2004. Every NFL franchise wanting to sign me would have insisted on a stringent medical exam before offering a contract, and I couldn't have passed it. This might have cost me the football future I wanted and tens of millions of dollars.

I found myself wondering if the Niners were content to take the, at best, slower approach to treating my injury because they didn't want me to be healthy going into free agency. Then other teams might have passed on me, and they could have re-signed me for far less money than we wanted. No wonder the players union fought for the right to get a second opinion.

XXXVII

IT WAS UP TO ME to decide whether or not I wanted to choose free agency and leave the 49ers behind. It was up to the franchise to make me an offer before March 2, 2004, when the football year officially ended. In January 2004, the Niners brass hadn't spoken with my agent about a new deal since the last June, and they'd never come forward with an offer. It appeared the team was going to put the franchise tag on linebacker Julian Peterson that year, so the door was open for me to go. I had very mixed feelings about departing the Bay Area but very clear feelings about wanting to play for a winner. The whole thing felt like a long marriage that was crumbling. As with most shaky relationships, the story line was not simple, and the outcome was uncertain. Egos were involved on every side. Personalities weren't going to change, and painful differences wouldn't completely mend. Jeff Garcia had been to the Pro Bowl three times in the past three years. So had I, and I was elected to go again in 2004, the fourth year in a row. I couldn't play in the Pro Bowl, but I went to Hawaii for the game and had a great time hanging with Donovan McNabb and other players.

In the past season, I'd gained more than 1,000 yards and had joined Jerry Rice on the 49ers list of those who'd scored more than 300 points, but none of this took away the sting of missing the playoffs. I was unhappy, and something or somebody had to give. It didn't help my confidence in my team or my quarterback when in January 2004, Jeff got picked up in the Bay Area for DUI.

One night in late January, I was fiddling around on my Web site, TerrellOwens.com, when I decided to answer some of the questions that fans had sent me. We'd created the site so we could put out our story instead of relying on the media to report on things and get them right. I don't get the time to log on to the site very often, but I was re- cuperating from my surgery and had some down time, and I thought it might be fun. Naturally, people wanted to know about my relation- ship with Jeff and my upcoming free agency. Without pausing to con- sider all the consequences, I started typing. I did what I always do: I tried to answer people honestly and openly. This was my first experi- ence with the true power of the Internet, and it was a great education. I wrote, in part: "I'm willing 2 work out a contract if the Niners cn get a QB 2 match my skills as a receiver! I want to win a Super Bowl & can be a big part of that, a receiver is only as good as his QB!"

In response to a fan asking about my leaving the 49ers, I wrote, "Hopefully, I dn't go anywhere but it dn't look good plus we need a QB 2 make a run @ the Superbowl."

I joked that if Jeff needed a ride after my Super Bowl party, I could provide him with a limousine to make sure he got home safely.

And I wrote, "I'm nt blaming the whole season on him. But bein a QB holds big responsibilities!!!! Havin said that, how about his DUI situation? Everybody wants 2 criticize me 4 this & that, but hv I represented the 49ers n tht fashion, nope—I dn't think so! I'm nt the problem, I'm the answer! If I cn't get a QB 2 help us win the Su- perbowl—I wn't b back!"

Football stirs up basic passions, which is why we love the game, but it can also make some people crazy. *Fan* is short for *fanatic*. It took only a day or two for the feedback to start rolling in about what I'd written, and the response was overwhelming. In the next seven days, we got 235,000 hits on our site, and some of the messages were supportive, but many were unbelievably ugly. Here are a few examples of what showed up in my e-mail box:

"Watch your back owens. You are racist and you want to start a race war . . . bring it on. Your comments that you made about Garcia's DUI were personal ones. Evidently you want to bring down Hispanics."

"Hey Terrell, it's not Garcia that has the problem. By far you are the most selfish piece of shit in the NFL. No matter how much money and fame you acquire you will always be a self centered, egotistical self promoting jerk. Hopefully you will sign with a team that plays San Fran next year. This way maybe somebody will try to blowout your knees."

"On the website, it says Mr. Owens lives in California. But, I seem to remember calling him a few times and talking to him and actually seeing his house in Georgia. Tell him he should be wary of giving his number out as everyone knows it now."

"You insult Jeff Garcia about how bad he is, and yet, you were not any better. As a matter of fact, you should take a pay cut for pathetic performance this year. While you are at it, grow up. If it wasn't for football, which an education is not needed, you'd be selling drugs like the rest of your homeboys. You got to be one of the stupidest niggers ever."

"Hey you gutless, spineless SOB . . . don't have the courage to talk to Garcia to his face? Have to do it in your bullshit website. Get a clue dude. You're the one dropping passes that are thrown right at you. You're the one that is too chicken shit to go thru the middle for a pass like Jerry Rice, or up in the air like Randy Moss. Not once did you have the guts to go up in the air and extend yourself like Moss, and you call yourself great, what a joke. McNabb wants nothing to do with you, Vick don't want you . . . nobody does cause you're a legend in your own mind. Get the fuck out of the SF you sorry ass loser!"

After these messages came in, David and I put out a lot of information on my site to restate my positions regarding the Niners and Jeff and free agency. This seemed to help, and the hateful e-mails stopped coming in, but that didn't prevent me from hiring a bodyguard or two at $600 per guard per day. A little protection wasn't a bad thing. In the end, though, the damage to my relationship with Jeff and to the 49ers had been done, and there was no way to repair it. The time had come for me to leave San Francisco. According to my contract, I had until March 2, 2004, to inform the 49ers that I was voiding the remaining years on the agreement. The big question was: Would another team give me a long-term contract with the kind of signing bonus I was looking for? In early February, David talked to ESPN football guru John Clayton, and he said he didn't think I could command more than $6 million as a signing bonus. We were looking for much more than this, but Clayton said that offer wasn't out there.

In the past, I'd gambled on my talent and won by making it as a receiver in the NFL. Since signing my multimillion-dollar contract in 1999, I'd taken larger risks by deciding to be myself on and off the field and not to act like a PC robot the way some other star players did. I'd chosen to challenge the NFL and its owners and management head-on. Could I buck the system and win again? Could I celebrate when I felt like it and how I felt like it, or was I going to be punished for that now when I became a free agent looking for a new contract? Could I speak the truth and get away with it, or was that unacceptable in pro football, where everything is about control and conformity? Would my talent take me where I wanted to go, or had I upset too many people in the past?

This was the bigger game I'd been playing since 1999, when I'd looked around the league and figured out that trying to be Jerry Rice or anyone else was never going to work for me. I wanted to succeed on my own terms, and if that meant rocking the boat, then let it rock. I was strong enough to deal with the consequences because of my foundation of family and faith. Everything in my background had prepared me for this challenge. By late February 2004, as I prepared to declare free agency, nobody knew what the outcome of all this was going to be—or just how crazy things would get before it was all over.

XXXVIII

ON FEBRUARY 25, seven days before I was to become an unrestricted free agent, the unbelievable happened. After I'd burned just about every bridge in the Bay Area, the league tried to stop me from leaving San Francisco. Talk about getting blindsided by circumstances—after we'd done everything possible to prevent something like this from occurring.

On Friday, February 20, David and Jason Knight were in Indianapolis at the NFL combine and annual agents meeting. Weeks before, David had called the NFLPA and asked if my void date had been moved or if any other contract changes were in the works. The answer was no. The union had told him that a free agent list was coming out on February 8, and they would phone me if I was on it, but they never made this call. Being very diligent, David called them and learned that the list had come out, and I was on it, which meant that I was probably subject to be stuck with the franchise tag by the Niners (the NFLPA was not 100 percent sure of this though), but no one said this would have any effect on my void date. In Indianapolis, David and Jason spoke with a union official and laid out our plan to void the contract after the franchise transition period had expired on February 24. We wanted to make sure that the Niners didn't tag me as they had back in 1999, because that would make everything more complicated and uncertain. The union representative listened to

David's strategy and said nothing except "Good luck." On Monday, February 23, the 49ers put the franchise tag on linebacker Julian Peterson, removing the last potential block to my free agency—or so I thought. About three P.M. on Wednesday, the 25th, David faxed a letter to the San Francisco front office, officially voiding the last three years on my contract. The deal was done, and a few hours later, David went home for the day.

After waiting until past closing time on the East Coast, Niners general manager Terry Donahue faxed David back. His letter said, "Your notice is untimely," and added, "Terrell remains under contract to the 49ers through the 2006 season." He ended with, "I hope this letter finds you and your family well, and we will look forward to working with you in the future."

The next morning was snowy and cold in Greensboro, a very dreary day. Traffic jams crowded the streets, and it took longer to get to work. David's secretary, Jodi Miller, came into the office first and found the fax waiting for us. As soon as David arrived, she handed it to him. He read it and did not feel well at all. Everything we'd worked for throughout the past eight years—getting me into free agency and onto a team that was a legitimate Super Bowl contender—was falling apart.

With a look of shock on his face, David handed to fax the Jason and said, "What in the hell is this?"

David immediately called a lawyer with the players' union and asked him what was going on. He had no immediate explanation. After many hours of research and discussion, it became apparent that the NFL was claiming that my deadline to void had been moved up to February 23, stealing nine days from me.

In January 2001, the NFL and the players' union agreed that they needed to permanently set certain dates, such as the start of the new league year and the Franchise/Transition Period. However, by setting these dates going forward they also recognized that certain dates that had been previously been negotiated into NFL players' contracts, such as void deadlines, could lose their effectiveness.

Thus, the NFL and the players' union added another clause to the collective bargaining agreement to ensure that dates previously negotiated would remain at their intended place in the process and not lose effectiveness. For example, if you had negotiated a void deadline in the middle of the Franchise/Transition Period and the deadline ended up being after the period, the new clause would move it back to where it needed to be in order to give it its intended effect.

The NFL misapplied these clauses to my void deadline and moved my date into the Franchise/Transition Period. The deadline to void as stated in my contract was March 2, 2004, a date that was always after the Franchise/Transition Period. Thus, it was *never* subject to being moved into the Franchise Period by the NFL. As soon as we determined this, David and I told anyone and everyone who would listen that my void deadline never moved and that I effectively voided my contract on February 25. I knew I was right and that I deserved to be a free agent as of March 3. Yet again no one would listen to what I was actually saying, and thus again I was subject to a period of intense criticism and ridicule. I had been through this before, but this time it went beyond me and included David.

In the meantime, Terry Donahue and the Niners were certain that they could either keep me under my old contract or trade me away, and they were in a housecleaning mood. The same day we learned about the dispute with my void notice, February 26, the team cut loose veteran tackle Derrick Deese, defensive lineman Sean Moran, and Garrison Hearst. The rumor mill said they were also getting ready to let Jeff Garcia go because they didn't want to carry his $10-million salary into the 2004 season.

David requested that the NFLPA file a grievance on my behalf, but they balked. Gene Upshaw, the head of the union, and Harold Henderson, executive vice president for labor relations of the NFL Management Council, thought they might be able to talk this over and work something out. In the meantime, they asked David's office not to speak to the press about this, basically putting them under a gag order, but Michael Signora, an NFL spokesman, already had released this statement: "Terrell Owens did not exercise his option in a timely fashion, which is what is required." The story that was going out to the media was that this was my fault and my agent's fault, and we were completely in the wrong. We'd blown the deadline and now had to pay for it by missing our shot at free agency. The media, of course, ran as hard with this version of events as they could, not caring if it was true or false. The opinion makers were busy doing what they did best: making opinions, regardless of whether or not they had any connection to reality. Everyone who'd ever held a grudge against me was dialing in and lining up to take a good whack at David and me.

All of this was somehow just perfect. In the past, the NFL had reprimanded me for not having my shirt tucked in during games and fined me for wearing a wristband that read "The Answer" on *Monday Night Football.* Every time I got fined, I got a letter informing me of it, but this time, they forgot to send us the letter saying they were changing the free agency rules. The No Fun League had found another way to keep players from exercising their options and earning what they had the right to earn on the open market.

The airwaves were instantly filled with people from coast to coast attacking David and me for our "mistake." Commentators everywhere were telling me to fire my agent immediately because he was an idiot. It seemed every sports reporter in America called us for an explanation of our failure, and for several days it was pure chaos. One journalist showed up at David's parents' home in Greensboro, demanding an interview with his father. Then the guy drove over to David's house and knocked on his door. David's wife answered the door and told him to leave them alone. Worried about his family's safety, David called the reporter, who continued to say that if we wouldn't talk he would just have to fabricate a story about us.

As stated, David called the union numerous times on February 26, but it took them several hours just to find the letter that apparently changed my void deadline. Their lawyers also had no clue about this change in the void date. Once they found the letter, they told us that the NFL Management Council's position was correct: my void date had passed. David erupted, telling the union lawyers that he'd been talking with them for weeks, and no one had ever mentioned this issue to him. Not only were we getting hammered by the league and in the media, but the union wasn't standing up for me in a crisis. On the evening of that awful first day, things got just a little worse when a union attorney called David and insisted that the NFLPA had faxed a copy of the letter to David on or around February 10.

For the next five or six hours, David and Jason turned their offices inside out and upside down looking for this fax. It wasn't there. They also checked their fax log for February 10 and found nothing. It had never come in. They'd done nothing wrong, but a few days later, Gene Upshaw spoke to the *New York Times* about all this.

"We faxed the notice to TO's agent on February 10," he said. "We have confirmation of the note. We faxed pages. Now he claims he wasn't notified. I'm not going to sit around and take the blame for a mistake he made."

Truth be told, there was no letter ever received by David's office, or one ever sent to my house, either.

While the union was taking cover, my agent was going through hell. On the 26th, he and Jason stayed at work past midnight and then kept talking. David knew he wasn't going to sleep that night, and Jason did not feel that his boss should be left alone. David was devastated, but I tried to stay cool. He called me throughout the 26th, and I just kept telling him, "I didn't get a letter, and you didn't get a letter. We didn't do anything wrong, and we're going to win." When my mother heard what was going on, she told him the same thing, not to give up and not to lose faith, because we were going to win. She'd been through way too much in her life to worry about faxes and paper notification.

As much as David wanted to believe us, he was having a very rough time. I was used to being kicked around by the press, but he wasn't, and he was the one taking the heat now from ESPN and Jim Rome. David felt absolutely terrible and all alone, even though he wasn't. He thought I might listen to other people now and fire him, but he really didn't understand what the last eight years had meant. We were family now, David and I. He'd had my back for years, through Dallas and Sharpie and everything else, and I had his now. If you don't do this when it really counts, then you don't know what family means. Or faith. Or love. David was in the meat grinder, and I needed to be there for him until this got resolved. He'd already started losing weight and would drop from 158 pounds to 133 during the next three weeks. At 133, he looked like a Bobblehead doll.

In the morning, David and Jason hired a law firm. They needed a different perspective and brought on two attorneys, including a labor law expert. The way it looked to them was that regardless of the NFL's claims I had until March 2, 2004, to void my contract and that I had properly voided it on February 25. That was our legal position. The NFLPA, the NFL, and the media were all focused on this alleged fax, which made us question whether they understood their own collective-bargaining agreement or were just covering their you-know-whats. Even though no one would listen to him, David was confident that my date never changed under the collective-bargaining agreement and that the NFL could not simply change a term in my contract just because it was the NFL.

David and Jason worked on legal strategy all weekend and went to church on Sunday. They usually attended church in Greensboro, but that day, they made a point of it: their faith was growing stronger with each passing hour. On Monday, March 1, David got a call from a lawyer at Dewey Ballantine, the union's outside law firm, who said they were looking into grounds for filing a grievance on my behalf. We were encouraged until he said that as a union member, I'd given away my rights regarding the new void date. He basically told David and Jason that because they weren't labor lawyers, they didn't know what they were doing or talking about. David tried to talk to him about contract law and how my void date could not have changed, but they would not and did not want to hear from us. After this conversation, David was so angry that he couldn't talk; he knew that without the union's backing, it would be very difficult to pursue a grievance.

On midnight of March 1, David called Jason and told him that a deal was in the works: ESPN.com was reporting that the Niners were going to get the thirty-third pick of the upcoming draft, and I was going to get free agency. We were encouraged once again but not for long. The 49ers and the NFL had been waiting for the opportunity to punish me for years, and now they were ready to act. What had turned ugly was only going to get uglier.

On Tuesday, March 2, the Niners released Jeff Garcia and told David that things had changed once more. They were not granting me free agency in return for a draft pick. Instead, they agreed to give David seventy-two hours to work out a trade for me. If he could put together a deal, I could leave San Francisco. He immediately contacted the Bucs, Broncos, Jets, Falcons, Eagles, Ravens, and Dolphins. By Wednesday, we could see that the strongest interest was from Atlanta, Baltimore, and Philly. I soon got a call from the Ravens linebacking great, Ray Lewis, who said he wanted to play with me, but the Ravens were worried about my character issues. He must have forgotten his own trial a few years before.

It wasn't a very long conversation.

Ravens general manager Ozzie Newsome wanted me to come to Baltimore but told David that I needed to play under my old contract that first year. If I performed well in the first half of the 2004 season, he said, he would tear up that contract and write a new one. David wasn't impressed.

"TO has eight years in the league," he told Ozzie. "He doesn't do auditions."

I really didn't want to go to Baltimore, anyway. Philly was my first choice. For years, I'd wanted to play with Donovan McNabb, and after the Eagles lost their third straight NFC title game in the 2003 playoffs, Donovan started publicly asking for more offensive weapons. David called Philadelphia's team president, Joe Banner, who sounded willing to make the trade under the right conditions. What had appeared to be a disaster just six days earlier was looking better now. Baltimore and Philly were contenders, and David made it clear to both of them not to try and trade me until a new contract was in place. Late Wednesday afternoon, David sent some numbers to Ozzie Newsome, and Ozzie quickly called back, saying he thought we could get a deal done.

On Thursday morning, Ozzie called David and hooked him up with the Ravens' contract negotiator, Pat Moriarty. Things had changed yet again. The Ravens were not only offering us $10 million less than the deal we had discussed before, but Moriarty wouldn't budge a nickel. For ninety minutes, he and David butted heads on the phone. This time, when David hung up, he picked up the receiver and threw it against the wall. After cooling off, he called the Eagles to see if they had a better offer. While they were talking, the Cleveland Browns phoned and said they wanted to possibly do a deal. David told the Browns that the Eagles and the Ravens were ready to close, so if the Browns were serious, they needed to put money on the table now. As soon as David got off the line, Joe Banner of the Eagles called and said he was ready to make us a firm offer. It was a good one: Philly's entire bonus package would come to about $15 million. David faxed me the numbers in Atlanta and then called the Ravens' Moriarty to tell him about the new developments. As I looked at the fax, I was very excited by the prospect of playing with the Eagles.

David called Joe Banner back, at around three P.M. and proposed several additional changes to the contract. The Eagles were holding a press conference announcing the signing of defensive end Jevon Kearse, and Banner told David he would get back to him after the press conference.

Shortly thereafter, he called David and asked bluntly, "Have you agreed to a trade with the Ravens?"

David said no, but Banner told him to go look at ESPN.com.

He did, and there in black and white, it said that the 49ers, without ever talking to David or me, had dealt me to Baltimore for a second-round pick. That morning, while Ozzie Newsome had gotten David locked in a meaningless conversation with Moriarty for ninety minutes, he'd been talking behind our backs to Terry Donahue. The seventy-two hours that San Francisco had given David to put together a trade wasn't close to expiring, but that didn't matter to the Niners. They were out for revenge. The time had come to get even with TO—time to sell me out.

This is the cutthroat part of the NFL image that you never see when you watch the league's TV promos for itself. This is the stuff they hope you never hear about. Or read.

David now called Ozzie, who'd asked me a couple of months earlier at the Michael Jordan celebrity golf tournament if he could trust me. Oz was confused. He should have looked in the mirror and asked himself that question. He'd just committed the cardinal sin in TO's book: he'd kicked the *T* word right in the teeth.

"You don't know what you've done," David told Ozzie in tones that could not be described as friendly. "You've violated TO's trust, and you'll never get it back. That's the worst thing you can do with him."

Ozzie tried to calm David down and tell him how much I was going to like playing in Baltimore, but David hung up on him.

Then he called Donahue and really cut loose. All the bad blood that had been building between the two men ever since David had tried to open negotiations with the 49ers the previous summer was out in the open.

"You lied to me," David told him. "You gave us seventy-two hours to work a trade, and we were close to a deal with Philly, and you pulled the rug out from under us."

Donahue said that the Eagles weren't really serious about making a trade, and he didn't want their deal anyway, because it offered him only a fifth-round pick and receiver James Thrash. By now, Donahue was screaming at David, who was giving it right back. When the men stopped yelling, David hung up on *him*.

He called Ozzie again and played a new card, telling Newsome that the Niners had not revealed the whole truth to him about my contract.

The Ravens thought they were getting me for the remaining three years on my contract, but if I went to Baltimore, I could void the last two years left on my deal with the 49ers and become a free agent after the 2004 season. Ozzie didn't want to hear this and tried to soft-pedal everything, saying that he and David would work out new terms.

"I'll make TO love me," he said. "I'm gonna show him so much love that he won't know what to do. Everybody loves playing in Baltimore."

It was at this point that David decided, as he later put it, "to make the Ravens so fucking miserable they would never forget it."

He may have been under a gag order not to talk about this conflict, but I wasn't. I was ready to go public with my feelings and started telling people, through my Web site and the media, that my agent hadn't done anything wrong, that I wanted to be in Philadelphia, not Baltimore, and that I wanted to play with Donovan McNabb and not Ravens QB Kyle Boller. Nobody was going to shut me up or trash my agent without me getting in a few good licks. Within a day or two, the *Baltimore Sun* was filled with stories and opinions about the Ravens screwing up the deal for TO. Ozzie was in the line of fire now, and so was the whole organization. I'd had enough, and people out there were responding to what I had to say, big-time. In one week in early March, my Web site had more than 4.6 million hits. Things were getting hot. The more I spoke out, the more the commentators told the world that I had no chance of getting what I wanted, and the happier they seemed saying this. While they were talking trash, I hunkered down with my three best friends in Atlanta—Coop, Pablo, and Shaw—and we stayed up late shooting pool and swimming and playing hoops. We hung together tight.

On Friday, March 5, Ozzie called David and said he was coming down to North Carolina for the Duke-UNC basketball game in Chapel Hill that weekend. He wanted to see David and smooth things over, but David said no. He told the Ravens GM that he—Ozzie—had created a very big problem for himself, and it was up to him to fix it.

Ozzie finally stopped talking about love.

He began to go on about how he was a black man from Alabama, just like TO, and how he played thirteen years in the NFL, and was now in the Hall of Fame. And then he said that sometimes, a black man's gotta be slapped.

David was so stunned that he didn't say anything for a moment or two. Then he responded with, "What did you say?"

And he said it again, that sometimes, a black man's gotta be slapped.

Since David didn't want to see him in North Carolina, Ozzie said that he was going to call me and patch everything up. David didn't think that was a very good idea, but Ozzie phoned me anyway. I hung up on him.

XXXIX

WHEN I HIT the airwaves saying I didn't want to play in Baltimore, a shift seemed to take place in the players union. David and I had asked earlier to speak to Gene Upshaw directly, but that hadn't happened. In fact, it seemed the union hadn't done much at all. It wasn't until I started talking publicly and presenting our side in the media that the NFLPA stood up and took the matter seriously. Maybe they realized that we weren't going to back down, ever, so they might as well get on board. On Monday, March 8, the union filed a grievance, asking for a Special Master (Stephen Burbank) to hear my case. He was originally scheduled to consider the evidence by phone on Saturday, March 13, and give his ruling the next day. Burbank's decision would then have to be approved by U.S. District Judge David Doty of Minneapolis, who'd overseen a 1993 class-action settlement between the NFL and the players union. If Burbank ruled for me, I could still be a free agent and sign with the Eagles. If he didn't, I'd appeal, but if I lost the appeal, I'd have to make a very tough decision about going to Baltimore or holding out. The next-to-last thing I wanted to do was hold out. The last thing I wanted was to play football for Ozzie Newsome.

The hearing was rescheduled to be held in person on Monday, March 15, in Philadelphia, where Burbank met with representatives of the NFLPA, the NFL Management Council, the Ravens, and the

49ers. Neither David nor I had been invited. David waited for the decision in Greensboro while I was in Atlanta, and it was a very long day (it was also a long day for Jeff Garcia, who was about to be sentenced on the West Coast for his DUI). For several hours, nothing shook loose, although the hearing had ended well before noon. At two-thirty P.M., David got a call from Erik Albright, one of the lawyers we had hired, who'd just heard from David Feher, a union attorney who'd been at the hearing. Feher told Erik that he had no feeling for which way Burbank was leaning. David was trying to stay cool, but he was upset by this call, because he felt that both his fate and mine were on the line and nobody was telling us anything. He was so nervous that he and Jason left the office. For days, they'd been taking lengthy drives together just to escape the reporters and the tension and to clear their heads.

Around four forty-five David's cell phone rang. Joe Banner from the Eagles was on the line. This wasn't the call they'd been expecting. Something must have changed.

"Does TO really want to come to Philadelphia?" the Eagles president asked David. "Do we have a deal?"

David didn't commit but said he had to talk to me first.

That was fine, Joe said, but he needed an answer as fast as possible, which meant that day.

Why the hurry? David wanted to know.

Shortly after the hearing ended, Banner explained, he'd gotten a call from the NFL Management Council asking him if he had a deal with me and if he could get it done in the next few hours. Joe said he could try.

While David and Jason had been driving around the North Carolina countryside desperately waiting for information, the Eagles, the Ravens, the Niners, and the NFL were apparently calling one another trying to resolve the issue.

It seemed that by the end of the hearing, it had become obvious that the NFL did not want the Special Master to issue his ruling because they knew they were going to lose and lose big! The NFL, which had taken a very hard line against me since all this began, was now backpedaling as fast as it could. Its case had crumbled in front of Burbank and the only way for the NFL to save face was to prevent the Special Master from issuing his decision declaring me a free agent. The NFL was frantically trying to arrange a deal with the Ravens, the Eagles, and the Niners that would allow me to sign with Philly before Burbank could deliver his opinion the next morning—and they wanted David and me to help them out. That was why Joe Banner was under so much pressure to get the deal done by sundown.

David tried to reach me with this news, but there was a foul-up. He didn't have my new cell-phone number and couldn't get me on the old one. He called my best friend and my mother, but nobody could get me on the phone.

Without speaking to me, David called Banner back and told him to do whatever was necessary to make the trade work. As Banner moved forward, David and Jason went back to the office and crunched some numbers, studying the deal they'd been talking about with Philly before the Niners had traded me to the Ravens. Late that night, David and Banner came to terms: I would get $16 million in signing bonuses and guaranteed money, plus a seven-year contract with the Eagles worth approximatley $49 million. I'd get to fulfill my dream of playing with Donovan McNabb. The Eagles would send a fifth-round pick to the Ravens, who would get their second-round pick back from the Niners. Philly would trade defensive end Brandon Whiting to San Francisco—if everyone could agree to this deal. Everyone did agree quickly, except Ozzie Newsome. While David and Joe were negotiating all this, Ozzie apparently went to dinner in Baltimore and spent two and a half hours lingering over his meal. When he got back to David and Joe, he let them know that he wanted to sleep on the deal and make a decision by nine the next morning. Then he went home. Ozzie may have slept that night, but David and Jason and Joe didn't. They were in the office by seven A.M., waiting for two hours for the phone to ring.

At nine-thirty, Banner called and said the Ravens had accepted the trade; the long ordeal seemed to be coming to an end at last. David and Joe spent the next couple of hours going over the details, but the Eagles wanted to hold a press conference that afternoon and wanted all of us to fly in for it. It was snowing in Greensboro, so David and Jason had trouble getting a commercial flight to Philly. While they were trying to book one, the union's lawyers phoned and told them to hold off putting our signatures on the contract until certain things regarding my signing bonus had been changed. The deal wasn't done yet, even though I was on my way to Pennsylvania.

A small private plane, sent by the Eagles, picked me up in Atlanta, and it now flew to North Carolina to get the two agents. As we went farther north, the weather got worse. When we approached Philly, it was snowing hard and the wind was whipping the seven-seat plane sideways; it felt as if we were flying on black ice, our nerves were shaking, and we had to circle the airport for thirty minutes before touching down. At the airport, a limo met us, and we were driven to the Eagles' headquarters with a police escort. When we arrived, fans were holding up signs with my picture that read, "Free TO" and "TO's an Eagle!" They were cheering as we stepped out of the car.

The press conference was supposed to start at five-thirty, but David and Jason went upstairs and began renegotiating the fine points of the bonus arrangement. Both sides locked horns, and it looked as if everything could still be canceled and we'd go home empty-handed, but we'd come too far to quit now. After more than two hours of wrangling, the Eagles agreed to change three words in the contract, which would provide me with more financial protection, and those three words were the final hurdle. Neither snowstorms nor stubborn lawyers could keep this deal from going through.

At seven P.M., the press conference got under way, and I was officially a Philadelphia Eagle. All the critics had been wrong—once again. David and I hadn't made a mistake that was going to cost me my football desires and millions in cash. The league couldn't force me to stay in San Francisco or to play for the Ravens. I was going where I most wanted to be and for the money that I'd earned through eight years of hard work. It didn't matter what John Clayton or anybody else had said about my prospects for getting out of a bad situation and into a better one. David and I weren't going to be stopped by a few opinions or potholes in the road. We weren't going to be defeated by gossip, any more than my grandmother or my mother had been. They knew what real strength was, and I was so fortunate that these two women had passed some of theirs along to me.

The last three weeks of turmoil were in line with everything else that had happened in my career. Since leaving Alex City and entering college, I'd had to keep showing people over and over again that they didn't get to define me or limit me or tell me what I could or couldn't do. Just because they said something a thousand times didn't make it true. That was my story—and this bizarre free agency episode had made the point once more. Talk was cheap. Talk was easy. Sports, at least pro sports, was about your ability to go out onto the field or the court and perform when it counted. The critics could keep on talking; I was going to keep playing football and try to help the Eagles win their first Super Bowl.

Despite this huge win in March 2004, I was right back where I'd been in high school, at UTC, and when I'd first gone to the Niners. I'd have to prove myself once more to the doubters and to those who said that I would bring more problems to my new team than I was worth. I've got just two words of advice for all of you: *Watch me.* Watch me, and see if history repeats itself. Watch me closely, and you might just learn something about the heart of a true competitor still looking for a ring. Watch me, and see how hungry I still am. I won't rest till I get there.

Appendix

Testimony of Terrell Owens, Fremont, California,
Presented to the Subcommittee on Labor, Health & Human Services,
and Education and Related Agencies Committee on Appropriations,
United States Senate, April 1, 2003.

Good morning, Senator Specter and Senator Harkin. I am honored to be here. My name is Terrell Owens. I am here to talk to you about an incredible woman named Alice Black. Alice is my grandmother, and she has Alzheimer's disease. While I'm here in Washington, she is in a nursing home in Talladega, Alabama. At this point, she remembers mainly me, her late husband, and the woman who is here with me today, Marilyn Heard, her daughter and my mother. Professionally, I have achieved one of my dreams; I play football in the National Football League. I am a wide receiver for the San Francisco 49ers. In my seven seasons in the NFL, I have caught hundreds of passes, scored many touchdowns, set numerous 49ers and NFL records, and been to the Pro Bowl three times. Despite this success, I am basically powerless to help a woman I love dearly.

She's not as sluggish-looking when I go over there. She's not in like a mummy-type state. She used to stay with my mom, and I would go over there. She would just sit there, with her head slumped down. She would sit in that chair all day. I would sit in that house and look at her. What is she thinking? Is she thinking? I know the time will come when she doesn't remember me. But I swear, within the last three or four years, or however long it has been since she was diagnosed, she's been able to say my name. It's probably only like that for three people: her late husband, my mom, and myself. She just says, "Terrell."

Sometimes, she has to think for a second. You can tell she is in a thought process, her version of brainstorming. But soon she'd get it. "Is that Terrell?" She's sixty-eight. Maybe. She's not old. Not too old at all.

She doesn't realize the magnitude, or the level, of success I have reached. That's what makes me go stronger. That's why it doesn't bother me when the media criticizes me about doing this or that. That's why it didn't bother me when Mooch and I were going through our thing. He didn't understand. He was the head coach. He was in a situation where he was supposed to understand his players, but, for whatever reasons, we didn't get along. It didn't bother me. I think it bothered other people, though, because I would go off in my own little world. I didn't have to say anything to anybody. But when it came down to Sundays, I was able to block out all of that and still be able to be productive on the field. But that was the thing with a lot of people. They didn't understand.

They probably say, "How does he do it?"

It doesn't matter. They can put me in a box. I won't be there long. And unless they've experienced someone close to them suffering from Alzheimer's, they'll never have a clue.

Football has provided me with a certain amount of fame and privilege; however, no amount of fame or privilege can heal my grandmother. While I gladly pay her medical and health-care expenses, I cannot change the fact that she has Alzheimer's and continues to suffer. My grandmother helped mold me into the person I am today. She helped raise me, my brother, and my sisters while my mother worked numerous jobs and sewed clothes on the side. Through the way she lived her life, my grandmother passed many special gifts to me. She was strict when necessary but always caring and often playful. She taught me to work hard, to be proud of who I am, and never to back down or take a backseat to anyone. Many of her so-called old-fashioned beliefs became the bedrock for my success—self-discipline, work ethic, and focus.

Moreover, because of my grandmother's and my mother's steadfast convictions, I am never afraid to speak my mind honestly about matters that are important to me. Finally, my grandmother's indomitable spirit (she would often cite scripture, sing hymns, and make sure that I attended church) created a similar spirit within me that gives me the strength to carry on as she continues to suffer.

One of the real tragedies of Alzheimer's is the isolation it produces. The woman who helped raise me is barely aware of my accomplishments or my position in life. I am proud to be Alice Black's grandson, and I simply wish that she was able to celebrate what we have become, where were are going, all the while remembering where we have been. I know there are millions of others who have suffered with a loved one stricken with Alzheimer's, just as my family and I have suffered. I am truly humbled to have been chosen to represent many of those persons here today. I believe I speak for all of us when I ask this committee to help us help those who cannot help themselves. I know what it takes to be successful in sports. My success is a direct result of the hard work that I put in during the off-season and off the field during the NFL season. When a game is on the line, I want to be the player my teammates look to to make a big play or to score a touchdown for my team.

Unfortunately, I cannot go out and make a big play or score a touchdown that will cure my grandmother and the millions of others who suffer from Alzheimer's. However, I am here today as part of a team that can work together to defeat Alzheimer's. I am asking the senators on this committee, and President Bush, to help me, Coach Martz, and the millions of persons we represent to team with us to defeat Alzheimer's. Together, we can make a difference and defeat this horrible disease once and for all.

There is really only one thing I care about in this world: my family. It has been devastating for me and my family to watch my grand-mother slip into the ravages of Alzheimer's. I know that you have many difficult decisions to make and that you must always balance many competing priorities and interests. Part of the reason I decided to appear today in front of this committee is because of the enormous respect I have for it and the work it does. Thus, I urge you, for my grandmother and for all of the other families that have been affected by this terrible disease, to increase the funding for Alzheimer's research by $200 million this year and to keep Congress on track toward the goal of $1 billion for research.

About the Authors

TERRELL OWENS grew up in Alexander City, Alabama. He attended the University of Tennessee–Chattanooga and in 1996 was drafted by the San Francisco 49ers in the third round. Although never expected to become a starter, since 1999 he has been selected to four straight Pro Bowls and holds the NFL record for most catches (20) in a single game. In 2004 he left San Francisco to become a member of the Philadelphia Eagles.

STEPHEN SINGULAR is an investigative journalist and the author of fifteen nonfiction books. He has written extensively on sports, crime, business, and the entertainment world. He lives in Denver, Colorado.